Who Is My Neighbor?

Social Affinity in a Modern World

James A. Vela-McConnell

STATE UNIVERSITY OF NEW YORK PRESS

Published by
State University of New York Press, Albany

© 1999 State University of New York

For information, address State University of New York Press,
State University Plaza, Albany, N.Y., 12246

Production by Cathleen Collins
Marketing by Dana Yanulavich

Library of Congress Cataloging-in-Publication Data

Vela-McConnell, James A., 1967–
    Who is my neighbor? : social affinity in a modern world / James A.
Vela-McConnell.
        p.   cm.
    Includes bibliographical references and index.
    ISBN 0-7914-4311-6 (alk. paper). — ISBN 0-7914-4312-4 (pbk. :
alk. paper
    1. Social interaction. 2. Affiliation (Psychology) 3. Community.
4. Social action. 5. Social perception. 6. Civilization,
Modern—20th century—Psychological aspects. I. Title.
HM291.V36 1999
302—dc21   98-56093
                                                                      CIP

10 9 8 7 6 5 4 3 2 1

*To all of those who
take the time to step beyond
the boundaries of their own lives.*

Contents

Figures

Tables

Foreword

There may be no more fundamental sociological question than "What do persons in a society feel they owe each other?" Sociologists have long emphasized that reciprocity and exchange are among the essential normative underpinnings of social order. Georg Simmel observed that "If every grateful action that lingered on from good turns received in the past were suddenly eliminated, society would disappear" and Adam Smith wrote that "To feel much for others and little for ourselves . . . to restrain our selfish, and to indulge our benevolent affections, constitutes the perfection of human nature." It is no wonder, then, that classical sociological theorists were absorbed by the changing character of the "social bond" as agrarian societies were transformed into the urban world wrought by the industrial revolution that enveloped mid-nineteenth-century Europe.

Although their visions differed in important respects, these writers were united in their view that people's connections to each other and to society itself were increasingly loosened as societies modernized. They were unanimous in their assessment that people were less morally constrained in urban societies because their commitments to communities of all sorts had become far more tenuous. With some exceptions, contemporary theorists sustain the same view, emphasizing the degree to which an ethic of "expressive individualism" minimizes persons' felt obligation to each other. Robert Bellah writes that "individualism lies at the very core of American culture. . . . We believe in the dignity, indeed the sacredness, of the individual."

Postmodern theorists also typically claim that contemporary American society is defined by increasingly short-lived and superficial relationships, geographic mobility that diminishes our commitment to place, and a mass media that confronts us with multiple and contradictory points of view on nearly everything. Zygmunt Bauman has described the "postmodern self" as composed of "momentary identities, identities 'for today', until further notice identities." Such momentary and fluid identities, which are furthermore dedicated to self-enhancement, conspire to minimize our sense of responsibility to each other. Thus, the prevailing opinion of sociologists from the nineteenth century to the present seems to be that we may live in a world with others, but an ethic of individualism makes it increasingly difficult to live for others.

Beginning in the 1960s, a significant stream of social psychological research was concerned with gathering data to unravel the social circumstances under which people would help others in trouble. After Kitty Genovese was murdered on a street in New York's borough of Queens while dozens of people watched and did nothing, researchers became intrigued by the phenomenon of "bystander apathy." Although the essential finding of multiple studies was provocative and counterintuitive—the *more* people who simultaneously witness a person in trouble, the *less* likely is anyone to intervene (presumably because of a "diffusion of responsibility")—the empirical materials offered were never used in an especially satisfying way to connect broadly based sociological theories with concrete helping behaviors. Certainly, these studies did nothing to explain why some people's lives are bounded by an ethic of service and care for their less fortunate fellows.

To understand apathy and activism, we need a rigorous effort to join accumulated theoretical insights with carefully collected data on the motives of those who, in varying degrees, have opted for a life of helping others in trouble. Bold in conception, breathtaking because of the range of writing it draws together, scrupulously careful in execution, and elegantly parsimonious in its explanation, Professor Vela-McConnell has written a book that is at once deeply satisfying intellectually and hugely valuable to anyone interested in linking theory to public policy. All whose political and moral sensibilities lie in the direction of maximizing a sense of neighborliness—in the immediate social contexts of our lives, within the boundaries of the United States, and in our increasingly global village—should read this book.

I especially admire this work because of the author's conceptual courage. The central thread that holds this enterprise together is Professor Vela-McConnell's elaboration of the notion of "social affinity." Any time a writer commits himself or herself to an idea that intersects with a myriad of related ideas, there is the danger of falling into a crippling analytical morass. Because the notion of social affinity is so closely aligned with ideas like attachment, connection, empathy, sympathy, cohesion, kindness, generosity, and compassion, the author risked generating confusion rather than clarity. The book is a triumph partly because Professor Vela-McConnell so skillfully navigates exceedingly complicated theoretical terrain, eventually to show how powerfully the social affinity concept bridges "key ideas within classical sociological theory and contemporary social psychology." With a skill akin to a brilliant surgeon, Professor Vela-McConnell dissects the components of social affinity in early chapters and then later reconstitutes them to explain how thirty-six people, intensively interviewed, relate to the issues of hunger, AIDS, and any other social problem that most concerned each.

As it should be, respondents' voices are at the book's center. They are plentiful and eloquent in elaborating the evolution of individuals' social consciousness. Using the data in a fully inductive way to discover just what distinguishes the level of a person's activism, Professor Vela-McConnell identifies four "ideal types" along a continuum—those who are nonreferenced, self-referenced, relationally referenced, and socially referenced. His treatment of each affirms the great value of describing complex human realities with typologies. Any device for ordering data will miss the full complexity of respondents' idiosyncratic subjective experience. The question is whether a researcher's theory, model, categories, typologies, or themes do enough justice to the complexity of things while displaying the essential and repeating dimensions of a phenomenon. The best social science writing achieves a delicate balance between capturing regularities in human behavior and paying attention to each interviewee's distinctive subjectivity as reflected in their particular narrative. *Who is My Neighbor?*, by presenting detailed "case studies" of each of the four types, maintains an artful balance between thick description and analysis.

These days, an increasing number of social scientists are experimenting with personal narrative as a mode of data presentation. Discussion of narrative analysis is part of a new and emerging language of qualitative research that seeks to be more responsive to the richness of people's experiences. Advocates for narrative analysis worry that traditional modes of data presentation (using short excerpts from several respondents to illustrate a theme) inappropriately decontextualize the life experiences of those we study. Professor Vela-McConnell's book shows that we need not choose between these two modes of data presentation. The credibility of much of his explanation rests on the traditional approach to qualitative data analysis by presenting quotes from multiple respondents. In addition, though, we come to know several of those interviewed far more intimately. Not only does this make for engaging reading, it informs us about the range of life circumstances that inhibit social activism or propel it.

The last chapter of this book is titled Becoming "Fully Human." Of course, the question of what it means to be fully human animates volumes of literature, philosophy, and social science. Consistent with the underlying argument of previous chapters, Professor Vela-McConnell aligns himself with Leon Eisenberg who writes that "[only] the adult whose concerns extend beyond family and beyond nation to mankind has become fully human." The bad, albeit expected, news in this book is that only a precious few persons have, by this criterion, achieved full humanness. The good news is that the sort of finely grained, persuasive, and insightful social psychological writing in *Who Is My Neighbor?* provides a potential blueprint "for overcoming the limits of social location and creating an environment which is conducive to the emergence of social affinity from the local to the global levels." In this regard, *Who Is My Neighbor?* is a profoundly human and hopeful document. Its careful treatment of the bases of social affinity points the way toward a world in which we might feel more connected to and responsible for each other. It is, therefore, an exceedingly important contribution to a long history of dialogue about the requirements for a more just and caring world.

David A. Karp, Ph.D.
Boston College
April 1998

Acknowledgments

First and foremost, I would like to acknowledge all of those who made a point of asking, whenever they saw me and usually before anything else, "Are you done yet?" You helped keep me on track, even if it was just to silence the question! And then there are the many people who feigned interest after making the mistake of asking me about my research at dinner parties. Thanks for humoring me! I hope to see you again sometime!

On a more serious note, the completion of this project would not have been possible without the support of others, whether it be in the form of funding, inspiration, or especially the "neighborliness" of colleagues, friends, and family. The Ford Foundation, the National Research Council, and Boston College all provided the necessary funds to complete this research. Without their support, I would probably still be collecting data. The words of poet Marianne Williamson provided much inspiration: "Our deepest fear is not that we are inadequate. Our deepest fear is that we are powerful beyond measure" (*A Return to Love*, 1996). These and the words that follow were taped to my desk next to the computer as I was writing. In fact, they're still there.

I would like to thank the members of my research writing group—Lyn Rhenisch, Uli Boehmer, Patty Bergin, and especially Kathleen Odell Korgen—for all of their support, encouragement, feedback, and—yes—criticism each step of the way. This group proved invaluable in setting deadlines and providing a forum in which to discuss ideas, debrief, and work out the challenges of writing. Kathleen deserves special thanks for being there even outside the context of the group, as in our innumerable telephone "conferences." She also had the sense to "make me" *write down* my own short-term writing goals. These goals are still staring at me from my desk, every one of them with a check mark and a completion date. Kathleen helped me to surpass even my long-term goal for completing this project. Uli provided some key insights during that fertile period between data collection and writing. That was one helpful walk on the beach of Provincetown! Linda Schworm also deserves recognition in this context. While not a member of the group, she actually took time out of her own busy schedule to read each chapter and provide additional feedback and encouragement, as well as much-needed conversation on topics other than my research.

The Coutsoukis family—Platon, Sandy, and my "nephew" Christopher—were an amazing source of support, helping me to celebrate all of the triumphs—small and large—along the way. I am honored and deeply touched by being made a part of their family. Their goodness and beauty constantly reminded me of the spirit beyond the mere "facts" that are the subject matter of social science. Platon also sat and listened to me present my research and, while still providing the feedback I needed, showed his enthusiasm by engaging in a discussion that bounced off between both our perspectives. Moreover, he always found "yet another" article that I "might find interesting and relevant." They were! Any more?

Then there is my own family—David and Allan McConnell, Fran Dodd McConnell, Hortensia Vela, Sylvia Vela, and the many others—who had faith in me every step of the way. To Dad and Grandmother Vela, who never failed to say how proud they are, I cannot possibly convey how important those words were and still are to me. As often as you said them, they never lost their strengthening power. Your moral support and love were crucial. Grandmother, you also reminded me that "all work and no play makes James a dull boy." Striking this balance between work and leisure helped give me the energy to press on toward completion. Thank you for helping me keep the joy of life in a place of prominence.

Above all, I would like to express my deepest gratitude to my mother—Adrienne Vela McConnell. Despite your much grieved absence, you have made your presence and love known to me. You have demonstrated that individuals are capable of crossing the greatest distances and the most formidable boundaries—a theme running throughout my writing—even if only in spirit and in prayer. You have shown me how to live, and I am truly blessed and grateful.

ONE

A Society of Strangers

A human being is a part of the whole, called by us 'Universe;' a part limited in time and space. He [*sic*] experiences himself, his thoughts and feelings as something separated from the rest—a kind of optical delusion of his consciousness. This delusion is a kind of prison for us, restricting us to our personal desires and to affection for a few persons nearest us. Our task must be to free ourselves from this prison by widening our circle of compassion to embrace all living creatures and the whole of nature in its beauty.

—Albert Einstein

Getting lost within a labyrinthine "automated voice system" is an all too typical experience in our culture today. When phoning an insurance company, a financial institution, a hospital, a school, or even the local phone company, we are greeted with a recorded voice asking us to choose one of several options. After pressing the appropriate number, we are confronted with yet another list of options. Eventually, if we are lucky, we are placed on hold in order to talk to an operator. Heaven forbid they need to transfer us to another department! But oftentimes we never communicate with a "real person." In our culture today, it is increasingly difficult to avoid scenarios such as this, and it only seems to be getting worse: there are some banks that now charge their customers extra in order to see a "real" bank teller rather than use an ATM or their automated voice system. It is now possible to go grocery shopping over the computer, to get gas for our cars without speaking to an attendant, or even to send and receive "virtual flowers." Technology has "set us free" from the constraints of personally interacting with others.

With technology, the world and its peoples are brought closer together than ever before; and yet many of us also feel more disconnected

1

than ever—cut off from others and overwhelmed by all of the problems facing society. In this global context, how are the intimate ties of community possible? In a society historically dominated by the Judeo-Christian tradition, among the most basic values we are taught is the value of loving our neighbors as ourselves. But in this global context, what does such a guideline mean for us? And in a world that oftentimes is labeled a "global village," who exactly is our neighbor? Ideally, we would say "everyone is our neighbor." And, indeed, with globalization and technology, we can see within a matter of minutes events that occur all over the world. On television, we saw the Berlin Wall come down, "smart bombs" wrecking havoc in Desert Storm, and the aftermath of the Oklahoma City bombing. "Everyday" acts of violence from domestic abuse to street crime to war impinge themselves upon our consciousness: people going hungry throughout the world, people living with and dying of disease, people fighting for their rights and standing up against oppression—the lone student standing in the path of tanks in Tiananmen Square. But oftentimes, the more we see, the smaller we feel in terms of being able to do something because there is just so much going on "out there" and so much to be done.

Globalization and technology are like a double-edged sword. In many ways, they make the world a "smaller place." For those who are privileged enough to afford it, modernization has brought the whole world to our fingertips; but our grasp remains the same. The demands placed on our attention, sympathy, and social obligations are greater than ever. No one person could address all of the issues demanding our attention, so we are forced to choose. Out of all the possibilities before us, where do our sympathies lie? Which issues grab our attention and prompt us to get involved? In other words, how do we conceive of and express our obligations to society? How do we overcome this feeling of "smallness" and widen our "circle of compassion?"

The answer to the question of "Who is my neighbor?" is crucial to our understanding of moral obligation—the responsibilities individuals and organizations have to contribute to the health of society and that serve to hold society together. Moreover, it is directly relevant to an understanding of the moral crisis that many of our intellectual, political, and religious leaders note faces our society today and that is evident in the breakdown of society: the collapse of the family, community, and social responsibility as well as the rise in crime, from the street to the seats of political and economic power. Social thinkers such as Alan Wolfe—in his award-winning book *Whose Keeper?* (1989)—note that the moral code that defines the obligations of individuals and organizations to one another and to society has become lost amid the social, political, and economic developments of modernization.

The Problem of Modern Consciousness

Human existence and consciousness have radically changed as a consequence of the process of modernization. Consciousness within contemporary society is characteristically different from that which is premodern—an idea that was of great interest to classical sociological theorists. As societies become more complex—carried along by such things as technology, the global economy, the bureaucratic state, and urbanism—a qualitative transformation occurs within our consciousness. What we know—and more importantly, how we know it—changes.

This subject of study is anything but new. However, among those who have sought to understand these changes, there are myriad interpretations of the causes and implications of this transformation. Some of these perspectives are positive in their outlook; many are negative. Many social commentators view some aspects of modernization as detrimental to social solidarity. At the same time, however, they do not argue for a return to a premodern form of consciousness. Modernization is not inherently negative. It can be a tremendous force of liberation, but the path is not an easy one.

A central question arising out of this issue concerns the impact of modernity on human consciousness and its concomitant effect on social relations in general. Take the World Wide Web as an example. On the one hand, some argue that it has the potential to be a tremendous force of liberation by making it possible for more people than ever to get involved in activism and community organizing (Nader 1995). The Internet gives individuals the opportunity to "sign" virtual petitions and easily send letters—many of which are already written for you—expressing their views on legislation to local, state, and national politicians. Moreover, the Internet has been lauded for its ability to bring diverse peoples from across the globe together into virtual communities (Rheingold 1995).

On the other hand, while it is easy to acknowledge the virtue of virtual activism as a *supplement* to other forms of involvement, can virtual activism really become a *substitute* for actual activism? It is easier to dismiss a host of e-mail messages than to ignore a handful of demonstrators. Even assuming that the addressee reads the messages, they still lack a "human face." Moreover, while demonstrators may get little or no media attention and exposure to the general public, at least it is an issue that can be addressed—as Charlotte Ryan describes in her book *Prime Time Activism* (1991)—whereas *by its very nature*, virtual activism is invisible to the media as well as the public. Such exposure is critical. And while the Web may be a way to meet interesting people, how diverse can a virtual community be when most of those in communication with one another already share that similar interest or curiosity that brought them "together" in the first place? Moreover, there is the issue of access to the Web, which is limited to those individuals and parts of the world that have the appropriate technological and economic resources (see Kadi 1995; Stuart 1995). Does not this further limit the diversity of virtual communities? Community itself is characterized by interdependence and mutual obligations. How obligated are we to virtual others?

The impact of technology such as the World Wide Web on individuals and society has been a topic of much interest for social scientists such as Kenneth Gergen (1991). He argues that, in the postmodern world, we are faced with a "saturation" of self. Because we are in contact with ever-increasing numbers and varieties of people through our technology, our identities become populated by these many others, resulting in a multiplicity of often contradictory values, self-doubts, and rationalities. While he sees such contradictions as somewhat problematic, his view is rather optimistic. He says that,

> [A]s such technologies [of social saturation] become increasingly effective, we become increasingly populated with the identities of others, and come increasingly to recognize the extent of our relational embeddedness. As this occurs, the separation between self and other becomes diminished, and warfare becomes a nonsensical proposition. (1991: 257)

In other words, technology makes us more aware of our interdependence. However, Gergen seems to confuse the quantity of our relationships with the quality (i.e., an increase in the quantity of our relationships does not necessarily mean that the quality of these relationships has improved as well). In fact, in many instances, the opposite may well be the case.

Pursuing the example of the Internet, it is easy to forget that the words appearing on a computer screen actually came from another human being with all of the hardships, joys, strengths, and weaknesses that characterize each one of us. Berger, Berger, and Kellner (1973: 31–35) describe such "virtual" relationships as "anonymous social relations" in which there is a distinct abstraction from the personal qualities of interaction. Direct, personal contact is no longer relevant to our social relations. The relative anonymity of these virtual encounters implies that one's personal identity becomes irrelevant to social relations. For instance, when we no longer deal with people so much as we deal with answering machines, automated tellers, written contracts, computers, and the ubiquitous automated voice system, one's self—one's identity—is no longer important for such abstract relations. Instead of personal contact, we have developed procedures for lending a superficial level of personalization to these anonymous interactions so that we *appear* to be personally concerned for another's welfare when, in fact, we are not.

At the most basic level, we have become a "society of strangers." Sociologist Georg Simmel (1971) describes the "stranger" as someone who is both near and remote at the same time, a description that is most appropriate for understanding this dilemma of modernity. Technology gives us the illusion of proximity while the actual distance between ourselves has not changed. Thus, for Simmel, "spatial relations not only are determining conditions of relationships among men [and women], but are also symbolic of those relationships" (1971: 143). The spatial relations of proximity and distance are symbolic of the relative attachment and detachment between individuals, and one who is a stranger is "not bound up organically, through established ties . . . , with any single [person]" (1971: 145). In other words, in a society—such as our own—that is increasingly dominated by superficial contacts between relatively anonymous others, we are losing those social ties that hold us together. We increasingly rely on the interventions of technology to assist in broadening and deepening our *relationships*, much like a crutch. Without the closer intimacy of face-to-face interaction, it is merely our social *contacts* that are multiplying.

Simmel also points out that intimate ties are characterized by the similarity of those in the relationship. Recognizing these similarities is most easily achieved when only two people are involved. For example, when two people first start dating, they are in all likelihood going to give much attention to finding and appreciating all those things they have in common. However, when extending this principle of similarity beyond a relationship between two people to include entire populations and, given our global context, the entire world, the ability to find such commonalities thins out with the size of the group. Feelings of connection dwindle: "To the extent to which the similarities assume a universal nature, the warmth of the connection based on them will acquire an element of coolness . . . the connecting forces have lost their specific, centripetal character" (1971: 147). In other words, given our modern and global context, we are caught within the tension between two different trends. Globalization and technology are bringing the world closer together, forcing us into contact with others with whom we never before would have interacted, at the same time that the sheer numbers—the overwhelming quantity of contacts—actually strains our capacity to maintain anything but the most superficial and "cool" relationships.

As a society of strangers, the ability to connect with one another in traditional relations based on similarity is strained. Individuals feel increasingly disconnected from the rest of society despite the quantity of their social contacts. If, in an effort to unite the world's peoples, we look only at the most broad and abstract source of commonality—our humanity—Simmel points out that it actually has the effect of highlighting all of the things we do not have in common. The end result is that we do not perceive others as whole individuals any longer. Instead, we see them as strangers of a different "type" (1971: 148).

In contrast with Gergen's optimism, the effect of living in a society of strangers can be chilling. As quoted earlier, Gergen believes that by bringing the world closer together, warfare becomes "nonsensical." However, the superficiality of such broad social ties with little basis in concrete forms of similarity can easily become a source of dehumanization. Sam Keen, in his book *Faces of the Enemy* (1991), argues that the advent of technology has made it possible for us to avoid seeing the human face of the world's peoples entirely, making warfare and widespread brutality psychologically easier for the perpetrators. In the past, governments dehumanized their enemies in order to legitimate war by comparing them to barbarians, demons, wild beasts, and vermin. Today, without the need to ever see the enemy while destroying them, we do not even have to acknowledge their "actual" existence. With technology, we only need to press a button to destroy millions of lives. We never have to see the carnage we inflict and we never have live with the guilt and the horror over what we have done.

One military officer reflected on the impact that losing sight of the individuals who suffer the effects of war has on the consciousness of those who never have personal contact with them:

> It's something generals and presidents can never understand—
> only mothers, fathers, brothers, sons and daughters, and
> wives. . . . [Starting with Vietnam], we reduced the blood and
> suffering and the death and destruction to mere ciphers, and in
> so doing we reduced our own souls. Numbers don't die; peo-
> ple do. Columns of figures don't disintegrate in the explosion
> of a bomb; human beings do. Statistics don't bleed, and if you
> can make your war a war of numbers, you have no trouble
> sleeping. Most generals and presidents sleep well. (1991: 84)

The presidents and generals who decide to "go" to war never have to live
with the direct effects of their decisions and to deal with the pain of war
because they have less contact with the battlefield and those who actually
die. They are distant, removed—emotionally, psychologically, and even literally. Directing a war today is quite similar to moving pawns on a chess
board or playing a video game: there are no emotional consequences or
personal losses in games or in war because there are no "real people" at
stake. We only see "blips" on a screen, just as on the Internet we only see
words on a computer monitor. The human face and all that it stands for is
easily "lost in transmission." When we never have to see the abstract others
"out there," it is easy to overlook all the things we have in common with
them. It is easier to overlook, ignore, dismiss, and even kill a stranger than
it is to do the same to someone whom we actually know.

Thus, the nature of social ties between diverse and distant peoples is
highly problematic in a modern and globalized world. At the same time
that we are in contact with ever-increasing numbers of people from all
over the world, we feel more disconnected from those around us. At the
same time that technology makes it possible for us to be informed of events
happening across the globe, we feel increasingly overwhelmed by all of the
claims upon our attention and sympathy. And at the same time that the
world is brought virtually into our living rooms, the personal ties are still
missing. We are caught up in the paradox of the stranger—we are simultaneously proximate and distant with the world's population and even our
next-door neighbors. So, again, we come to the question: In a world
increasingly known as a global village, who exactly is our neighbor?

The research presented in the following chapters is an effort to
understand this paradox of simultaneous connection and disconnection—
the impact of modernity on social cohesion and moral obligation. However, this is obviously a broad line of inquiry. In order to study such an

abstract topic, it is first necessary to narrow the scope by focusing on its most essential elements. The concept that embodies the sentiment underlying social cohesion I have labeled "social affinity."

Toward an Understanding of "Social Affinity"

The term *affinity* has several closely related meanings that are relevant here, each one adding more depth to our overall understanding. At a surface level, it indicates resemblance—those who have an affinity are those who share some similarity, likeness, association, or correspondence. At a slightly deeper level, affinity suggests fondness—a bond or feeling of affection, attachment, liking, closeness, or alliance between those who enjoy such a bond. Finally, at a still deeper level, affinity implies kinship—a strong tie or union, a feeling of connection, or a relationship in the deepest sense of the word. More generally, social affinity encompasses the empathy and identification between individuals or groups that lies at the heart of the classic notion of social cohesion—and that which undermines affinity undermines the basic cohesiveness of society.

As already noted, the challenge in our global context is to establish social affinity between diverse and disparate individuals in order to reinforce the cohesiveness of society. At heart, the paradox of modernity is symbolized by the tension between proximity and distance. In a modern world, we are simultaneously close and removed—attached and detached from one another. The question is, "How do we reconcile the two?" At the same time, there are several different ways of being proximate and distant: *spatial, temporal,* and *social proximity/distance.* Each of these variables describe our individual social location in relation to other individuals (i.e., every individual is located spatially, temporally, and socially, and this social location is unique to the individual).

The most obvious of these social location variables is spatial proximity, which pertains to the literal geographical distance between two or more individuals or groups. People can be as distant as those dwelling on different continents or as proximate as lovers in their tenderest moments. Such proximity can minimize or maximize the personal contact between individuals, groups, or institutions with far-reaching implications. Let us take war as an example. In the United States, it has not been since the Civil War that we have fought extensively on our own soil. War is something which happens in Vietnam, Iraq, the former Yugoslavia, and so on. It happens in parts of the world unfamiliar to the majority of us living in this country. We do not see for ourselves what the realities of life are like for those living and dying in these other parts of the world. It is difficult to be compassionate across such geographical distances, especially when one does not know anyone "over there." Thus, it comes as no surprise that it took so long for the United States to intervene in the war-torn former Yugoslavia when it was not in our interest to do so. By contrast, Desert Storm was in our country's interests and so we did not hesitate to get involved. Considerations of self-interest are able to circumvent the limitations of proximity and distance.

As the name implies, temporal proximity refers to the amount of time separating two or more individuals or groups. The most obvious example is the distance or length of time between those living in the world today and those in generations yet to come, or the proximity of those who are of the same age—the same cohort—and who experience many of the same historical events: in other words, the "generation gap." Returning to the war example, take World War II and the Holocaust. These events happened over fifty years ago. Apart from the dry and impersonal accounts one can find in the history books, and despite the personalizing tendencies of, for example, movies like *Schindler's List* and the exhibits at the Holocaust Museum in Washington, D.C., many people have no understanding of the impact this event had on those who experienced it first hand. Thus, we find today that some people deny that the Holocaust even happened—that it was a hoax. With time, it is easy to forget and the atrocities of the past are likely to be repeated.

Moreover, we may make decisions today as individuals, as groups, as institutions, and so on that may have results extending well into the future. In this sense, temporal proximity also includes the passage of time before the full impact of a decision is felt and the course of its implications become realized and known. Are we aware of the consequences—either positive or negative—of our actions today for our own future and for the future of those yet unborn? Such a question goes beyond a discussion of intended versus unintended consequences by focusing on whether such a question even enters our mind when making a decision. In our individual daily lives, we make our plans or agendas for the day and for the week. However, fewer people make plans extending into the distant future, setting goals for five, ten, twenty, or a lifetime of years. And many organizations, concerned more with "short-term" gains than long-term commitments, willingly sacrifice our environment for profit without worrying about the long-term effects.

Such effects have little or no relevance in the present, so it is not in our interest to concern ourselves with them.

Finally, there is social proximity or distance—a term that must be carefully distinguished from social affinity. In the tradition of Simmel, social proximity refers to the degree of similarity or dissimilarity between individuals or groups. Thus, the term involves those characteristics with which we are born—*ascribed* attributes—such as gender, race, ethnicity, sexual orientation, and so on. These are the attributes of social status that individuals possess and "over which they have no control" (Karp and Yoels 1986: 65, 86). Yet social distance, as understood here, also includes what social psychologists refer to as *achieved* attributes—those that we have earned through our own efforts. One's level of education, occupation, and social position are examples of these attributes (1986: 65, 86). Returning once again to war as an example, the Iraqis, the North Vietnamese, and so on were "another people." The were not "us." Instead, they represent cultures that are foreign to us, and so it is easy to dehumanize them in the sense described by Sam Keen. We legitimate hostility by focusing on our differences with others.

Social distance is different from social affinity in that it denotes those factors that serve to differentiate between or separate individuals (as in distance) in terms of status or level of personal intercourse. On the other hand, social affinity refers to the sentiments underlying the social bonds bridging the gap between individuals. The object of this distinction is to hypothesize that affinity is a sentiment that is *affected by* social distance. To the degree that these factors of gender, race, education, and so on affect the decision of who to include in one's circle of neighbors, friends, and family, social distance has an impact upon affinity. Indeed, social affinity is affected by all three forms of distance: temporal, spatial, and social. As the distance between ourselves and others increases, the possibility of establishing social affinity with those others is strained, undermining the basic cohesiveness of an increasingly global society. This relationship between social affinity and social location is further developed in chapter 2.

The influence of social location on social affinity runs through the entire discussion of the problem facing modern society presented in the previous section. The modern world has become very impersonal. We have become detached from those around us. We value the competition that drives us apart rather than the complementarity that could bind us together. The very attributes that forge social bonds—kindness, generosity, patience, tolerance, cooperation, and compassion—are those that are undervalued in our society, while those that further the distance between us—competition, self-interest, and individualism—are esteemed. We have become *strangers* in our own society, in our own communities, in our own homes. We have become alienated from one another and from society and its institutions. We have become mere automatons in a world where civil society is increasingly elusive. It is with fear and trembling that we wonder about the consequences of this breakdown of civil society, and we seem reluctant to hope that there may be solutions.

With globalization and modernity, the rules of the game have changed, but the way in which we think remains the same. Phenomenologists Berger and Luckmann point out that, even in today's global context, much of "reality" in everyday life is determined by its pragmatic application. The "here and now" that each person experiences, and that is represented by his or her social location, is his or her highest reality because it has practical importance and is readily available to the individual (1967: 22). For example, when a person is working at his or her job in a library, whatever is going on at the nearest fire station is not a part of his or her immediate reality—unless, of course, the library is on fire; then the nearest fire station takes on a whole new significance. This example highlights two important points. First, one's social location is inherently caught up with one's self-interests: we are more likely to be interested in those things that have a direct and proximate impact on our lives. Second, social interaction is a major part of everyday reality. People best experience others in face-to-face interaction. Through interaction, the "here and now" of two people overlap and there is a continuous reciprocity between them (1967: 28–29). Without these direct and personalized interactions, the emergence of social affinity—the sentiment of interconnectedness—is jeopardized.

The Empirical Exploration of Social Affinity

Given this understanding of social affinity and its relation with social location, it is possible to study the idea of "neighbor" from the perspective of the social sciences. The aim of the research presented here is to explore the criteria for the emergence of social affinity. This research will demonstrate how social-contextual variables shape social affinity and the meaning our values have for us. But how do we study something so intangible as social affinity? While social affinity is not something one can see and touch directly, it is possible to study its manifestations—how we *act* upon our commitment to society. By studying our outward behavior—something that is observable and measurable—it is possible to understand the inner sentiments that underlie such behavior.

Within the social sciences, there is a tradition of studying what is called "prosocial behavior"—actions that are directed toward the benefit of others. These actions include everything from helping someone in need to voluntarism to activism. All of these forms of behavior on behalf of others are concrete manifestations of the abstract notions of social affinity, social commitment, and moral obligation. With this in mind, prosocial behavior toward social issues (such as hunger, AIDS, racism, violence, civil rights, abortion, and so on) is an indicator of these unobservable sentiments.

There are two general trends in the prosocial behavior literature of social psychology. On the one hand are those who argue that prosocial behavior arises out of personality variables, such as our value system and ethical beliefs, our ability to empathize with others, our socialization process, our moral development, and so forth. On the other hand, social psychologists point out that situational variables play an important role: How many people are there to witness an event calling for a helping response? Is the potential helper in a hurry? Is the situation an emergency or not? The research presented here, by exploring the impact of our social location as well as including the construction of social consciousness, empathetic role-taking ability, and so forth, acknowledges both literatures within the field.

To study social affinity, I began with a survey in which respondents were asked a series of questions about three different social issues: the hunger issue, the AIDS issue, and the issue each individual respondent listed as being of utmost concern. (The rationale for choosing these particular issues appears at the beginning of chapter 3, at which point the issues are discussed in more detail.) In this way, I was able to draw comparisons between those issues respondents felt were important with those they may or may not feel were as important. However, a conscious effort was made not to focus on activists and activism, *per se*. Much research has already been done in that area (such as Flacks 1971). This work is more comparative in that it covers the full range of involvement, from non-activism to activism, from the perspective of social affinity. There were 426 people (46.81%) who responded to the survey. From this initial sample, I took a sub-sample of thirty-six people for intensive interviews that averaged about two hours in length each. These interviews focused on the three issues in much more detail and were intended to elicit each individual's perceptions of and experiences with the issues and those affected by the issues. This qualitative data forms the heart of my research and is supplemented with the quantitative survey data as needed throughout the chapters that follow. The analysis of this data provides a useful hueristic tool for understanding moral obligations within a global context. (See Appendix A for a much more detailed description of the methodological procedures and challenges faced in conducting this study. For those with a strong interest in the more technical aspects of the methodology, be sure to read all of the endnotes.)

The reason I chose to study social affinity from the angle of social issues and prosocial behavior is due to my own personal background. Growing up, I was taught the Judeo-Christian values of loving your neighbor and helping those in need. However, despite my socialization in traditional religious and secular values—as represented by my Catholic upbringing on the one hand and my participation in Cub Scouts and Boy Scouts on the other—I was not really taught to "go out of my way" in expressing my commitment to others, especially if they were outside of my own life sphere (i.e., if they were distant from myself). Taking cues from our culture, I restricted my definition of "neighbor" to those with whom I came into direct contact and gave precedence to those who were already familiar to me, such as family, friends, and acquaintances. In other words, my "circle of compassion" for others was restricted to those closest to myself, indicating that there is a certain amount of tension between the value of loving one's neighbor and the self-interest imparted by our culture of individualism. I—along with most of us in our society—ended up being pulled in two different and opposing directions.

When I moved from home for college, I ended up joining a community action program and volunteering in a shelter for battered women and their children. I did not join because I felt that domestic violence was an important issue. I did not know much about it at the time. Instead, I joined because I wanted to meet people and those in the community action program seemed like the kind of people I would enjoy getting to know. In other words, my motivation was one of pure self-interest even though it meant that I would be reaching out to others. However, my worldview began to change because of my experiences as a volunteer. Through my volunteer work, I was made more aware of domestic abuse—and not just the simple facts, but the everyday, lived realities of those suffering from abuse. By viewing life from their perspective, my own point of view began to change. While I had originally become involved in order to meet people, I soon became committed to volunteering out of a sense of responsibility to the people I served. Through these experiences, I began to develop a commitment to social involvement that has continued ever since. To the surprise of many, I even set aside time now and while in graduate school to be involved in the community. So, taking this angle in my own research—focusing on social issues and prosocial behavior as a manifestation of social affinity—meant that I could understand more about my own journey from pure self-interest to a greater sense of social responsibility.

However, as will be seen in the chapters that follow, the attainment of such a sense of social responsibility does not necessarily endure forever. As our life circumstances change, so does our commitment—for better or for worse, but hopefully for better. At the same time, our social context—what Simmel calls our "spatial relations"—is not so deterministic as he seems to suggest. Individuals, groups, organizations, and institutions each have the ability to manipulate the social location variables of social, spatial, and temporal proximity and distance. In other words, we are able to overcome the limitations of our social context and extend our social affinity well beyond the boundaries of self-interest and our own life spheres. The processes involved in the emergence of social affinity as well as how we are both shaped by and overcome our social location form the heart of the analysis that follows.

Outlining What Is To Follow

The concept of social affinity is not a new notion so much as it is a bridging of key ideas within classical sociological theory and contemporary social psychology. With this in mind, we will begin with a broad overview of the theoretical roots of social affinity. Chapter 2 traces those roots and the relationship between social affinity and social location through the classical literature, contemporary writings within that classical tradition, and research within contemporary social psychology. The classical roots focus largely on the idea of social cohesion, but they also contain a subtext that describes the social location factors that affect that cohesion. Social, spatial, and temporal proximity and distance each have implications for the empathy and identification required for affinity. While contemporary social psychology focuses much more explicitly on these variables of social location, they are typically treated separately—one within the field of group formation, another within the topic of attraction, and so forth. Our consideration of social affinity brings them together and, in combination with one another, the implications for social cohesion are both readily apparent and of undeniable importance.

Before breaking down the development of social affinity into its most basic elements, the terrain is mapped by exploring individual attitudes and responses to two very different social issues: hunger and AIDS. After a brief presentation of why social issues in general, and these two issues in particular, make a good case study for examining social affinity, we turn to a more direct analysis of this topic. A useful way to begin such an analysis is to distinguish between those who are "low" in this quality of social affinity versus those who are "high." With this in mind, I begin by delineating a four-point typology that extends from low to high social affinity. While at a surface level, this typology represents differing orientations toward social issues, at a deeper level these types represent the successive degrees of commitment associated with social affinity and moral obligation.

Chapter 3 outlines the first two types, the *nonreferenced* and the *self-referenced*, and chapter 4 continues the presentation of the typology, focusing on the *relationally referenced* and the *socially referenced* types. These chapters present a first-person narrative portraying each of these types, focusing either on hunger or AIDS. These case studies will then serve as a resource to draw upon when analyzing the process of the development of social affinity in subsequent chapters. Chapter 4 concludes with a discussion of the dynamic nature of this typology and its usefulness when comparing distributions of individuals within the typology from one social issue to another.

Together, chapters 2 through 4 paint a picture of social affinity in broad strokes. The following three chapters break down social affinity into three dimensions and then further disassemble them into their constituent elements. In other words, learning about the emergence of social affinity is much like viewing a large and intricate mosaic. After viewing the picture as a whole, we then scrutinize each of the individual pieces. Such a focus on detail is very much a part of my own social psychological training. While it is easy to lose sight of the "big picture" when looking so closely—the proverbial "can't see the forest for the trees"—the reward will be a greater appreciation for the overall intricacy and complexity of design in our mosaic of social affinity when the pieces are put back together in chapter 8.

With this image of the mosaic in mind, our analysis of the emergence of social affinity begins with a focus on each of its three dimensions. Social consciousness, sentiment, and action are the topics of chapters 5 through 7. "The 'Other Side of Silence'" explores the processes by which individuals come to some level of social awareness. In many ways, our place in society determines the breadth and content of our consciousness. Society's dynamics and cultural values further influence our consciousness. However, individuals also have the power to shrink or extend the boundaries of their awareness. What are the mechanisms at work here? What impact do these mechanisms have on an individual's perceptions of the social world? We first focus on the process of filtering, arguing that individuals filter information in and out of their awareness just as readily as do the institutions that are traditionally the focus of such analysis. Information is also framed within one's consciousness. Frames that are applicable across a variety of social issues are presented. Finally, individuals seek to confirm the reality they have constructed. However, some individuals—particularly if or when they are socially referenced—do not need to rely on public opinion to verify their perceptions of reality.

In "A 'Sentimental Journey,'" we examine the feeling component of social affinity—that *feeling* of connectedness with others. Emotions are a highly personal phenomena; however, they also provide a crucial link between the individual and society. With this link in mind, we discuss the role of emotions in society, focusing particularly on empathy and the role-taking that is so central to the emergence of social affinity. At what point does empathy emerge? To what effect? Those factors that serve to enhance or inhibit the emergence of an empathetic response to a given situation will be explored. What are the limitations of our empathy? Is it necessary to be empathetic to be socially responsible? We then move beyond a consideration of emotions at the individual level and focus on emotions within the context of social issues. How do we negotiate sympathy claims with something so abstract as a social issue or so large as an outreach organization?

As many an activist has lamented, there is often a great disparity between being aware of the social world and actually taking part in it, not to mention the disparity between one's values and one's behavior. "A Call to Action" will explore the component of action—or inaction—as the culmination of the development of social affinity (although action is not necessarily the last in the sequence). Action oftentimes has been thought of in "either/or" terms: either individuals are active in addressing social issues or they are not. However, this understanding of action is highly limiting. Not surprisingly, there are many different forms of action and even nonaction.

Under what conditions is each of these likely to emerge? And with what implications? Four types of action are described, as well as the mobilizing potential of each of the frames presented in chapter 5. We also explore some factors that promote or hinder taking action toward social issues. Finally, we bring together each of the three dimensions of social affinity—consciousness, sentiment, and action—into a single model of social affinity.

Throughout chapters 5, 6, and 7, I borrow from a wide variety of theoretical perspectives within the tradition of sociology. The reason is twofold. In the first place, I find myself continually frustrated—particularly within the field of social psychology—with the profusion of miniscule theories offered as explanation for highly circumspect social phenomonena. Those focusing on theories of attraction, for example, rarely look at theories of motivation. Prosocial behavior, socialization, moral development, emotions, collective behavior, and so on are all too often treated as if they are separate and distinct social processes with absolutely no bearing on one another. I believe such disparate theorizing is highly misleading. Instead, it is my intention to place a wide variety of literatures in conversation with one another, to build bridges between otherwise isolated theoretical perspectives. Individually, these theories present a rather simplistic view of the social world. Together, they give us more of an appreciation of the underlying complexity of the world in which we live. Thus, there is a certain amount of complexity conveyed in chapters 5 through 7. However, the utility of such a nuanced analysis will become fully apparent in chapter 8 when the variety of perspectives are brought together for the purpose of analyzing personal biographies in order to understand the "big picture" of the emergence of social affinity.

Secondly, I include multiple theoretical perspectives because I am a person who avoids espousing any single point of view. Each perspective lends important insights into our understanding of the social world and is valuable in that respect. Imposing a single, overarching theory is dogmatic and ends up shaping the data rather than allowing the data to shape the theory. In short, I believe that a single theoretical perspective misrepresents the data and I take an eclectic approach in order to avoid such an outcome. The use of a single perspective also presents a relatively deterministic view in which individuals are mere automatons carrying out the machinations of some "grand theory" (Mills 1959: 25–49). As already mentioned, individuals are creative agents who do not blindly follow the rules of some abstract theory implanted within their subconscious minds. Deterministic models do not reflect individual variations and their ability to step outside of such external constraints—an ability that is central to our understanding of the emergence of social affinity.

At the same time, however, it is incumbant upon me as a researcher to make clear to the reader my own theoretical biases. Given my own sociological training, I find that I am influenced by phenomenology and symbolic interactionism. These perspectives are particularly apparent in chapter 5, as evident by its subtitle of "The Construction of Social Consciousness." At the most basic level, these perspectives begin with the assumption that human beings inhabit a symbolic world that they creatively and cooperatively assist in constructing. Individuals act according to their assumptions and understandings of the social world—how they define and construct reality. Phenomenologists Peter Berger and Thomas Luckman take such a perspective and argue that, by establishing patterned ways of interacting with one another, individuals construct and reconstruct the social world around them. In other words, individuals play an active role in society and determining their own lives. At the same time, however, society is reified—it "assumes a life of its own"—and acts back upon individuals. Individual behavior becomes regulated. We are constrained and are no longer free to do absolutely anything we wish to without some consideration of the consequences. In other words, individuals have the power to construct society and that power is both enabling and constraining (Giddens 1984: 14–16).

Utilizing the phenomenological and symbolic interactionist perspectives provides the theoretical background for this research. However, these views are only loosely presented in order to lend a greater degree of flexibility to the specific perspectives presented in chapters 5 through 7 and that comprise the foreground of the analysis. Together, these multiple theoretical perspectives give us a more complete and nuanced picture of the emergence of social affinity.

In addition to the issues of hunger and AIDS, and as I already noted, I gathered data regarding those issues the respondents themselves identified as of utmost importance to society. In chapter 8, I use the concept of social affinity and the delineation of its development and experience, as detailed in the preceding three chapters, to analyze individuals' responses to those social issues of most concern to them. At this point, I reassemble all of the individual pieces in the mosaic and we take a step back to look at the overall picture. I then analyze two new case studies—one representing each extremity on the continuum of social affinity—in order to demonstrate the various outcomes of the process of moving from social consciousness to social action, including an instance in which social affinity is not reached.

At this point, I reintroduce the social location variables of social, spatial, and temporal distance to the analysis. At root, these variables are indicative of the self-interest that permeates our culture. What is the impact of self-interest on the development of social affinity in the context of social issues?

The implications of this study of social affinity are far-reaching within the context of the modern world. While technology has made our world a smaller place, bringing diverse populations together like never before, our ability to bridge the distance between ourselves and distant others has not necessarily kept pace. In fact, given the potentially limitless scope of moral claims on individuals within the media age, the demands on our social responsibility are greater than ever. In chapter 9, we take another step back from the mosaic in order to see how the picture of social affinity we have drawn fits into this global context: What are the implications of what we have learned for the cohesiveness of an increasingly global "community?" By breaking down the overall picture into its constituent elements and then reconstructing the whole, the reader will gain a greater appreciation of both the complexity and the overall picture of the emergence of social affinity. After discussing the uniqueness of the relationship between self-interest and social affinity is to the United States, I apply the findings of the previous chapters to an analysis of urban planning and its impact on the emergence of community as well as an analysis of the globalization of the economy within the context of social affinity. Finally, we turn to the question of "Who is My Neighbor?" and how such a precept applies in a modern, global context.

The goal of this research is not to speculate as to the status of social affinity in our society (i.e., whether we have a problem due to a lack of affinity) so much as it is an attempt to lay out what is meant by affinity, how it is manifest in our orientations toward social issues, and, most importantly, the way in which it emerges within individuals. As is apparent in this introduction, questions surrounding the deterioration of social affinity inspire this research. However, it is only after we have a thorough understanding of the nature of social affinity and its emergence that it will be possible to discuss the implications of its presence or absence in society. The concluding chapter outlines initial steps in such a direction, but the research presented here concentrates primarily on constructing a firm foundation from which to proceed. I hope that the theory of social affinity presented in the following chapters leads to much discussion and research regarding its status within our society and the emerging global culture.

It is also important for the reader to understand that the goal of the following analysis is not to construct a single formula or "grand theory" that may be universally applied as an explanation for how social affinity develops or even how individuals do or do not get involved in addressing social issues. Such a model implies a level of determinism, which is misleading given that individuals have the capacity to act as self-determined agents and break out of any positivist and deterministic mold a researcher may propose, although, admittedly, whether a particular individual claims this agency is another question altogether. Instead, the focus is on giving voice to those interviewed and tearing apart all of the small pieces that are then reconstructed into a larger whole.

Moreover, understanding social affinity in terms of consciousness, sentiment, and action—and how it is influenced by self-interest and one's social location—is by no means the only way to understand the topic of social cohesion. It is only one of many possible perspectives for understanding how society is held together. However, just because it is one among many does not mean that the viewpoint presented here is any less valuable. Every perspective has its limitations. Each perspective available provides unique and distinct insights into the subject matter. As such, the elements of social affinity presented in the following chapters provide a set of tools that the reader will find useful in making sense of the personal biographies presented in chapters 3, 4, and 8. It will also provide valuable insights when applying what we have learned to the process of globalization and the current struggle to construct a truly global *community*.

TWO

The Roots of Social Affinity

What is it that holds society together? This is a central question in sociology. Early efforts to understand social cohesiveness were at the societal level as captured, for example, by Tönnies's distinction between *gemeinschaft* and *gesellschaft,* or Durkheim's notions of solidarity. Since that time, this issue has also been taken up by those who focus more on the individual within society: social psychologists. They have looked at social cohesiveness in terms of concepts such as social distance, propinquity, similarity, and so forth. The concept of social affinity combines these macro- and micro-sociological trends into a more nuanced analysis of social cohesion.

Since the birth of the field, sociologists have constructed typologies of societies in an effort to understand their characteristics, underlying principles, and especially the bonds that hold these societies together. Such typologies have generally fallen into dichotomies between what have been broadly interpreted as "simple" and "complex" societies. One of the oldest and most notable was Ferdinand Tönnies's distinction between *Gemeinschaft* and *Gesellschaft*—"community" and "society." This dichotomy has inspired many successors. Following close behind Tönnies was Émile Durkheim, who couched his typology in terms of "mechanical solidarity" and "organic solidarity." As we move forward in the history of sociology, we come across Charles Horton Cooley, who distinguished between "primary" and what have been labeled "secondary" groups, and Stanley Milgram, who relied upon a rural/urban distinction. In each case, the typology revolved around the qualities inherent in each kind of social arrangement.

The "qualities" in question are primarily associated with the *form* and *intensity* of social cohesion within each type. Social affinity is a concept that applies to these qualities. Thus, it is not in itself a "type" of society or group.

Instead, it is an attempt to look at our social affiliation and nonaffiliation with a hope of understanding their consequences for social cohesion and society in general. Interestingly, the concept of social affinity bridges the classical notion of social cohesion represented by Tönnies with micro-sociological notions of empathy and identification, placing these bodies of theoretical thought in conversation with one another. At the same time, it is important to note that these two bodies of thought were never really so far removed from each other. This is evidenced by the fact that traces of those same micro-sociological notions of empathy and identification can be found within the classical tradition of social theory just as traces of the notion of social cohesion can be found within social psychology.

The Classical Foundation

Tönnies (1855–1936) set out to distinguish between what can roughly be translated as "community" and "society." These are two different types of social organization accompanied by two corresponding types of human mentality and behavior. The first, *Gemeinschaft,* is dominated by "natural will"—a "mode of thought" that is passed down and internalized by each succeeding generation and that emphasizes close relations between individuals. Tönnies's ideal example of *Gemeinschaft* was the social organization of the family, but included that of the rural, premodern village—both of which are societies of "organic" formation. This type of social organization is based upon fellowship and authority rooted in the protection of the group.

Taking a close look at simple societies, we readily notice that there is a societal emphasis on "connectedness." Anthropologist David Maybury-Lewis (1992) notes that within tribal societies, the connectedness of all things—human as well as nonhuman—is the foundation of life. Furthermore, connectedness implies mutual—reciprocal—obligations. For everything we "take" from society, we are obliged to give in return. These obligations create the bonds that hold society together. Peoples within a tribe are bound to one another and bound to the people of other tribes as well as to nature itself.

In simple societies, this bond with others and with nature often proves to be more important than individual autonomy. It is the bonds that go beyond the tribe to others and to nature that are most fundamental in that, without them, the human social world would be impossible. If one upsets the balance between tribes, between humanity and nature, one's own self is placed at risk. The well-being of each person and each tribe is *dependent upon* the well-being of others. Each individual's well-being is placed in the hands not only of himself or herself, but of others as well. The tribal worldview includes a deep respect for the interdependence of all tribes, and this sense of connectedness carries over to the mutual obligations existing between one person and another—between one people and another.

Gesellschaft, on the other hand, is dominated by "rational will"—that mode of thought that is characterized by conscious, individual thinking and decision making and that emphasizes more distant social relations. In contrast to the wholeness and organic nature of *Gemeinschaft, Gesellschaft* is conceived of by Tönnies as a mechanical construction.[1] This type of social organization is based upon the authority of social contracts agreed upon by individuals in a more characteristically modern and urban society. As social groups grow larger, *Gemeinschaft* is succeeded by *Gesellschaft* and the community and its intimate ties are lost within an impersonal, individualistic world based on contracts with strangers. There is a strong element of nostalgia in Tönnies's writings on this subject, even though he acknowledges that *Gemeinschaft* is still found within some associations of *Gesellschaft.* Tönnies's tacit implication in the loss of *Gemeinschaft* is a resulting breakdown in "moral obligation." Within *Gesellschaft,* we perceive ourselves as independent of others and enjoying great freedom when, in fact, we are actually interdependent—bound, to some extent, to the welfare of others.

> The condition of being bound to others . . . [implies] a moral obligation, a moral imperative, or a prohibition. There exist a great variety of such "ties," which involve an individual through different types of relationships. These ties may also be called types of social entities *(soziale Wesenheiten)* or forms which link him to his fellow beings. He is bound in these social entities *if he is conscious of being linked to them.* His consciousness of the tie is either predominantly emotional or predominantly intellectual. From this consciousness there results a feeling or a realization of moral obligation, moral imperative, or prohibition, and a righteous aversion to the consequences of incorrect, illegal, and unlawful, as well as of immoral and indecent conduct and action. (1988: 242; emphasis mine)

Feelings of moral obligation are dependent upon an individual's conscious awareness of being interdependent with others. Purely mechanical links between separate individuals dissolve the modern individual's awareness of interdependence. For example, when shopping for food in a grocery or department store, it is easy to lose sight of the fact that it took the labor of thousands of individuals, many with families, to bring those products to us. As a consequence, feelings of moral obligation and the resulting benefits for social cohesion are jeopardized when our social consciousness is limited in this way. It is thus quite easy to overlook the mistreatment and exploitation of migrant workers or those who work in sweatshops within our own borders, or to be oblivious to the fact that many common products, such as soccer balls or Oriental rugs were made by the hands of children, many of whom are actually owned by their "employers" (Schanberg 1996). Moral outrage at such realities has no chance to be triggered as we hunt for bargains or view "snazzy" packaging and advertisements.

Maybury-Lewis argues that, while the tribal ethic focuses on interdependence, those within industrial society are concerned primarily with *mastery*. This attitude of dominance is directed in the first place toward the environment, and such dominance has been found profitable for modern economies. Such a sense of mastery is alien to tribal peoples. For the industrialized world, land—nature itself—has become a mere commodity. However, as alluded to in the previous paragraph, not only does industrialized society thrive on the mastery of the environment, but it also thrives upon the domination of other peoples. This domination, too, is found profitable. Society and the relations within it have become rationalized such that the possession of *quantifiable* objects becomes more important than the more spiritual emphasis on the *quality* of relationships among people and the environment.

While the tendency toward mastery may not always be so extreme within modern democratic societies as to result in outright oppression, the underlying sentiment remains.[2] Because individuals are set one against another, the emergence of the modern, complex society involves a breakdown of the social ties that bind people together. With the loss of *Gemeinschaft* is a concomitant breakdown of what we today call "civil society" and the moral obligations that are the basis of social affiliation in simple societies.[3]

With this in mind, we come to the problem of modern, complex societies as understood by such intellectuals as Alan Wolfe (1989). Wolfe argues that modernity is accompanied by interdependence on ever widening circles of strangers. Contemporary society's increasingly complex forms of social organization challenge us with obligations that go beyond the family and immediate community. This is the context in which the concept of social affinity becomes relevant. Moreover, the impact of the social location variables—social, spatial, and temporal proximity/distance—comprise a subtext throughout his book and even the work of Tönnies.

Wolfe's approach to time, space, and sociality is easily summed up in one simple statement: "Modern people usually find themselves in three situations in particular: they live in time; they occupy space; and the rules that define their interactions are the product of a specific culture" (1989: 43). For Wolfe, these factors are inseparably linked to the problem of moral obligation[4] and modernity. The following passage captures the essence of his argument concerning this problem:

> Both the scope and the specificity of moral obligations change as societies become more modern. The sheer complexity of modern forms of social organization creates an ever-widening circle of newer obligations beyond those of family and locality. Modern liberal democrats, for one, have obligations to perfect strangers. . . . They have further obligations, at yet another remove from the traditional milieu, to what has been called the "generalized other," a term that might include, for example, those who will live in the future and will therefore be dependent on decisions made by the present generation. To be modern is to face the consequences of decisions made by complete strangers while making decisions that will affect the lives of people one will never know. The scope of moral obligation— especially at a time when issues of possible nuclear war, limitations on economic growth, and ecological destruction are public concerns—seems to be without limits. (1989: 2–3)

While for Wolfe, the *Gemeinschaft* idealized by Tönnies is too extreme and tends to be stifling, he contrasts this problem with one at the other extreme—the almost overpowering distance that accompanies modernity. In the modern world, we must constantly live with consequences of decisions made by total strangers while making decisions of our own that will have an impact on the lives of still more strangers.

In referring to the "generalized other," Wolfe speaks in terms of all three aspects of social location: he speaks of social distance, those outside of the "family"; of spatial distance, those beyond the immediate locality;

and temporal distance, those of future generations. While those within a premodern society were not called upon to act as individual moral agents because of the social ties that did not leave room for individuality, those within a modern society are faced with a burden of moral obligation that is overwhelming—"without limits." While in a traditional society there is a fixed moral framework to which its members are obligated to adhere, in a modern society there is no such overarching framework and the individual is left to determine moral courses of action on an almost situational basis.

The technology of modernity—especially in communications technology—has effected a qualitative transformation of the world with a far-reaching impact across both time and space. The modern condition requires that its inhabitants extend their concern—their awareness, their consciousness, their affinity—beyond the limits we have heretofore reached. As individuals within modern society, we must think about the impact of our actions well beyond the immediate here and now; we must be concerned about the consequences of our actions for different peoples in other parts of the world, including those beyond even the next generation.

Although he uses different terminology, the question of social affinity is one of the central aspects of Tönnies's discussion of *Gemeinschaft* and *Gesellschaft*. Like Simmel, Tönnies begins his discussion of affinity through a consideration of what it means to be a stranger. This discussion centers on the distinction between those we know, those we do not know, and the qualitative difference in our relations with each. For instance, when walking down a city street, we are much more likely to stop and talk to an acquaintance—assuming we come across one—than we are to talk to a stranger (Tönnies 1988: 237–238; this book was first published in 1887). Tönnies also discusses some of the factors that influence with whom one does or does not become acquainted. These factors include such things as language differences (1988: 238), which may accompany differences in race and ethnicity, or social status: "Sympathy may . . . be engendered by the fact that individuals belong to the same estate [or situation in life]. . . . In the same way there exists, on the other hand, some antipathy toward all those who are in the opposite camp" (1988: 239).[5] The antipathy to which Tönnies refers can take two forms: hatred or indifference—both of which will be addressed later.

Yet another aspect of social distance that affects the emergence of social ties is one's outward appearance. Tönnies notes that such things as one's "figure, his [sic] face and expression, his dress, his behavior, his manners, his way of speech, even the sound of his voice" (1988: 239) all influence the establishment of a relationship, especially—as is well known among social psychologists—with regard to first impressions. Yet, Tönnies acknowledges that first impressions are subject to change as one gets to know the person who had once been a stranger:

> Immediate and instinctive sympathy or antipathy may, however, be counteracted in actual experience, by a more intimate knowledge of the hitherto strange person. One finds, for instance, that someone who gave one an unfavorable impression at first turns out to be quite a nice person, perhaps interesting or positively charming. . . . In many cases experience may prove the first impression to have been correct; but the reverse is also well known and practically a daily occurrence. An excellent impression may so bias one in favor of an individual that after more intimate acquaintance one may reproach oneself for having been taken in by a brilliant outward appearance. (1988: 239)

This passage points out another source of variation in affinity as it is influenced by social distance: the impact of "actual experience." Thus, the passage of time—an intervening variable, if you will—either helps or hinders the development of a relationship, allowing one to refine one's initial judgment. This example illustrates how social distance and temporal distance may act in concert to influence the development of affinity.

Without it being the focus of his analysis, Tönnies alludes to a "theory" of the relationship between social distance and affinity that may be summed up as follows:

> Understanding is based upon intimate knowledge of each other in so far as this is conditioned and advanced by direct interest of one being in the life of the other, and readiness to take part in his joy and sorrow. For that reason, the more the constitution and experience or natural disposition, character, and intellectual attitude are similar or harmonize, the more probable is understanding. (1988: 47)

"Similarity"—a form of social proximity—has a positive effect upon the development of social affinity.

Tönnies did not directly address the concomitant impact of spatial or temporal distance, although their relevance may be inferred by different parts of his treatise, such as the influence of time in relation to "actual experience" as discussed herein. He also gives fleeting references to the role of spatial distance.

> The real foundation of unity, and consequently the possibility of *Gemeinschaft,* in the first place is closeness of blood relationship and mixture of blood [social proximity]; secondly, physical proximity [spatial proximity]; and, finally, for human beings, intellectual proximity [another form of social proximity]. In this gradation, therefore, are to be found the sources of all kinds of understanding. (1988: 48)

It is thus apparent that Tönnies placed his finger upon the relationships between consciousness, the three social location variables, and affinity and emphasized their necessity for the sense of mutual or moral obligation inherent in a healthy society. In his delineation of such concepts as "similarity" and "physical proximity," he also prefigures the work of social psychologists. With regard to the concept of social affinity, it is here that the dialogue between the two bodies of literature begins.

The Social Psychological Foundation

The social location variables affecting social affinity have received much more attention within the field of social psychology. While social psychology focuses explicitly on the dimensions of social, spatial, and temporal proximity and distance, in this discipline they are typically treated separately—within the fields of group formation, attraction, and so on. In understanding the emergence of social affinity and its relation with self-interest, it is essential to bring these traditions and the social location variables together. In combination with one another, the implications for social cohesion are both readily apparent and of undeniable importance.

Social Proximity and Distance

The concept of "social distance" has been the focus of much research within the field of social psychology. On the other hand, its counterpart—social *proximity*—has received comparatively less attention. However, in looking at the link between classical and contemporary thought, the issue of social proximity is apparent. Classic theorists are not the only ones who have made distinctions between types of groups and the nature of the social cohesiveness within these groups. As will be seen in the distinctions between primary and secondary groups, and ingroups and outgroups, social psychologists have done much the same thing. The difference is that there is much more direct attention paid to social proximity and distance. They even show us how and why both social proximity and distance can be manufactured by the members of the groups.

In much the same vein as Tönnies's distinction between *Gemeinschaft and Gesellschaft,* or Durkheim's distinction between "mechanical" and "organic" solidarity, Charles Horton Cooley distinguished between primary and secondary groups; and the qualitative differences between these are much like the differences between social proximity and social distance. The primary group characteristically involves a sense of "we-ness" and "the sort of *sympathy* and *mutual identification* for which 'we' is the natural expression" (Cooley, 1909: 24; emphases mine). Primary groups include the family, a group of friends, a work group, and so on. They are noted for their closeness in terms of the intimacy of contact—a characteristic that is enhanced by both physical proximity and the temporal frequency and continuity of that contact.[6] We tend to be close by our loved ones—figuratively, if not literally—and interact on a very personal level. Who we are as individuals matters to the other members of the primary group. Because of the intensity of involvement within these groups, social psychologist James Vander Zanden notes that these intimate associations are limited to smaller groups (1987: 412–413).[7] In short, primary groups are representative of the qualities inherent to social proximity.

Secondary groups involve more distant relations characterized by a less intimate and more impersonal atmosphere. These groups tend to be much larger, so the individual self is irrelevant to the practical purpose of the group. In fact, we may never meet most of the members of this group. Social contact is less direct, less frequent, and of shorter duration, so social relations are formalized in specific roles and tasks aimed at achieving the goals of the group. Secondary groups include institutions such as schools, churches, corporations, and the military—all of which are institutions that mediate the relationships occurring within them. To this list, and at a more distant level, it is possible to add the nation-state and the community of states. In any case, within secondary groups, we experience that sense of alienation we typically find within a bureaucracy where we are more likely to be known by number than by name. This sense of alienation is a direct result of the social distance characterizing secondary groups.

The distinction between primary and secondary groups has received much attention in the social psychological literature. A closely related distinction is that between "ingroups" and "outgroups," which is essentially a distinction between "us" and "them." Ingroups are defined by a sense of "we-ness," which entails a *sympathetic identification* with the other members of the group (Allport 1954: 29–46). This sympathetic identification is the basis of social cohesion within groups from dyads to societies; and it is a common or *similar* identity that lends itself to such identification. Ingroups are characterized by a sense of familiarity and similarity, loyalty, and a feeling of belonging. For this reason, an ingroup bears many similarities with Tönnies's description of *Gemeinschaft*. Where group identities differ, there are likely to be divisions between the groups, thereby creating an "outgroup." For example, if race is defined as an important aspect of the group's identity, any variations in race become problematic and a source of divisiveness. If whites hold the power within such a group, anyone who is "nonwhite" is marginalized. In other words, nonwhites become members of an outgroup, which is then separate and distinct from the white ingroup.

Those of the outgroup share a different collective identity from ourselves; in other words, they are socially distant. In the example just noted, they are *different* in terms of race. Interestingly, it is the existence of a group that is different from us that helps to solidify our own collective identity, strengthening our own group cohesiveness (Lauderdale et al. 1984; Wilder and Shapiro 1984). Knowing what we *are not*—people with dark skin, for example—allows us to be more sure of what we *are*—people with light skin. It is but a short step between seeing mere differences and perceiving them as a threat to one's way of life because the presence of differences tends to delegitimize the ingroup's identity. In the case of the race example, the mere existence of "nonwhites" implies that being white is not necessarily the "best," much less "only" way to be. For a group that has defined whiteness as important to the group's collective identity as a "white group," such alternatives are seen as threatening. Feeling threatened in this way opens the door to actual hostility (Speier 1941).

Phenomenologically speaking, these differences between the two groups become objectified through the use of labels—"white" and "nonwhite"—and can take on a reality of our own making. We not only come to expect differences between us and them, but as we will see later, we can actually *create* differences that were not there before (Sherif et al. 1961; Markides and Cohn, 1982). And by making these distinctions between the ingroup and the outgroup, the collective identities and social cohesiveness within each group are solidified: "We Are Whites."

Ingroups and outgroups become polarized through this perception of difference *between* groups and a simultaneous perception of similarity—a form of social proximity—*within* groups (Shibutani and Kwan 1965). Even when there are differences within our own group, we tend to smooth over these "minor" differences in favor of the more "major" differences *between* groups. For example, in a society such as our own that is often divided by race, even "whites" as a group have differences in opinions and experiences, gender, class, and so on. But these differences are minimized because being white is the uniting factor in such a group. In other words, we have a tendency to see similarities within our group even when they do not necessarily exist. We expect these similarities and actually create them when needed.

This perception of similarity seems to play an even more central role in the *development* of social ties. We are much more likely to be involved on a social level with those who are like us in many different respects, including race, class, attractiveness, beliefs or attitudes, religion, nationality, education, age, and so on (Gonzales et al. 1983). It has been hypothesized that people are attracted to those who are similar because it minimizes cognitive dissonance—inconsistencies in one's life that produce psychological tension (Newcomb 1956, 1961, 1963).[8] Choosing to have relationships with those who are similar to ourselves validates our sense of our own identities (Byrne 1971). Newcomb also shows that, while physical proximity is important in the initial development of friendships, it is later superseded by similarities in beliefs and values. Because of these similarities—real or imagined—we are more sympathetic toward members of our ingroup.

> When social [proximity is high], people can enter imaginatively into one another's minds and *share their experiences;* they are able to sympathize with one another's pains, joys, sorrows, hopes, and fears. Those who feel close to each other are more relaxed and tend to be less defensive, for each feels that he [sic] can understand those around him. He feels "at home," that he "belongs" in this company. (Shibutani and Kwan 1965; emphasis mine)

Similarity creates a sense of comfort when we are within our own ingroup and we feel positive toward our fellow group members.

On the other hand, we tend to exhibit a certain degree of negativity toward outgroup members (Moreland 1985). Oftentimes, the emphasis on the distinctiveness of one's own group promotes the downgrading of the other group, giving rise to stereotypes and prejudice, as well as ethnic slurs and other labels.[9] The ingroup and outgroup do not even have to be in direct contact for such prejudice to develop (Greenberg and Pyszczynski 1985). The result is an experience of social distance between us and them. Understood in this way, "social distance . . . [refers to] a subjective sense of being set *apart from* (as opposed to being *near to*) certain people" (Vander Zanden 1987: 408; emphases mine; see also Allport 1954: 38–39).

> When social distance is high, the other individual is seen as representative of a *different* category. We feel apprehensive before a creature unlike ourselves, for we are not sure of what he will do. Even after acquaintance there remains a residue of *uncertainty*— a vague apprehension, especially if the stranger maintains his reserve. (Shibutani and Kwan 1965; emphases mine)

It is this apprehension and uncertainty that give rise to the perception, noted earlier, that the outgroup represents a threat. The differences between the groups have then taken on a reality independent of the groups themselves.[10]

The stereotypes, ethnic slurs, and labels mentioned earlier also serve to create a social distance between the groups that was not there before— in much the same way as a self-fulfilling prophesy (Blanchard, Weigel, and Cook 1975). It is thus possible for us to *manufacture* the social distance between ourselves and others. One way in which this is accomplished is through "deindividuation." Vander Zanden defines this term as "a psychological state of diminished identity and self-awareness. *Anonymity* contributes to deindividuation" (1987: 342). Such deindividuation was demonstrated in a study in which the individual identities of subjects were wiped out by avoiding the use of names, covering their faces, dressing them in identical uniforms, and so on. These anonymous people were much more likely to act aggressively toward others than those who maintained their individual identity. Because they were anonymous, blame could not be attached (Zimbardo 1969) and they did not take personal responsibility for their actions. We are also much more likely to act aggressively to anonymous others than to those who have individual identities (Keen 1991).[11] In this case, those who are anonymous are distanced from ourselves by the very fact that they cannot be readily identified as individuals and can easily be conceived of as less than human, thus justifying our aggression. As already described in the introduction, anonymity infiltrates our lives in more subtle ways as well, as when we converse with one another via answering machines, automated telephone answering systems, e-mail, and so on. Such anonymity lends a certain degree of superficiality to the relationship in that the salient aspects of an individual's identity are no longer relevant to interaction. In other words, there is a tendency to cloak our social relations with the qualities inherent in primary groups while a more careful scrutiny of these relations reveals that they exhibit the more impersonal characteristics of the secondary group. Those who are trained in the service industry—such as flight attendants and restaurant wait staff—are especially familiar with the idea of putting on a friendly smile and attitude no matter what one's personal feelings may be.

Institutions also result in the manufacture of social distance. In discussing the concept of "stimulus overload," Milgram (1970) argues that we can handle only so much personal contact. He points out that there is so much going on around us within complex societies that we cannot possibly attend to everything. One adaptive response is to place institutions between ourselves and those in our society who want personalized attention and who need our help. When such an institution exists, the social and moral responsibility to those in need is transferred from our shoulders to the institution. For example, when we know that homeless shelters exist within our community, we feel less obligated to give to a homeless person asking for money on the street. One of the many things likely to go through our minds when given such a request is the idea that someone else has the responsibility to address this problem, thus legitimating our hesitation to act. In other words, the institution "simultaneously protects and *estranges* the individual from his [sic] social environment" because we are deprived of "a sense of *direct contact*" with those in need (1970: 1462; emphases mine). Even those within that institution are buffered from responsibility to the needy. At risk of making a gross generalization, all they are *personally* responsible for is "shuffling the papers" on their own desk.

In sum, the classical distinction between *Gemeinschaft* and *Gesellschaft* find their echo within the field of social psychology, specifically within the distinctions between primary and secondary groups, and ingroups and outgroups. Moreover, social psychologists explain the relevance of social proximity and distance to the social cohesion described by Tönnies in much greater detail. Social proximity and distance at the micro level, and especially our ability to *create* both, have far-reaching consequences for the social cohesiveness of society. But again, this variable is not alone in its importance.

Spatial and Temporal Proximity and Distance

While social proximity/distance is the primary social location variable involved, spatial and temporal proximity/distance also exert much influence on the emergence of social affinity. Within social psychology, issues of spatial proximity have been studied primarily with regard to the subject of attraction. Research has shown that such proximity is a major factor in the development of relationships (Festinger, Schachter, and Back 1950; Segal 1974).

The role of spatial proximity and face-to-face interaction is especially apparent in smaller, more simple societies. In large, complex societies, it is possible to get to know people through alternative means, such as letters or the Internet, without ever having seen them. On the other hand, one might not even know one's own neighbors: "A person with numerous close friends in different parts of the city may not know the occupant of an adjacent apartment" (Milgram 1970: 1462). Physical proximity is no longer a necessary or even a sufficient condition for the development of social ties. In fact, the physical aspect of this proximity is relative. In some cases, the *perceived* spatial proximity is more relevant than the *actual* distance involved (Priest and Sawyer 1967). However, spatial proximity does provide circumstances that are *conducive* to the establishment of such relationships by increasing the opportunities available. Even so, once social contact has been made, physical proximity becomes less central an issue, although the case may be arguable when considering long distance relationships such as friendships and marriages that did not start out as long distance. Such relationships must change in fundamental ways in order to cope with the new conditions or risk fading away with the passage of time.

Milgram's study on obedience to authority provides a more in-depth example of the problem of spatial proximity (1963 and 1974). In his classic—though ethically suspect—experiment, Milgram had his subjects help him "teach" some material to a "student" (a paid actor) in another room. The student was supposedly hooked up to a machine that could deliver electrical shocks of different levels. The subject was told to shock the student when he got a question wrong. For the next wrong question, the voltage of the shock was increased, moving up a scale from "Slight Shock" (15 volts) to "Danger: Severe Shock" (450 volts) by increments of fifteen volts. If the subject refused to inflict more shocks, they were ordered by the experimenter to continue. Some subjects eventually stopped administering the shocks and refused to obey the experimenter; however, none of the subjects stopped before reaching the 300-volt level and over half continued to administer the shocks even to the maximum voltage level of 450.

Milgram then varied the proximity of the student (actor) and the teacher (subject) under four conditions. The "remote" proximity condition was the same as his original experiment. In this situation, the teacher could neither see nor hear the student's voice. However, as the subject reached a shock level of 300 volts, he (all participants were male) began to hear the "student" pounding on the floor, the interpretation of which was left to him. Under the "voice-feedback" condition, the teacher was able to hear the verbal protests of the student through the wall that divided them. In the next condition, the subject was more proximate to the student who was positioned in the same room as the teacher. Thus, the subject could see as well as hear the student while administering the shocks. In the fourth scenario, the teacher was expected to touch the student by forcing his hands onto a shock plate and strapping them there.

The results of these variations are interesting for the consideration of spatial proximity. Under the remote condition, only 12.5 percent of the forty subjects quit at 300 volts while 65 percent went all the way to 450 volts. However, under the other three conditions, the subjects generally quit at the much lower level of 165 volts and fewer went all the way to 450 volts (62.5%, 40%, and 30% respectively). These findings indicate that the closer the proximity of the student to the teacher, the less likely the teacher was to administer harmful levels of shock as punishment for incorrect responses.[12]

Milgram speculates as to the reason for these variations. One such hypothesis has to do with "empathic cues." In the distant conditions, the suffering of the student was not readily perceived by the subject. Even though he knew the student was in pain, it did not influence his behavior because this knowledge was incomplete. With a closer proximity, the subject could empathize with the student more readily because his suffering was immediately apparent (1974: 37–38). Thus, with regard to spatial proximity, what is "out of sight" is also "out of mind." Whether the individual's actions are intentional or not, the result is the same.

In the proximate conditions, it was not possible for the subject to put the suffering of the student "out of mind" because he and his suffering were "continuously visible." The obverse was the case for the distant conditions. "One subject in the Remote condition said, 'It's funny how you really begin to forget that there's a guy out there, even though you can hear him. For a long time I just concentrated on pressing the switches and reading the words'" (1974: 38). At the same time that the subject can see the victim, he can also be seen by the victim, thus coming under his scrutiny. Milgram speculates that "it is easier to harm a person when he is unable to observe our actions than when he can see what we are doing. His surveillance of the action directed against him may give rise to shame or guilt, which may then serve to curtail the action" (1974: 38).

This shame or guilt arises out of our role-taking ability—our ability to identify with another individual. George Herbert Mead informs us that, when we take the role of another, we are able to look back at ourselves *from the other's perspective.* At that point, we begin to evaluate our behavior and—depending on this evaluation—make any adjustments we think are necessary so that we will be more fully connected with the others in our society—our reference group (Mead 1934). However, our ability to role-take with others is hampered when they are distant and hidden from ourselves. As a result, the shame and guilt so necessary in regulating our behavior are cut off before they have a chance to emerge and exert their influence.

When we consider that we never come into contact with the vast majority of the world's population, the implications of these points are staggering. In a modern world where we live in globally interconnected systems of government and economy, decisions are made that have far-reaching ramifications for populations of people our leaders (much less we ourselves) will never see face-to-face; they only see the *representatives* (elected or not) of these masses of people, and even then the contact is not generally on a personal level. It is thus possible, for example, to view the victims of United States aggression as "collateral damage," as we did in the Gulf War with Iraq, rather than as unique individuals with lives and loved ones of their own.

As already noted, spatial proximity facilitates the development of relationships and group formation—a point that is easily waved aside because of its "obviousness." However, the *ramifications* of this point are potentially enormous. Milgram highlights the idea that a shared space can be a uniting force between different individuals or groups. In the remote condition, the experimenter and the subject were in the same room, allowing for the development of an "ingroup" set apart from the victim—an "outgroup:" "There is incipient group formation between the experimenter and the subject, from which the victim is excluded. The wall between the victim and the others deprives him of an intimacy which the experimenter and the subject could feel" (1974: 39–40). As soon as the victim was in the same room, the dynamics of group formation were radically changed and the subject was in a better position to align himself with the victim. Thus, the dynamics of ingroups and outgroups are affected by the spatial proximity or distance involved, actually a more complex relationship than what may at first be apparent.

Milgram's experiments highlighted the role of spatial proximity in the relations between a "student," a punishing "teacher," and a commanding experimenter. However, in reviewing his description of the possible factors that make spatial proximity so important, it is apparent that they could also apply to the other social location variables. We are more likely to receive the empathic cues from those who are close to us—spatially, temporally, and socially—than from those who are distant. Those who are close to us are less likely to be put "out of mind," more likely to observe our actions, and so on. We find it difficult to ignore what occurs in our presence, although whether we recognize its significance and chose to respond or not is another issue. Thus, in considering the relevant literature within social psychology, our consciousness and its impact on our social relations are of primary concern.[13] With this focus in mind, it is now possible to further delineate the concept of social affinity.

A Theoretical Elaboration of Social Affinity

Social affinity may be understood in terms of three dimensions: Social consciousness, sentiment, and action. In this respect, it bears some resemblance to an attitude—defined as "a learned and relatively enduring tendency or predisposition to evaluate a person, event, or situation in a certain way and to act in accordance with that evaluation" (Vander Zanden 1987: 173–174)—although it is much more involved. However, understanding something more simple—like an attitude—can prove to be enlightening when trying to comprehend a more complex process, such as the emergence of social affinity. With this in mind, drawing comparisons between an attitude and social affinity will be helpful.

As mentioned earlier in this chapter, an attitude involves three components: a cognitive, an affective, and a conative—or behavioral—component (Breckler 1984). The way in which we perceive a particular person, group, event, or situation, is referred to as the "cognitive component." The "affective component" refers to the emotions evoked by what we perceive. Given our perception and affective response, we have a tendency to act in a particular way toward that which we have perceived. This is the "behavioral component" of attitudes. However, because this is a tendency, we may or may not follow through with what we are inclined to do.

In a similar vein, social affinity comprises three dimensions that bear an interesting resemblance to the components of an attitude. Again, these dimensions include social consciousness, sentiment, and action. The meaning of the term "social consciousness" is a bit deeper than terms such as "cognition" or "perception." Social consciousness first implies that one is aware of or perceives something. Such is the extent of the definition of perception. However, the meaning of social consciousness goes even further in that it suggests that there is some understanding or grasp of that "something" by the one who perceives it. Thus, social consciousness involves becoming aware of a person, group, situation, or condition and having an understanding of its implications, connotations, meanings, and consequences. In this sense, it also implies more than the term "cognition." Social consciousness is the topic of chapter 5.

The "affective" component of social affinity is referred to as "sentiment"—a term that includes a wide variety of emotions. Among the most relevant of these emotions for our understanding of social affinity is empathy. Empathy is an "action of understanding, being aware of, being sensitive to, and vicariously experiencing the feelings, thoughts, and experience of another of either the past or present [and the projected future] without having the feelings, thoughts, and experience fully communicated in an objectively explicit manner."[14] In other words, while the "one" who is empathetic does not directly experience the situation or condition faced by the "other," the former is able to *identify with* the feelings, thoughts, and experiences of the latter.[15] Because empathy is able to transcend time—as well as space and difference—personal contact between the "one" and the "other" (or a similar experience of a similar situation or condition) is not *necessary*. Yet, as discussed with regard to the impact of one's social location, such personal contact *enhances* the likelihood of empathy. However, what is essential for empathy is that there be some *identification with* the situation or condition of an "other" and some *feeling* arising out of this identification.

Sociologically, empathy is an affective state that stems from our grasp of another's emotional state, and that is congruent with it (see Gruen and Mendelsohn 1986; Wispé 1986). In other words, the empathetic person is one who is feeling the same kind of emotions—whether they be sorrow, joy, anger, and so on—that others are feeling, although it may not be to the same degree.[16] With empathy we are genuinely experiencing the emotion, not just responding to another's emotion. Moreover, having a grasp of another's emotional state implies that we have a full understanding of what they are experiencing *from their perspective*—at least insofar as humanly possible. We have stepped into their shoes—engaged in role-taking—in order to see and experience the world as *they* do. The role of sentiments—and empathy in particular—in the emergence of social affinity is the topic of chapter 6.

The third dimension of social affinity is "action." Action not only implies "a thing done" but suggests that an alteration or change arises out of that behavior or experience. Focusing on the latter aspect of this definition, alterations or changes may occur at many different levels. Such a change may be as simple as a change in one's attitude or as complex as a social revolution. This suggests that there are many different types of action that fall on a sort of continuum from the internal (e.g., personal growth) to the external (e.g., intervention in social affairs), all of which are tied to social affinity. However, because social affinity includes the sentiments underlying moral obligation, action in the context of social affinity at least includes an internal transformation. Without such a change, all further actions are empty of empathy—the basic sentiment allowing for affinity. Yet, this continuum between internal and external action further suggests that, once social affinity is established, the likelihood of external actions are enhanced or reinforced. Action is the topic of chapter 7.

Social consciousness, sentiment, and action together comprise a useful analytical tool for understanding the emergence of social affinity. Moreover, they are mutually interdependent, each one enhancing or diminishing the strength of the others. In fact, it may be helpful to think of them as necessary conditions for the presence of social affinity, although none of them (alone) is a *sufficient* condition. One may be fully aware of a situation and act on behalf of an "other," but without the feeling of empathy, social affinity is not present. A rather simplistic example is the person who may be aware of the condition of muscular dystrophy and may give money to the March of Dimes without feeling an affinity toward those who have muscular dystrophy. Such an act is purely external and mechanical. Thus, social affinity requires an internal action—a transformation that cannot be perceived through behavior alone. As an even more extreme example, another person may have a lot of old clothes that she gives to the Salvation Army so that she may deduct the donation from her taxes. It is not possible to say that this person shows an affinity for those who wear the clothes she donated. Based on the information given here, there is no indication that she perceived the condition of poverty, that she empathized with those who are impoverished, and there is no evidence of an internal action or change. In neither case is it apparent that the individual is acting upon feelings of moral obligation. Thus, to reiterate, all three dimensions act in concert with one another. From the previous examples, it is possible to summarize our understanding of social affinity with the following equation:

Social Consciousness + Sentiment + Action = Social Affinity

However, as is further elaborated in chapter 7, these dimensions do not have to occur in a particular, linear order. In fact, they exist in a circular relationship such that each condition is built upon and reinforces the others.

A full understanding of social affinity requires a concomitant understanding of its opposite: apathy.[17] While recognizing that a problem or situation exists, those who are apathetic lack any feeling or emotion in response. In addition, the apathetic are unresponsive to that problem or situation. There is a lack of interest in it, and a lack of concern for those involved. While there are certain necessary conditions for there to be social affinity, it is the *lack* of these conditions that may be labeled "apathy." From this definition, it is possible to assert that, while an apathetic person *perceives* a problem or situation, he or she does not fully grasp its underlying implications or consequences. An individual who sees a homeless person begging for money on the street may not be aware of the social factors involved in homelessness and therefore blame the homeless for their circumstances. In other words, just because someone is aware of the homeless does not mean that he or she is fully conscious of homelessness itself. Because social consciousness is necessary for the development of social affinity, such a potential is cut off at the root when a person does nothing more than perceive a problem or situation.

The definition of apathy given here also makes clear that there can be no empathy on the part of the apathetic. Setting aside the fact that social consciousness is conducive to the emergence of empathy, the apathetic show a general lack of concern or even interest in the given situation. Such an attitude, as already noted, undermines the possibility of an internal change or action making social affinity fully realized. Interestingly, it may be argued that inaction is in itself a form of action—a decision to "not act"—although as a form of "negative action," it is qualitatively different from that of a person who has an affinity. While the apathetic do nothing in response to a given problem or situation, the person with an affinity allows that situation to affect him or her in such a way as to bring about an internal change (action) that can, in turn, lead to external actions—changes in behavior.

The model pictured in Figure 2.1 summarizes the distinctions made in the discussion of social affinity and apathy. As noted, apathy is charac-

FIG. 2.1.
Affinity and its relation with apathy and hostility.

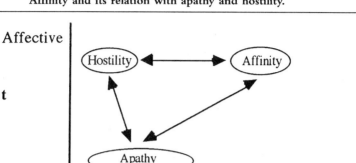

Action

terized by indifference and a lack of interest, concern, and emotion. As such, it falls at the "affectless" end of the vertical, "affect" axis. Because it can include anything from neutral inaction (i.e., "unbiased" or "value-neutral") to a form of negative action, or action through inaction (e.g., a "sin of omission") apathy extends from the "negative" to the neutral points along the horizontal, "action" axis. Hostility is characterized by enmity and thus falls at the "affective" end of the affect axis. In addition, hostility takes the form of such things as prejudice, discrimination, and war, thus falling at the "negative" end of the action axis. Because affinity is characterized by empathy, it too falls at the "affective" end of the affect axis. However, because it is exhibited in compassionate action, affinity lies at the "positive" end of the action axis.[18]

Moreover, there are continuums between each of the three categories. In other words, there is a continuum extending from apathy to hostility, from hostility to affinity, and from affinity to apathy. This research focuses on the last continuum (see Fig. 2.2), with occasional references to the hostility category. With this continuum in mind, a helpful way to begin an analysis of social affinity is to compare those who are low in this quality with those who are high. The next two chapters present a four-point typology extending from low to high social affinity, each type representing a different level of social commitment. After the typology is introduced, we break social affinity down into its three dimensions, focusing on each in more detail. Finally, the social location variables of social, spatial, and temporal proximity and distance are reintroduced and their relationship with social affinity more fully explored.

FIG. 2.2.
The continuum between apathy and affinity.

Apathy   Affinity

THREE

The Construction of
Social Issues, Part I

Compartmentalizing the Self and Society

There are many ways to approach the study of social affinity. Perhaps one of the most informative is to look at social affinity within the context of social issues. Social issues provide compelling opportunities for individuals to expand their sympathies beyond the personal level to the societal level. They comprise a major area in which people have a forum to play out their commitment to the larger society. The most visible example of this commitment is reaching out and taking action on behalf of others. Such prosocial behavior is an observable manifestation of an individual's inner commitments. By reaching out to others around them, individuals exhibit their commitment to their social environs.

The realm of "social issues" is quite broad. In order to narrow the field from social issues in general, hunger, AIDS, and an issue selected by the respondent were chosen as comparative issues within which it is possible to examine the topic of social affinity. These social issues were strategically chosen. The two issues of AIDS and hunger were selected as the focus because their social meanings complement one another. While AIDS is a rather recent development historically, hunger is comparatively timeless as an issue (i.e., involving temporal proximity and distance). It is a worldwide phenomenon, although somewhat removed from the attention of the average American in that its domestic manifestations do not receive much media attention. Such coverage is usually restricted to famines in other parts of the world (i.e., social and spatial distance). In addition, and somewhat ironically given the breadth of the hunger issue described later,

Americans are less likely to know someone who is hungry than someone who has AIDS unless they make a conscious effort to reach out to the hungry.[1] Unlike AIDS, hunger is an issue that does not cross differences in social class and potentially affect everybody (i.e., it is socially distant).

By comparison, AIDS in the United States has received widespread media attention. AIDS is an issue that has some stigma attached to it while it still has the potential of directly or indirectly affecting everybody (i.e., it is both socially distant and proximate). It knows no geographical borders (i.e., both spatial distance and proximity). In addition, it has many long-term and short-term implications (i.e., involving both temporal distance and proximity) beginning at the individual level and extending out to include broad social policy issues (i.e., social and spatial distance/proximity)—both domestic and international.

As is discussed later, individuals view different issues in very distinct ways depending upon their own personal experiences. In a world as large and complicated as our own, it is not possible for an individual to have an affinity for everything and everyone, or even toward every social issue. Even an individual who sees all social issues as equally worthy cannot address all of them with the same degree of commitment. It is necessary to pick and choose where one is to express his or her affinity. Some issues are quite broad and comprehensive, such as human rights, while others are quite focused, such as the Cuban refugee crisis. Even if one focuses on human rights, other issues such as racism, which can be classified under the "human rights" umbrella, are left for others to address. Since not everyone is drawn to the issues of hunger or AIDS, research participants were also asked about the issue that they felt was most important at this time. In other words, they were given the opportunity to describe where their affinities lay. It was therefore possible to compare an issue in which they were interested with one in which they were not. Of course, some respondents selected hunger or AIDS as their top issue. This was also necessary in order to compare them with those who were not focused on these issues.

For the purposes of this and the following four chapters, the examples are limited to hunger and AIDS. The issues listed as most important by the research respondents are the focus of chapter 8, in which the concept of social affinity and the delineation of its development and experience—as detailed in chapters 5, 6, and 7—are used as a basis for analyzing these issues.

Very few comparative studies between different social issues have been conducted. Most research focuses on single issues, such as Gordon Allport's classic *The Nature of Prejudice* (1954) and Jay MacLeod's work on poverty and youth culture, *Ain't No Makin' It* (1987). Assertions can and have been made about how a particular issue is portrayed in society and thought of by individuals. These studies are very important; however, by juxtaposing two or more issues, it is possible to highlight the unique characteristics of each issue as well as what characterizes social issues in general in terms of how they are thought of and portrayed. Since there are innumerable books on the issues of hunger, AIDS, and so on, this chapter is not an examination of the unique qualities of each social issue *per se,* but focuses on those things that social issues have in common in terms of how they are viewed by individuals. However, in order to give the reader a basic picture of each of these issues, it is necessary to introduce each in turn.

The Hunger Issue

> Someone must raise the bar, and urge us to reach higher—because when emergency food requests grow by 26 percent in a year and shelter requests by 13 percent, something is very wrong in America.
> —Boston Mayor Raymond L. Flynn, 1991

Hunger is as timeless an issue as AIDS is recent. It is defined as "a group of symptoms that come about because of a shortage of food in the body. It goes deeper than an empty stomach. Hunger weakens the body and slows down its activities."[2] When hunger reaches the point of starvation, "the body begins to devour its vital proteins in a desperate attempt to get the nutrients it needs." However, hunger is much more than a medical problem in that it is a manifestation of the even larger issue of poverty. As poverty grows in the United States, so does hunger. As of late 1993, 36.9 million Americans were living in poverty, representing 14.5 percent of our country's total population and an increase of 1.2 million over the previous year. Moreover, the number of poor increased at three times the rate of the rise in population. Together, poverty and hunger are the two leading factors in the poor health of infants and children in the United States.

Within the United States today, hunger is more prevalent than it was even a mere ten to fifteen years ago. Every night, 30 million Americans go to bed hungry. It is estimated that between 20 and 30 million people in this country are malnourished. In fact, in 1990 the United States ranked nineteenth in the world with regard to infant mortality rates, due in part to "our lack of prenatal concern for hungry/malnourished mothers." Children under eighteen years of age account for 12 million of the hungry in our country, and 12 million more are considered to be "at risk" for hunger. Hunger also disproportionately affects people of color. Blacks and Latinos are three times more likely to go hungry than Caucasians, while Native Americans are six times more likely. The elderly are also adversely affected; 30 percent of them skip meals on a daily basis due to lack of money. There are between 500,000 and 1 million malnourished seniors and another 5 million considered to be at risk for hunger.

While there is enough food to feed the world's population three times over, 40 million people die of hunger each year, and 15 million of these are children under the age of five. Contrary to popular belief, only a small proportion of these deaths were due to famine. Ninety percent of deaths attributed to hunger "result from chronic, persistent hunger rather than famine."[3] Moreover, for those who do not die as a result of chronic hunger, the condition also leads to excessive medical difficulties throughout the individual's life because the immune system may be impaired, increasing susceptibility to infectious diseases. The lack of nutrients can affect all organs of the body. For example, 250,000 children go blind every year because of a lack of Vitamin A. Without proper nourishment, even common conditions such as a cold or diarrhea can be fatal. As a result, "more people have died of hunger in the last five years than died in all the wars, revolutions, and murders in the last 150 years," making hunger the world's number one single killer; and lurking underneath this issue of hunger is the question of economic injustice.

The AIDS Issue

> How many people have to die to make it cost efficient
> for you people to do something about it? . . . Give us a
> number so we won't annoy you again until the amount
> of money you begin spending on lawsuits makes it more
> profitable for you to save people than to kill them.
> —Dr. Don Francis, Centers for Disease Control

Since 1981, AIDS has emerged as the leading cause of death among Americans between the ages of twenty-five and forty-four.[4] At that time, AIDS was referred to as the "gay cancer." There were eighty known cases and twenty-six deaths attributed to this disease (Shilts 1993). This new disease was later known as GRID—Gay-Related Immune Deficiency—even though it was already apparent that people other than gay men had contracted the virus, namely Haitian immigrants, intravenous drug users and their infants, hemophiliacs, and those receiving blood transfusions from a tainted blood supply. This initial association between AIDS and gay men was to suffuse the epidemic with issues of morality and civil rights. While it is known that heterosexuals are just as susceptible to the disease, the initial stigma remains.

As of January 1, 1996, there were 513,486 people diagnosed with AIDS and more than 315,000 fatalities attributed to AIDS-related complications in the United States. Moreover, there are an estimated 650,000 to 900,000 Americans who are HIV positive.[5] Seventy percent of those infected do not know their HIV status, and one person is newly diagnosed with AIDS every seven minutes. One in four of all new HIV infections occur among those who are twenty-one years old or younger, leading to projections of an "AIDS boom" within this age group. Among men, it is estimated that one in ninety-two between the ages of twenty-seven and thirty-nine is already infected with HIV. As a result, more women diagnosed with AIDS in 1995 were infected through sex with a male partner than through injection drug use. Among African-American men, HIV-related illnesses account for 33.3 percent of deaths.

In the United States, we are oftentimes so focused on AIDS within our borders that we forget it is a worldwide epidemic. In this study, not one person interviewed referred to AIDS outside of the United States. And yet, as of October 1995, more than 22 million people were already infected worldwide,[6] and it is estimated that by the year 2000 between 30 and 40 million people will be HIV positive.[7] Around the globe, two men and two women are infected with HIV every minute and, in many countries, an estimated 60 percent of new HIV infections are among fifteen to twenty-four year olds. Ten years ago, there were few women infected with HIV; today women represent 50 percent of all new cases. Further underscoring the fact that AIDS is not a gay-related disease is the fact that heterosexual sex accounts for over 90 percent of all newly infected adults. Clearly, AIDS is a social issue of some urgency, both nationally and globally.

A Typology of Individual Orientations Toward Social Issues

Upon close examination of the interview data, it became quite apparent that individuals fall into one of several broad categories or types in terms of how they view a particular social issue, whether it be hunger, AIDS, or some other issue, such as the one the interviewees picked as being most important. When discussing an issue, individuals relate to it within the context of their lives and experiences. In doing so, they reveal a part of their innermost consciousness—the way in which they have constructed the issue in their minds, their feelings about the issue, and their behaviors toward the issue. Within these three broad areas, there are wide variations in the particulars from individual to individual. And yet, as an outside observer, it is possible to take a step back and see the similarities as well as the differences. At that point, it becomes possible to categorize individuals in terms of their orientation toward the issue, although it must be emphasized that the boundaries between each type are not so distinct in the majority of cases as they are presented here.

These types—of which there are four—each represent a different level of commitment toward a particular social issue. However, these different types also represent—at a more abstract level—the individual's level of attachment to society within a specific context. This typology serves as an indicator of one's degree of social affinity within the context of social issues—one's commitment to individuals, the community, and society beyond the individual's self. In other words, these four types represent different points along the continuum from low to high social affinity. While an individual's placement in the typology represents a form of judgment, it must be emphasized that this is not a moral assessment of the individual himself or herself. As is discussed in more detail later, an individual's location within the typology varies from issue to issue. Moreover, an individual's orientation toward an issue fluctuates over time and under different circumstances. No overall judgment of the individual is intended or implied. Instead, an examination of this typology is a useful tool for understanding the way in which such an orientation toward an issue is socially constructed and is a concrete means for examining the abstract concept of social affinity.

The first two types represent those who have not made a link between a social issue and the society outside of themselves. The types that reflect this orientation toward social issues are the *nonreferenced* type and the *self-referenced* type. The next two elements of the typology—the *relationally referenced* type and the *socially referenced* type—represent those who have begun to step outside of their own life sphere and focus on the impact of a given social issue on others. In this and the following chapter, each of these types is discussed in turn, focusing first on the nonreferenced and the self-referenced and then, in chapter 4, on the relationally referenced and the socially referenced. A detailed case study is provided for each—either in the context of hunger or AIDS. Following each case study, there is additional commentary linking the narrative with the type it represents. In that way, the details of each type will be more fully explored. These case studies—as well as additional interview and other materials—and the types they represent will be used as a springboard for the analysis of social affinity in subsequent chapters.

The Nonreferenced Type—"It's Not My Problem!"

Those falling into the nonreferenced type do not focus their attention on the issue at all. A commitment to the issue or those affected by it has not developed at any level. As such, the nonreferenced type represents a low degree of social affinity. Sometimes, as is seen in the case of Leslie, this lack of commitment is a conscious decision. Many times it is largely unconscious. The individuals do not think the issue can realistically affect themselves or those they know and so they do not think about it at any great length. Moreover, they are not concerned with the impact the issue has or may have on society itself and feel that it is not a part of their sphere of responsibility. In fact, it may not even have occurred to them to consider this possibility in the first place.

LESLIE MUSCOVITZ

Leslie is a young, white woman training as a physical therapist with an emphasis on sports medicine. She presented a relaxed and noncommittal demeanor during the interview and took the same approach to social issues in general, except for her top issue of health care. While she talked about her concern for hunger and AIDS, it became apparent that it was at a very superficial level.

She lived in many different places while she was growing up because her father would move from one job to another. He stayed in the same field of manufacturing throughout, but he was never really happy with the jobs themselves. Her mother also worked, but never in a career-oriented position. Leslie has an older brother and a younger sister. The older brother is considered the "black sheep" of the family. Leslie mentioned that he's a waiter, but says he's very lazy, hates to work, drinks heavily, and does a lot of drugs. He frequently ends up getting evicted and "bumming off" of Leslie and her sister. This experience with her brother plays a significant role in Leslie's attitudes regarding the issue of hunger.[8]

The first kind of thing that comes into my mind when I think of hunger is Ethiopia and stuff—those kinds of things that were always drilled into your head: people starving in Third World countries. That's usually what I think when I hear of hunger. People keep telling you, "Oh, there's all this poverty and all this hunger out there." And so you hear that and you just kind of know that it's there. Maybe, for all I know, it's not there at all! I've just been told that it's there. It's not like I saw it first hand or anything. It seems so abstract. It's kind of like not there for me, although you would think that it should be. It doesn't affect me, so I don't really think about it so much. I know that's really awful to say, but it's such a big issue that I just don't think too much about it. I feel bad and stuff, but I'm like, "Well, what am I going to do about it?" And that's kind of what everyone does and then nothing gets done. But that's kind of how it is.

But also, there's such a problem here as well as in other countries. I see it in Boston—the people on the streets and stuff like that. Although, being in this neighborhood, I think I have a bad impression of what kind of people are hungry. I think there's respectable bums and then regular bums and I just think all the people around here are druggies. I think of that as their fault, although it's not always necessarily theirs. And then I think of families, kids starving, inner city children and stuff like that. They're born into it. So, when I think about hunger around here, I tend to place blame on certain people. It's not very fair, but . . . I have a really big thing for people who are drug and alcohol users. It's a problem and I see that they got themselves into it, even though it might not necessarily be true. So, it's kind of like I discriminate against those types of people. But when I think about the children—once in a while you see somebody with a kid around here, but not too often—I start to think, "Well, then they're hungry." That kind of bothers me.

Another reason why I kind of have a prejudice against people around here is because I have tried to give food. We'll be out on the front steps or something and we'll offer a piece of pizza to somebody who asks us for a buck. "Well, have a slice of pizza. I don't have a dollar." And they say, "No, I want a dollar." They want drugs. That's all they want. My sister will walk home from a restaurant and she'll give her leftovers to somebody who's on the street. I've done that a few times, trying to get people food. They don't usually take it around here. Usually they want money. I don't have a problem giving people money for food. It all depends on what they're going to use it for. And how do you know how they're going to use the money? You don't know, so I'd rather give them food because I know that's going to directly take care of the problem at hand.

With food drives and stuff, I'll give cans and stuff like that. It's not like I go out of my way to search for them though! If there's things that you can do and it's easy—if it's there—then you do it. "Oh, I don't need these cans of corn anyways, so I think I'll give them to somebody else." It's not a big deal. I don't know if it's necessarily because it makes me feel good or because I just do things like that. Although, you never know what gets to where. I've always heard stories that it doesn't necessarily end up where you think it's going to end up. That makes me angry. It's just another big system thing. There's so much bureaucratic stuff going on that it just never gets to where it's supposed to go. It's kind of sad.

I just don't know how effective it is unless I personally go out and give the food to somebody. If I give somebody around here food, then I feel effective; but if I give it to some place, I don't know how effective it is. I imagine it gets to where it's gotta go, but I don't know. I'm not so trusting of those things. I guess it depends on how much you know about the organization. I mean, if it was my organization, then I would prefer to give to it over giving to someone on the street. Feeding people and stuff like that—if you do it more personally—it's a little bit easier to know what's going on and there's less red tape and fewer people being paid for this or something. Nonprofit organizations still have to support the people who work there and so it's just kind of like there's an extra middleman who's getting a little something. It's not like they're making all this money, but there's still extra money involved and it's not going directly to feeding people. It's just doesn't seem right. Who's to trust all these other people? I don't know. You see all these frauds going on with food stamps and stuff and it just amazes you. I saw that on 20/20. People buy food stamps off of people so that they have money to buy drugs. Wonderful! That's nice! It's amazing.

I've never really known anyone who's gone hungry—just college students! That's not really hungry. I've known when money's gotten real tight with people and stuff like that. It's scary because then it can really get to be a problem. Sometimes I worry about my brother because he's probably on the streets for all I know. He just gets kicked out of places and stuff, so he could definitely be one who goes hungry. But I don't really think about it unless it gets real bad. Recently, I was working with him and he got fired. Then he went to another place and he got fired from there. He was kicked out of his apartment, he didn't have any money, and he was kind of bugging my sister a lot. See, he's like one of those bad people: he had money to go out and get drunk, yet he didn't have money for food or for rent. I can still be prejudiced against that because I just feel like it's his own fault. He bums money off of us. Lately, it's been a concern just because he was bothering my sister so much and my sister had to deal with it and she was freaking out. She said, "Don's coming over drunk and he's trying to get food and trying to get money." He'd rather not do something as opposed to do something. He's very lazy and it's just a pain in the butt to have to deal with it, but that's him. That's just kind of sad. It's not nice to think about your own brother being like that.

So, hunger is something that I feel I should be concerned about, but I'm not because there's so many other things to think about. Why bother your whole day worrying about everything when you can just focus on certain things that really just touch home. It would be great—an ideal world—if everybody could think about these things and cure them, but it's not going to happen. I wouldn't even know where to begin!

———————

Leslie opens by noting how abstract the hunger issue is for her, a point that is underscored by the fact that the first thing she thinks of with regard to hunger is Ethiopia—a country about which she has very little knowledge and no experience. She jokes around that it might not exist at all, saying "Maybe, for all I know, it's not there at all! I've just been told that it's there. It's not like I saw it first hand or anything. It seems so abstract. It's kind of like not there for me. . . ." This joking attitude indicates that, as far as she is concerned, global hunger really does not exist. It's not a part of her experience. Her only contact has been through media coverage of the famine there—information that is "drilled into your head." Leslie has a lot of knowledge with regard to the issue, but most of it exists only in her head. It has no independent reality for her and there is no personal emotional connection.

However, when it comes to domestic hunger, the issue becomes more real for Leslie. In fact, it is so real for her that she has an elaborate system of beliefs and opinions on the topic. In addition to her negative experiences on the street and with her brother, she falls back on stories she has heard to back up her views. While this knowledge is just as purely intellectual as her knowledge of Ethiopia, she accepts it uncritically as reality. Hunger does seem to bother Leslie at some level, but she concludes by saying that she is not concerned with the issue because it does not "touch home." And while her experience with her brother is about as "close to home" as this issue is for her, she does her best to push it and any claims of responsibility aside because of the inconvenience for her. As a result, and in relation to hunger, she can be characterized as belonging to the nonreferenced type.

By her own admission, she is not committed to the issue, even though she donates food on occasion—when it is convenient. It is also apparent that she has few, if any, positive feelings toward the hungry—with the notable exception of children—nor those organizations created to address the issue. While she says several times that, "it's sad," these phrases come across as having little meaning for her, almost as if she says them because that is what is expected of her. While her attempts at giving food to the homeless make her somewhat exceptional among the nonreferenced, these acts carry the same overtone, like they are mechanical attempts at helping when it is convenient for herself and so long as they play by her rules. She does not trust these individuals or organizations and is often frustrated and angered by them. Given these feelings, she has set up a barrier between herself and those who either are affected by or who are addressing the issue—a barrier apparent in her stories and even in her language, as the use of the words "bum" and "bumming" indicate. While Leslie is not concerned with the issue itself, it is apparent that she also is not concerned about or committed to those suffering from hunger or even those organizations attempting to relieve the problem.[9] She falls short of seeing the issue within a societal or even personal context.

An interesting twist to her story is that Leslie at least had the potential of being categorized as relationally referenced on this issue—a type that is discussed later. The figure of her older brother embodies her orientation to the issue. She sees what is going on in his life and knows why it is happening. Her response, however, is one of anger and resentment more than concern. While "it is sad," she refuses to sacrifice her own self in order to help him out. As she notes, her individuality and independence are paramount—and so it is with regard to hunger in general. Leslie will not allow herself to be committed to the issue or those it affects beyond what is convenient and best for herself. Her degree of social affinity in relation to the hunger issue is quite low.

The Self-Referenced Type— "It Could Be Anybody . . . Even Me!"

Individuals who are self-referenced with regard to an issue focus on that issue in terms of its impact on themselves. Other considerations, if they exist at all, are purely secondary. Their commitment to the issue exists insofar as it affects or has the potential to affect their own life. At this level, the individual has not gone beyond their selves when understanding an issue. They may be intellectually aware of the larger facts, but they remain focused on how the issue has or may have an effect on *them*. Thus, social ties have not yet entered the picture and they remain on the lower end of the continuum of social affinity.

This frequently happens with AIDS. Many heterosexuals were not concerned with it at all so long as it was a "gay disease." They were non-referenced. But when they found out it could be transmitted to *anybody*— including themselves—*then* they concerned themselves with the issue. In fact, Silva Suarez, whose views and experiences with hunger will be presented in the following case study, says it best:

> *I even had the stupid mentality that it only hit homosexuals. Now that I think about it, that's so stupid. How could you think that? . . . But then, when my knowledge of AIDS progressed and I found it happened to heterosexuals also, it changed a lot. Then it could hit me . . . so, I better do something about it. I'm going to protect myself.*

SILVA SUAREZ

Silva was born to a Cuban father and a Mexican-Aztec mother. She doesn't know her father that well because he was not around during much of her childhood. However, she is close to his family since they live only a half-hour drive away. While Silva is much closer to her mother, that side of the family has been thoroughly integrated into United States culture—something with which she is not enamored. Silva strongly identifies with her Cuban heritage, and, for this reason, she considers the Cuban refugee crisis to be her most important social issue.

However, she also has personal ties with the hunger issue. When her father left, her mother had to go to work. Her mother worked the graveyard shift because she wanted to be home with Silva during the day. Making ends meet was no easy task, and they were in a precarious economic position throughout much of Silva's childhood. Hunger was an issue she personally experienced, something that has left its mark on her outlook.

Emptiness. Hunger brings to mind emptiness, sorrow. It's just a feeling that no one should have. No human being should ever experience it because there's so much food in the whole world. No human being should be in hunger. I don't care what race they are. I don't care where they're from. So many countries are in poverty; but in America, there's also a lot of people who are in poverty. We forget that sometimes because we know there's so much food here. How could someone be hungry? Well, it happens a lot. A lot of people say, "Well, we feed other countries, why don't we feed America? Why don't we do both?" And it must be really sad when a parent can't provide that for a child. It must be the saddest thing. They must feel so incompetent to bring a child into this world, loving it, and then not being able to give it food. It must be the ultimate. . . . Hunger is something I've experienced; not to the extent that those people have, in the sense that I'm sure there's people who have been hungry for days on end. I've never experienced that hunger, but I've experienced my mother's not being able to give me milk or buy a thing like that in a society which we live in. It's pretty bad in itself. So, there's different degrees of hunger and I'm sure different people have experienced different degrees of it. There shouldn't be any degree, but obviously there is. It's just something that shouldn't happen.

When you're little, you look up to your parents and they're supposed to give everything. A child never thinks that a parent is not going to be able to give. And when a parent says they can't, it's devastating. "What do you mean you can't?" They don't understand. There was one situation I can remember when my mother didn't have money for milk. We didn't have money for food, for anything. My mother always had this tendency to leave money laying around. She'd always wrap it up and put it somewhere, but she never remembered where she put it. So, I was looking through my drawer one day and I found a hundred dollars. "Mommy, I found a hundred dollars!" She said, "Silva, stop playing around now, okay? because I'm thinking of how to do this." "But Mommy look, I got it." She wouldn't believe me. I was going on and she wouldn't believe me. She thought I was talking about Monopoly money—fake money—because I was so small. She said, "What do you mean? Silva, the paper money doesn't count. That doesn't work."

I finally gave her the money and she started weeping. She just started weeping right in front of me. She never cries. My mother cry? No way! But she started crying and crying and she hugged me and she kissed me. "Where did you find this?" "It was in the drawer." And she's like, "Oh, my gosh!" And she was extremely happy and of course we went out and got some food, she paid some bills, we were okay for about two or three weeks. "Somehow," she's always said, "God looks after us." And she's always said, "God put it in your mind to go into that drawer and go looking." I was such a small child. I was about four or five at the most and you just know to look through things. I could understand that my mother didn't have anything for me and I was going to look. She said, "How has that happened? God has always been a part of our life in the sense that, whenever we were in distress, He always came through." And so my hunger wasn't for more than a day or two. It was only for a few hours at the most, but I felt it anyway, that feeling of emptiness, of wanting to consume, of not wanting my belly to growl. I can't imagine a person having that feeling for three or four days. And ever since then, my mom's always stocked up the fridge. She's always said, "The basement's full of canned goods just in case the bomb drops." But it was amazing how something like that could happen to us.

I saw it in front of me. I understood it. But at the same time, I had to go to school and the people I went to school with never felt this. And as a child growing up, you sort of put that aside because the kids are not going to like me if I tell them what's going on. They're going to think I'm weird or far removed from them so they won't be my friend. So, on the one hand, you know what's going on in the world and you know there's poor people; you know the feeling, and that's good. But by the same token, you want to have friends, you want to be loved by other people, and you want to get involved and people don't want to hear it.

Once they give their money, that's it, they don't want to hear it anymore. If you preach about hunger all the time, you're not going to be liked, or you are, but not by the type of people you want to be. It was hard because I felt it; but I was raised in a town that didn't. So, I knew what was going on, but at the same time I didn't talk about it or anything because I knew the kids wouldn't like me and wouldn't hang out with me because of that—or at least that was my fear.

And actually, I have never told that story to anyone in my life except for you and my mother. That's because we live in a society where we're supposed to be afraid if we were ever hungry. That's our secret, mother and I. People don't know how it was for me growing up with my mother. We don't talk about that because our society teaches us not to. We shun away the poor and unwanted, so we don't talk about it. I think a lot of people are far removed from the issue. They feel pity for the people who have felt hunger, but they're far removed from it. They know the fact that if they didn't have food, they'd be very sad. They'd be very depressed and so forth. They feel pity and so they bring out the purse and take out a couple of quarters and dimes and go call that 1-800 number on the television and then they feel good because they fed 100 or 200 people in some country. So, they feel good and they go on with their lives and that's it. And then once they see another commercial, well then they'll call again and then the guilts will go away. That's a bit condescending. But in our society, people are like that and that's the reality. What hits home is when they see it on television, because they're so far removed from it. That's the only time they get sad—when they see it on television or maybe if someone talks to them about it, which is probably very rare.

I have mixed feelings on this issue. There's the people on the street. If I see an able man ask for money, I feel very angry. If I see a mother and two children ask for money, I'll give them money. Maybe it's because of the way my mother brought me up. She's always said, "If you're an able man, there's work for you. If you're a woman and you have two or three kids, that makes life harder." Not to say that you're not going to find a job because that can obviously happen; but it's harder and I have more sympathy for a woman who has kids who can't support herself than I do for a man who is 30 or 40 years old and begging for money. Maybe that's just me, but I don't have any sympathy for them. If you're an able man, I'm sure you can find a job. Maybe it will be garbage picking, but it's something.

There's a lot of bums asking for money where I live. Sometimes, I'll be in a good mood and I'll give them money, and other times I'll just be disgusted. My favorite ones though are the ones who play music.[10] *I love those. I'll give the ones who play the violin or the saxophone money because   feel as if they're doing something. They're not just begging. At least th i've actually taken the time to learn an instrument. And I kind of enjoy them a lot. I actually just sit there and listen sometimes because I find it so fascinating. I think that's really neat that they just sit there and play. Some of them are really good. It's amazing. They should actually be in an orchestra. They shouldn't be there. It's funny. At least they're doing something; whereas if someone's just standing there asking for money and you're an able man, then you can do something else. The time you're spending there asking for money, you could be earning money. That's what I always think.*

People also like to give money to organizations that feed the hungry, but you don't know if the food gets to them. What about going to a shelter and feeding these people with food instead of money? What they need is the food, not the money. I think of it, not as a money thing, but as a "get a pan and cook some beans" sort of thing, because that's what they need. They don't need money; they need food, substance, water. I've never sent money to those organizations for the simple reason that I thought, "Well, they don't need the money, they need the food." I would be more apt to go to a shelter and start cooking for someone than I would to give money to the organization. When my mother worked for the church, we'd cook for free. And there were a lot of poor Hispanic people who would come. They knew that the food was free and that was fine because it was a church thing and I think that made them feel good. So, I would help my mother in the kitchen and she'd be cooking her tacos. My mother is an excellent cook. And she'd cook and cook, and I'd help her.

But in something so public as a shelter, everybody knows what you're doing. I would be more comfortable inviting a poor couple into my home and feeding them. My mother has done this numerous times. She's invited people she knows who don't have money, who don't have food, to come over. "Oh, well, I'll make you something." At church she'll say, "Why don't you come over." She wouldn't say, "Do you want to come over and eat? because I know you're hungry." That would make them feel bad, especially a man and a wife who have two or three children. They don't want to feel pitied, and my mother knows that. So, she would say, "I have a present for the kids," or "why don't you bring the kids over to play with the cat?" They'll start conversations. "Well, maybe you can help with the church. Maybe you can come over and we can talk about what you can do for the next show we're doing." They feel better about it if it's something that they're doing for you more than something you're doing for them.

I see that as more admirable and more self-fulfilling than going to a shelter and feeding people because society knows what you're doing if you work at a shelter. In your home, that's more gratifying. You also get to know them better. I got to know them; whereas in a shelter, you're just going to be, "Bye. Next one. Food. Bye." If they're over to the house, you get to talk to them and say, "How are you doing? What are you doing? Is there a way I can help you?" It's more of a one-to-one, personal feeling. You get to know them and maybe you'll have a friend at the same time, which is good. I could see myself doing that more than I can see myself going to a shelter. Not to say that shelters and soup kitchens are bad, because they're wonderful institutions and someday maybe even I will do it; but I feel more comfortable in a private situation because my mom did it. It's so self-fulfilling—much more so than just feeding 50 million people a day, if you think about it.

So, I've never worked in a shelter or anything like that. I've always wanted to have the experience, but I've never really done it. Fear has held me back. Fear of meeting people who've been in the situation I have been in. Fear of knowing people who've felt what I had at one time and just knowing that there's people like that in the world. And sure, I can feed this one and feed the other one, but I can't feed all of them and I know that feeling's going to be there even though I'm helping. My mom says you can't do everything in the world, but I've always wanted to. Maybe some day I will; but I think what's holding me back is fear—fear of meeting those people and knowing . . . just knowing. They may think that this girl is just trying to be nice and in truth I know what they're feeling. That scares the hell out of me because I don't want to feel it again.

The case of Silva is a very complex one. She has experienced hunger first hand and this has brought the issue home to her in a way that Leslie cannot even imagine. When discussing the issue of hunger at the level of the big picture, Silva expresses a great deal of compassion and she struggles to relate with individuals on a more personal level. However, when she brings it down to a more concrete level, her compassion begins to become selective as she distinguishes between the deserving and undeserving poor, a characteristic very similar to Leslie.

Silva's mother provides an excellent role model in terms of reaching out to others at a personal level, and Silva idealizes this form of addressing the issue. This idealization is closely tied with her distrust of organizations—also quite similar to Leslie's perspective—and her concern with how it comes across to others. On the one hand, this concern reflects her understanding of how it might make the people being fed feel bad because of a condescending approach that strips them of their pride and dignity. On the other hand, she is quite caught up with how others perceive her. This is a theme that goes back to her childhood when she was afraid to bring up her experiences with hunger because of what the other children might think. At present, she worries that the homeless would not realize she went through the same thing, as if she were at the soup kitchen merely out of pity. In other words, Silva wants others—including the interviewer, only the second person to whom she has told this story—to know or not know of her experiences so that her self is perceived in the way she deems most beneficial to her. The hunger issue is secondary to her impression management.

As her conflicting feelings about becoming involved with the issue of hunger indicate, Silva's biggest hurdle is her fear. This is what prevents her from reaching out and growing attached to others experiencing hunger. She expresses an apparently genuine wish to feel and act more directly as her mother did, but fear holds her back. Her fear is not of them or of the issue. Her fear is of being in contact with people going through what she herself experienced. She is afraid of reliving that part of her life because of all the negative feelings that go with it—emptiness and sorrow.

Thus, Silva's focus with regard to the issue of hunger is on her self first and foremost, her own feelings and experiences. She expresses compassion for the anonymous masses, but this remains at an abstract level. She has not committed herself to anyone going hungry, although if her idealization of her mother's outreach takes hold and eventually prompts her to do the same, becoming relationally referenced is a strong possibility. At the same time, hunger is not a non-issue for her. Her own experiences have negated that possibility. Silva does realize that it can happen to her—it already did. Thus, her level of social affinity in the context of this issue is a bit higher than Leslie's.

The Confines of "Personal Troubles"

What those who are nonreferenced and self-referenced have in common is that they have compartmentalized their selves and their life spheres, setting themselves apart from the wider society. The broad ties of social affinity are cut off at the root. In terms of social issues, they do not see the connection between the social dimensions of the issue and the individual dimensions. In the tradition of sociologist C. Wright Mills, they have not translated their personal troubles into public issues. Personal troubles "have to do with his [or her] self and with those limited areas of social life of which he [or she] is directly and personally aware" (1959: 8). If an issue does not enter into this "limited area," then in the mind of the individual, it exists purely in abstraction and they are nonreferenced toward that issue. The self-referenced have a more concrete fix on the issue, but only in terms of how it affects themselves. The issue is more a personal trouble than a social or "public" issue.

Mills contrasts this focus on personal troubles with the focus on public issues. These issues "have to do with matters that transcend . . . local environments of the individual and the range of his [or her] inner life. They have to do with . . . the ways in which various milieu overlap and interpenetrate to form the larger structure of social and historical life. An issue is a public matter . . ." (1959: 8). Those who fall into the relationally referenced and the socially referenced types are conscious of these "overlapping milieux" and have begun to step outside of their personal troubles and focus on the impact of a given social issue on others. These two types represent more fully realized degrees of social affinity. They are the subject of the next chapter.

FOUR

The Construction of
Social Issues, Part II

Breaking the Boundaries Between Self and Other

As discussed in the previous chapter, those who are nonreferenced and self-referenced with regard to a particular social issue either do not focus on the issue at all or see it only in terms of how it affects themselves. Their attention is directed inward and is restricted to the boundaries of their individual life spheres. Personal troubles dominate their consciousness within the context of that issue. Their social affinity, at least within that context, is highly limited as a result. In contrast, those who focus on the social dimensions of an issue rather than its individual dimensions have actually broken the boundaries between their own life spheres and the society that exists outside. They have transcended the self and have begun to focus on the issue in terms of its effects on others and on society as a whole, reaching a higher degree of social affinity within that context. These individuals fall into two types: the *relationally referenced* and the *socially referenced*.

The Relationally Referenced Type—
"I Can't Believe This Happened To Someone I Know"

The focus of those who are relationally referenced is on understanding the issue in terms of someone they know. Those who fall into this type are committed to the issue insofar as it affects or has affected other individuals known to the interviewee. Their consciousness of the issue, while still proximate to their own life sphere, has extended beyond the boundaries of the self. These individuals begin to step outside of themselves and identify with another person. They create a link with the issue that is outside themselves, based on a relation—that which is *between* people. Social ties have entered the picture and the individual is at a higher point along the continuum of social affinity. Those who are relationally referenced may, at the same time—although not necessarily—be self-referenced. In other words, while they think of the issue in terms of how it affects those known to the individual, they may also think in terms of how the issue affects themselves.

Becoming relationally referenced is not just something that happens to everyone who knows someone affected by the issue. Garrett Gilmore, a gentle and shy white man, knows of someone with AIDS, but this person is the friend of a friend and knowing about this person did not prompt him to become relationally referenced.

> *A friend of a friend of mine . . . this guy who rents a room in their house . . . just found out two months ago that he has AIDS. I've met him a couple of times. I just feel bad for him. I mean, he's going to die. . . . Knowing him has just highlighted my fear of AIDS. I guess it's brought it closer to home. He's the only one I know of who has AIDS, but I don't think it's too likely I know anyone else who does.*

Garrett does not think of this as an issue that really affects him or the people he knows. At the same time, though, one can easily imagine that if a close family member acquired HIV, then Garrett would devote much of his time and attention to that person. It is thus possible to hypothesize that the strength and closeness of the relationship—its salience—has a major impact on whether or not an individual will be relationally referenced.

Moreover, the individual has to be open to allowing the relation and the issue to be united in their consciousness. For Reuben Singleton, a very thoughtful young black man just starting college, the fact that a close family member has AIDS is not enough for him to be relationally referenced. He says, "I have an aunt who has AIDS, and I have no sympathy for her because of the way she got it—drug use. No sympathy whatsoever. . . . I just have no compassion for anyone who's going to endanger their life in that situation, and they know exactly the consequences. None *whatsoever.*" His value system of individual responsibility is stronger than his tie to his aunt. Thus, becoming relationally referenced on an issue takes some individual effort to extend one's individual self—a point made especially clear in the case of Chad.

CHAD OLSON

Chad is a tall white man with a deep and rough voice. He is a very reflective kind of person—highly introspective. He was born in Boston, although he grew up in many other parts of the country, attending high school in Kansas City and currently calling Texas his home. Chad doesn't get along very well with his father, who works on the business side of the entertainment industry. He feels that he and his father are too much alike, sharing many of the same faults, including difficulty in showing affection to one another. His mother, on the other hand, he considers to be his best friend—someone he can talk to about anything. She is also a devout Catholic who, while not preaching anything to her children, did make sure that they were educated in their religion. However, she did not put Chad into a Catholic high school until she noticed that his grades were going down in the public school. She felt that he was being distracted too much and that an all-boys environment would help. His grades went up soon after he switched schools. It was there that he was first exposed to psychology—a field that strongly interests him because he likes to understand how people turn out the way they do. This may partially explain his desire to reconnect with his favorite and yet estranged uncle who has AIDS.

———————

When I think about AIDS, I guess it scares the hell out of me. One of my best friends could have AIDS and I wouldn't know because the statistics are so high now. It's just incredible. I think about how you get AIDS and it scares the hell out of me about sex and stuff. It made me a lot more conscious about messing around with people.

I have an uncle, actually, who has AIDS. He and I were very close when I was little. I can remember always asking for him. I just remember being around him and always wanting him to be around. When people brought up my other uncles and aunts, I was like, "Blah! Where's Uncle Joe? Uncle Joe, where's he?" Unfortunately, he kind of alienated himself from the family—kind of like the black sheep. I didn't really know him other than what I knew of him when I was little, so I just dismissed it. And then when I was in high school, I found out he was gay. I was just, "Oh, man! Forget this guy, he's . . ." I was playing hockey and was kind of a jock then—kind of set in my ways. I hadn't seen him since I was like five and decided I would never see him again. So, I kind of buried him, I guess. Later, I found out he had

*AIDS and that was another blow. But when I came to college, I just
kept thinking about him and about how we were. I realized I just had
a lot of negative energy stored up inside—energy he didn't really
deserve. So, I think that I matured a lot. Eventually, I wrote to him and
talked about how I felt and stuff like that and thanked him for how he
was to me when I was little and we've kind of become really good
friends since then.*

*Just talking to him . . . I don't know . . . I guess that's where
AIDS becomes really personal to me. Before I knew my uncle, AIDS
didn't really bother me. It didn't strike me as my problem. I was conscious of it, but not really overly conscious. But now I think about it
and about how much more I'd like to do with my life and stuff like
that. If I had AIDS, then I'd think about living in fear. It creates a sense
of paranoia which I really don't like. AIDS is almost like a death sentence. A lot of people think that way, and thinking of it as a death sentence kind of keeps you safe. You need a certain sense of paranoia in
order to get by. I'm definitely more aware of it now.*

*Since resuming contact with my uncle, I've also taken a lot of the
blame off people when it comes to thinking about AIDS. Before that, I
thought, "Those people that got it from blood transfusions can't be
blamed, and the kids who got it from their parents can't be blamed."
When I think about it now, I don't think that anyone should really be
blamed. When I think about sex and stuff, I've had it too. I don't know
about intravenous drug users, but when it comes to sex, there are a lot
of people who screw up. I don't think you can really put a lot of blame
on people's shoulders. If they're stupid once, then they're stupid; but I
try not to condemn people for that. I still think of AIDS as a death
sentence, but I don't believe that you should stop living. I don't think
that my uncle has changed a lot because of it. He doesn't sound like
he's crazy or anything now. He sounds like the same person I remember, but I just don't think that I should treat him or anybody any differently if they have it.*

*Beyond keeping in touch with my uncle, I don't know if I've been
given too much opportunity to really address the AIDS issue. You see
ads for fundraising. They had one for children's AIDS—and I usually
don't give to those—but I gave them a hundred bucks or something.
Something about that drew me to it immediately, but I don't really go
out and look for opportunities to help people with AIDS. I can provide
comfort and care for my uncle, but beyond that. . . . I've often thought*

out of desperation, "You've got to find a cure. You've got find a cure."
What does that do? It doesn't help the situation. There are people look-
ing for a cure now and I think they're doing their best. I can't force them
just because of my situation or his situation, because I care about him.
I kind of resign myself to the fact that he'll most likely die of it. But
for me to have known him, at least that's something. I don't know. I
don't know. I think that things are being done for it. I really believe
that. If I were to start doing research, I guess that would be a positive
step, but I don't think I have the first clue of where to start and it takes
thousands of years of medical school and then research. So, I think that
my activity goes as far as the personal level. My activity with the sub-
ject of AIDS goes that far. But even in our relationship, I don't talk
about AIDS too much. We talk more on a friendship level. I think
that's what my uncle needs as well as what I need. You don't need to
dwell on that. That's sort of like, "Well, you have AIDS, so I guess I'll
be your friend."

It's funny, but I never thought AIDS would have an impact on
my life. You hear about people and the fact that by the year 2000, 90
percent of us will know somebody with AIDS. And yet, I never thought
I would. But to hear about my uncle, it just blew my mind. It really
brought the disease out into the open for me. As much as we're indi-
viduals, I think that we like to have our security; and the people that
we care about are kind of like our security. So, when something happens
to them, it kind of brings everything home to you.

Chad's narrative is highly suggestive. There is no question that he is
relationally referenced on the AIDS issue. His concluding comments stand
in stark contrast with those falling into the nonreferenced and self-referenced categories. He acknowledges the importance of individuality, but
this independence does not come at the expense of one's relationships with
others. His model is one of interdependence—a significant step forward on
the scale of social affinity.

At the same time, Chad is also self-referenced on this issue. For Garrett, knowing someone with the disease "brings the issue home," but he still
thinks that the issue will not affect himself or his friends. However, Chad
does not make these exceptions. Instead, he talks about the positive impact
of living in fear of AIDS—being careful in his sexual behavior. Moreover, it
was his sudden knowledge of his uncle's HIV status that triggered this

change in Chad. Prior to that time, he did not take the issue of AIDS seriously. In addition, he blamed others for their irresponsibility, much as Reuben does. However, Chad's bond with his uncle is stronger than his belief in individual responsibility. His value system changed as a result of his relationship with his uncle and he has become compassionate toward those whom he previously blamed.

The issue of AIDS itself is not something that draws Chad's attention beyond himself or the context of his relationship with his uncle. The societal implications of AIDS are not discussed. In fact, he does not even talk about it with his uncle too much. His relationship with Uncle Joe is his priority and AIDS is simply a part of that relationship. For this reason, he notes that, while he has donated money for AIDS, he does not "go out and look for opportunities to help people with AIDS." In fact, Chad feels rather ineffective in the face of this issue. For him, to really address it implies being able to find a cure—something that he sees as beyond his capability. Instead, he focuses on being there for his uncle until death takes him away. But for Chad, "to have known him, at least that's something."

As hinted at in the beginning of this section, being relationally referenced toward an issue hinges on the nature of the relationship with the individual affected by the issue. Some relationships—as in the case of Garrett and the friend of his friend—are not strong enough to elicit the relational reference point. Other relations, while they might be strong in their own right, might also be secondary to a value system that is even stronger—as is Reuben's commitment to individual responsibility. Given the dependence on something so evolving and variant as a personal relationship, the relationally referenced type of orientation toward a social issue is pivotal in nature. Thus, there are several possible outcomes of this type.

In the first place, it is possible to remain relationally referenced. For example, we can imagine an individual who knows many people with AIDS or HIV. His or her attention and commitment moves from one to the next as some die and others are newly diagnosed. It is also possible for someone who is relationally referenced to eventually become self-referenced or even nonreferenced toward the given issue. For instance, we can ask "how will Chad's reference toward AIDS evolve after his uncle's death?" The clues in his narrative—his focus on his uncle more than on the issue, the fact that he does not seek out any involvement beyond what comes to him, and the fact that he takes AIDS seriously in terms of his own behavior—hint that Chad will in all likelihood move toward the self-referenced type. If he does not develop a commitment to the issue beyond his uncle and if he continues to be conscious of preventing AIDS in his own life, this outcome will certainly be the case. Whatever the outcome, Chad will be a more compassionate human being given his contact with an uncle he loves who also happens to have AIDS.

However, it is also possible to imagine individuals who have no commitment to the issue whatsoever, even in terms of themselves. Their sole focus is on the person they know. If, for example, they believe that AIDS is the "scourge of God" brought down on sinners and they do not count themselves as such a sinner, then they may devote themselves to that one person with AIDS whom they know—"love the sinner, hate the sin"—and revert to a nonreferenced state upon the death of that person. Finally, we can imagine a third outcome, further highlighting the pivotal nature of the relationally referenced category: it is possible to move toward the socially referenced type. We will see this in the case of Diane later.

Given this evidence, knowing someone who is affected by the issue is highly important in terms of one's positioning on the continuum of social affinity. Knowing someone is enough to yank one out of the nonreferenced category and make one highly aware that the issue does indeed affect one's own life. They begin to identify with that person and an affinity develops for him or her and what he or she is experiencing. Knowing someone can also boost one to becoming socially conscious and committed to changing the society that put their loved one in such a position. Being relationally referenced with regard to an issue is highly pivotal, leading to a full variety of outcomes along the entire continuum of social affinity.

The Socially Referenced Type— "It's Time for Society to Wake Up!"

Being socially referenced implies that an individual focuses on the issue in question in terms of its macro dimensions. Those who are socially referenced toward a particular issue have moved well beyond the boundaries of their own life spheres. Their awareness of the issue does not rely on an issue's impact on themselves or on someone close to them. They are committed to the issue insofar as it affects large numbers of individual human beings or even as it affects society in general. These individuals step outside of themselves and their immediate relationships. Their link with the issue is based on more than their own relations. It is based on a full series of relations between entire groups of people and even society at the broader levels of community, country, or world. This is social affinity at its deepest level. Whereas thinking at this societal level was too abstract and unreal for the nonreferenced such as Leslie, this abstract quality is no barrier for the socially referenced. For them, the large-scale social ties that have entered the picture are *just as tangible.*

As with the previous type, the socially referenced may also be self-referenced and/or relationally referenced. For example, an individual may be committed to the issue at a societal level, know someone who is directly affected by the issue, and be highly aware of how the issue does or may affect themselves. However, there are those who become committed to an issue without requiring personal or relational attachments to it.

DIANE BELLIVEAU

Diane is a person who would do anything for her friends and who places great value on her relationships outside her family. She was born in 1957 and grew up in a white neighborhood in New Bedford, Massachusetts, a small town outside of Boston and has lived in this area her entire life. She has one sister in Vermont with whom she keeps in touch; but she has not been in communication with her parents. Her father left when Diane was born and her mother was psychologically and financially incapable of raising her, so she was raised primarily by her grandmother. Despite being raised by a grandparent rather than her parents, Diane feels she had an extremely stable childhood.

Diane's mother has been in and out of institutions for as long as she can remember. For a while, she helped her mother out as much as she could. However, her mother was emotionally abusive and finally Diane felt compelled to break off the relationship. For a while, her mother was a bag lady; but Diane refused to take her in because she felt she could not put herself in the position of being psychologically manipulated and abused again. As a result, she feels she can be more caring of strangers on the street than of her own mother. Indeed, this has become a priority in her life.

Diane currently works at a Planned Parenthood office outside of Boston and is completing a nursing degree on a part-time basis. She would like to use the skills she learns to assist with people with AIDS. While AIDS plays a significant role in her life, it is homelessness and hunger—virtually inseparable issues in her eyes[1]—that she sees as being most important to her and an issue toward which she plans to contribute for a long time to come.

———————

I suppose homelessness and hunger are so important to me because they're so visible. You can see a person on the street and know that they're homeless. You can see someone else on the street and not realize that they're illiterate and they need to learn to read or that they have AIDS. It's really . . . it's so . . . it's there. It's right in your face. It's very obvious and it's like you feel for these people. My mother was homeless for a while. She was a bag woman on the streets of New Bedford, sleeping on people's front lawns. I remember one time when I first moved to Boston, it was mid-winter and I saw a homeless woman who looked rather insane, too. She didn't just look poor. She looked really out of it and I just heard a voice in my head clear as crystal: "There, but for the grace of God, go I." That homeless woman was one role model—something that I might have become if I had made different choices. I could be that person. So, feeling like it could have happened to me makes me feel more generous to people who it has happened to. I was the lucky one and I should spread the wealth a little bit or something . . . that kind of thing. I didn't end up being homeless, so I don't want anybody to be homeless.

While some people will say, "That's their choice. They don't have to do that. They can get a job," I know to some degree how narrowly I escaped that. I don't know what their lives have been like. I don't know what has happened to them. Once they were lovely children with rosy cheeks and now here they are. What happened? Something happened. Nobody chooses that. They lost all their options somewhere along the line. So, I just have a strong empathy for that.

That this is a pretty affluent society while there are people with nothing just seems unjust. It's just not right. There's something morally and ethically wrong with that. Also, on a more personal note, for me, my childhood home was sacred. There was that wacky period with my mother, but once I got my own apartment, it was like home. And to this day, home is this sacred place. It's my place. It's like my safe place. I would really flip out if anybody ever broke into my house. My sense of security would go right out the window. I love the word "home." It's one of my favorite words. It's my favorite place. It's as necessary as food and air, you know. It's where you go back to recharge the battery. To not have that space would be a horrible thought. So, I guess to some degree selfishness is involved. I love my things so much. I'm so sad that other people don't have a home as well.

As a child, I didn't really see the problems of homelessness and hunger. And when my mother was a bag lady, I don't think I had any real sensitivity to the issue. I just slapped a label on her. But during high school, I did see it because the high school was right by downtown and we'd hang around downtown a lot. I remember seeing homeless people and being shocked, you know. I guess the biggest shock was when one particular homeless person was defecating right there! I was like, "There's a man over there taking a shit! Right out in broad daylight! Just like that!" And it's like, "Wow!" And that's another thing: home is sacred, but so is the bathroom! That's a private place. You don't want a crowd going by. This is a place where I really seriously like to be alone. How horrible to have to take a dump outside. I can't imagine. I'd be mortified. I really felt bad for him; just shock—"Oh my God! Do I see that? Is that really happening?" Now, if I saw someone defecating, I don't think there'd be any shock around it.

I also remember a homeless woman—a bag lady—during my high school years—Depo Annie, as I called her—who would hang around the school sometimes with her shopping cart. She was really my first experience with a homeless person. Kids would tease her. I never teased her. I'd give her cigarettes. She'd bum cigarettes from me. At the same time, she was crazy and she scared me. She was kind of scary. But over the years, it's just . . . maybe the comfort of familiarity, just getting used to seeing it and understanding that these people might not have had the choices you've had in life. I remember having a conversation with a friend who thought, "But they don't have to live like that." It's like, "Look at where you grew up. Look at your family, how well-to-do it is. You were sent to a good college. It was taken for granted that you were going to college. And yet when I was a kid, it was taken for granted that I wasn't." And she had never really thought about it outside of her own reality. She was using her own measuring stick on everybody else and came up with the idea that, "They're just degenerates. They don't care." But it's like, "They didn't grow up in your house, and maybe if you had done that—if you were them—you'd think you were a degenerate. You would have been throwing your life away. You were given a lot of things. You don't know what their situation was." So, I just learned to be nonjudg-mental in my approach and avoid using my own yardstick.

Now, I get a lot of information about the issue from the local shel-ter and I've given them a lot of money in the past. Well, not a lot; but from my standards a lot. I generally donate every other year because I feel like one year I should be nice to my friends. I take all the money that I'm going to use to buy Christmas presents and send it to the shel-ter. Then I make nice handmade cards for my friends and tell them that, "We have so many things. We have everything that we need, really. I could get you another thing, but instead I gave the money to the peo-ple who don't have any things." My friends are very supportive of that. In fact, they like it; so it could become a yearly thing. Because of that, I'm on the shelter's mailing list and they've called me: "Are you sure you don't want us to send your friends cards in your name—'Diane has donated this money.'" "It's okay! I send them cards. You don't have to waste your money on a mailing!"

In addition to those donations, whenever I go into town or some-place where I know I will be in contact with the homeless, I always, always, always make sure I have change and single dollar bills in an accessible pocket. I always, always give them money. If I don't see any, fine; I'll go home with money—especially since I'm working part-time and still trying to pay the same bills that I paid when I was working full-time . . . my finances are more limited than they were. But I'm still going to waste money—it's never a waste going out to eat and having a fine glass of wine or going to a movie—but I still have money that I can play with. So, I will put that money aside into this pocket right here—accessible, easy to get to—and if I walk by somebody and they want some money, I can give it to them. Or if anybody is selling the homeless newspaper Spare Change, I always buy it. But friends—or just other people—will pull the old "they don't exist" thing. That is just so weird to me. It's just that they do exist. People think, "If I ignore it, it'll go away. . . . Geez! I hope I never get cancer!" Yeah, right! "If you ignore cancer, it's going to go away, honey!" But then afterwards they will always say, "You're so nice!" I just don't know where to put that. I try not to judge people who do the "ignore them, they aren't there" routine, but I don't understand it.

People will say, "You know they're just going to take that money and go and buy alcohol." But the minute you give money to somebody, it's not your money anymore. It's theirs; and what they do with it is *their business. Even if they're going to buy alcohol, think about their state of being. Think about how hard it is to be them and to be homeless and to be an alcoholic. I just try to think of the whole situation. It's almost like they need the money more because they're in so much pain that the little money they have, the tiniest amount of resources that they get, they have to use to self-medicate with alcohol so that they don't have to deal with something horrible. It's like, "Oh, for Christ's sake! Let them drink if they want. I would!"*

Obviously, there have been times when I haven't had any money to give—or I ran out of money. I really have to limit it or else I would literally keep giving it away. But when they ask me, I don't pretend they're not there. I say, "I'm so sorry. I'm out of money. I'm so sorry." I'll engage with them. I'll talk to them. I don't want to do the "see no evil, hear no evil" thing. But that's one of the nice things about becoming a nurse. I'll be able to help out organizations and individuals and volunteer as a nurse. It's a great skill to have to go into homeless shelters and just do health assessment on a volunteer basis. I really want to do that once I finish. I'm really looking forward to this—doing my life's work—as a job, but also on a volunteer basis . . . just to be in the community and actually doing something tangible and helpful, getting to know these people as people. I don't know whether I need to make these people more human—I already see them as human—but they're most human when dealing with them one on one, right there. The more you feel that, the more you're going to tell other people and the more it might enlighten them. It's like the old, "Think globally, act locally." Locally means just where you are.

I get a certain satisfaction out of helping. These problems aren't going to be helped if they're left alone. You have to attend to them. You have to pay attention to them and you have to do what you can, even if it's a tiny thing. If you see a little kid crying by itself, you're going to go over and say, "Where's your Mommy?" or "Who's taking care of you?" You're not going to ignore that. If you see someone hurt, hopefully you would go and check it out. Maybe not; I don't know. But it's almost morally and ethically your responsibility. I have a stake in this issue, at least on a moral and ethical level; and on a political level, too.

Diane's story is revealing of a mindset that is wholly different from the cases falling within the other three types. In contrast with Leslie, who characterizes hunger as being rather abstract, Diane characterizes the issue by its visibility. It is not something that is remote for her. It is right there in front of her everywhere she goes. She does not look past the homeless on the street. Moreover, she does not simply notice them. She actually role-takes with them, stepping outside of her own reality, imagining herself in their place, and realizing that this person on the street could very well have been her. And by taking the perspective of the other, she goes beyond feeling pity or sadness for them—she empathizes with them, feeling the helplessness and loss of having no place to call home, feeling their shame at having to relieve themselves in public places, and even feeling the need to anesthetize oneself with alcohol. Diane truly recognizes that, "There, but for the grace of God, go I." As a result of her insight gained in the process of role-taking, she does not use her own yardstick when measuring the worth of another person. Thus, in addition to being socially referenced toward hunger, she is also self-referenced.

Diane even takes a step further and mentions several times that there are moral and ethical dimensions to the hunger issue. She notes how unjust it is for people to have nothing in a society that has so much. She speaks of responsibility—not of individual responsibility, as does Reuben, but of *social* responsibility. The idea of a moral obligation to others within our society, while unspoken, permeates her narrative. In other words, she has stepped outside of herself and the boundaries of her own life space and thinks of the issue at a societal level while at the same time committing herself to assisting anonymous individuals, from donating all of her Christmas money to making a point of carrying money specifically for giving to people on the street. And while these individuals are anonymous—with the exception of her mother and Depo Annie—she still sees them as human beings equivalent to herself. If she does not have any more money to give people on the street, she does not simply ignore them as do the vast majority of passersby. Instead, she engages them—talking to them and explaining that she has nothing to spare. Thus, Diane is able to simultaneously see the moral and ethical dimensions at the societal level of the hunger issue and still focus on the individuals who are directly affected by the issue—most of whom she does not know.

"Anti-Affinity" . . . Hostility

It is also possible to speculate as to *negative* "affiliations." This goes beyond the mere absence of social affinity. In these cases, there is actual *hostility* toward others in the context of a given issue. Not only are social bonds nonexistent, actual boundaries have been set up between the individual and those concerned with or affected by the issue. The emergence of social ties is avoided and prevented. While the interview data did not reveal anyone who fell into such a type, there is evidence that such types exist.

For example, Jack Levin and Jack McDevitt, in their book *Hate Crimes: The Rising Tide of Bigotry and Bloodshed,* present a case of a "thrill-seeking" hate crime in which a group of friends sought out "a drug addict, a homo, or homeless" person to assault for the fun of it (1993: 73). The homeless and the hungry are often the targets of such violence and hatred. Charles Dickens, in *A Christmas Carol,* has immortalized such a perspective in the character of Scrooge, who takes a hostile approach toward the hungry, homeless, and impoverished. This is particularly evident when he comments that it would be better to let all these people die in order to "decrease the surplus population" (1935: 20). While the AIDS issue has not been around long enough to have similar characters immortalized in such a way, we do not need to look deep into the issue's history before coming across those who viewed it, or still view it in a similarly hostile manner.

Moralists on the religious right have been notorious in their depiction of AIDS as "God's Judgment" called down upon sinful homosexuals, drug users, and prostitutes.[2] In both of these examples, the underlying belief is that those affected by an issue are deserving of their fate. While hints of this sentiment were found in the cases presented earlier, they were not central in their overall orientation toward the issue. However, the presence of these attitudes lends credence to hypothesizing an additional type in which hostility *is* central. In later chapters, attention is given to evidence of setting up boundaries between oneself and others, effectively preventing the emergence of social affinity.

Utilizing the Typology as a Comparative Tool

Another interesting point regarding the typology that has been presented here has to do with the distribution of individuals across the four types within a particular issue. For example, Table 4.1 shows the distribution of individuals interviewed ($N = 36$) in each of the four types. Examining this distribution and comparing it across issues is an illuminating method for understanding the position of each issue within society. Most individuals were not self-referenced or relationally referenced toward hunger. However, those who were had been personally touched by hunger or saw themselves

TABLE 4.1.
Distribution of Individuals Across Types of Orientations
Toward Social Issues According to Issue

	Hunger	(N)	AIDS	(N)
Nonreferenced	72%	26	30%	11
Self-Referenced	8%	3	56%	20
Relationally Referenced	3%	1	11%	4
Socially Referenced	17%	6	3%	1
	100%	36	100%	36

at some point in their lives as being on the brink of hunger. Thus, they became highly aware of the issue within the context of their lives or the life of someone close to them. Again, however, they were in the minority. In another part of the world or at another point in our history—in other words, given a different social location in terms of the social, spatial, and temporal variables—these findings would most likely be very different.

The overwhelming majority of individuals in the sample are non-referenced toward the hunger issue. This fact indicates that this is an issue to which people are not really committed *even though* it receives much attention in our schools and churches. In other words, the interest in this issue is primarily at a surface level. However, 17 percent of individuals are socially referenced with regard to this issue, indicating that, despite only superficial attempts at addressing the issue by the majority, a significant minority are able to make the leap from being nonreferenced to being socially referenced. All of those falling within the latter category are socially referenced because of their contact with the hungry and their involvement with the issue. Thus, involvement has the potential to change one's position within the typology.

In contrast with hunger, the majority of individuals fall into the self-referenced type when it comes to the AIDS issue. One can hypothesize that this is due to the AIDS education taking place in our society. Almost everyone in the sample indicated that they had been given AIDS education in school while growing up. On the other hand, there are notable exceptions where, even if AIDS education is provided, it is only very sketchy at best. In some instances, it is deemed so controversial an issue that schools do not include it in their curriculum or it becomes the subject of much debate. For example, Michelle Meadows describes the reaction to AIDS education within her school:

My health teacher brought in a 20-year-old kid who was HIV posi-
tive to talk to the class and ended up getting calls from parents saying,
"How dare you upset my daughter like that!" And then we had
another speaker and there was a big thing in the paper that some groups
didn't want her to come, that she shouldn't be speaking to their chil-
dren. People were saying "How can you say that homosexuality is cor-
rect?" I thought, "Stop! She's not sitting here saying 'Okay, you have
to be gay, you have to be lesbian.' She's talking about AIDS." It was
crazy. It just turned into this big issue, so the Board of Education
almost pulled the plug on it. It was weird, almost like every TV show,
every movie, everything dramatic you've ever seen happening hap-
pened. We even had cops walking through the school in full uniform.

At the same time, the controversy surrounding the issue keeps it out
of most churches—the other institution most likely to include an outreach
program with regard to hunger. Steve Mitchell belongs to a conservative
Evangelical church that does a lot of outreach in terms of hunger, but none
in terms of AIDS.

I don't hear much about AIDS at church. We pray for it and everything,
but there are still people who believe it's their fault. People have little
debates. I mean, you can talk about it, but you don't want to press it too
much or else you end up having splits among people in the church.

Given the history of the AIDS issue in our society, its initial association with gay men—as evidenced in its early label of GRID (Gay-Related
Immune Deficiency)—and other populations deemed morally suspect by
society, such as drug users, prostitutes, and other sexually promiscuous individuals, these findings are not surprising. As is evident in the case studies
presented, many individuals still think in these terms. On the other hand,
11 percent of individuals were relationally referenced with regard to this
issue. This figure is likely to grow as the number of AIDS cases grows.
Interestingly, only 3 percent of individuals were socially referenced toward
AIDS. This issue is seen in our society as largely a matter of individual
responsibility for oneself—of monitoring one's own behavior. Very few
people associate AIDS with social responsibility.

Given these figures, it becomes apparent that, in our society, the
notion of social responsibility is highly bounded by the perceived legitimacy of both the issue and those affected by it. As a society, we value social
responsibility. And yet our individualistic culture pushes us in the direction

of individual accountability. The disparity between individual and social responsibility, as just noted, is particularly evident in the AIDS issue. However, it is also very apparent in the hunger issue. As a society, we value helping the underprivileged, so long as they are attempting to help themselves. For this reason, many people are contemptuous of the solicitor—the "bum"—asking for money on the street. Some, such as Silva and Leslie, are even distrustful of organizations meant to address the issue. However, the vast majority describe at least a surface level of compassion for the "deserving" poor—the children, the elderly, the handicapped, those unable to fend for themselves. These sentiments found in our society are reflected in the percentages of individuals falling into each of the four categories with regard to each issue. Thus, an examination of these figures is highly informative in drawing comparisons between social issues and how they are perceived in our society.

The Typology in Motion

A third point regarding the typology presented in this and the previous chapter focuses on its dynamic nature. Most typologies present a rather static view in that once an individual, group, or organization has been categorized, the categorization is unlikely to change. Like a psychiatric label, once given, it cannot be shaken.[3] However, this is not the case with the typology of orientations toward social issues. As briefly mentioned in the early part of this chapter, this typology is anything but a static set of categories into which individuals are forever placed. Instead, individuals are located in different types with regard to different issues. Moreover, individuals show an incredible degree of fluctuation in their orientations toward these issues, indicating that the typology should be seen as dynamic in character. And given that the typology represents—at a more concrete level—the individual's degree of social affinity within the context of that issue, it is possible to see that social affinity is also highly dynamic in character. One's commitment to individuals, the community, and society is constantly evolving and fluctuating and is highly dependent on the social context.

As individuals' lives, relations, and affiliations change, so can their type—and their affinity—with regard to any one issue. Several times in the case studies presented earlier, it has been apparent that the individual shifted from one type to another. Chad is one case in point. Prior to knowing of his uncle's HIV status, he did not take AIDS all that seriously. Upon finding out about his uncle, his consciousness of the issue and his reactions to it changed, thus changing his type of focus on the issue. Diane also recounts a time when she was not really all that aware of hunger and homelessness; but when she saw herself in a homeless woman, her orientation toward that issue changed.

In looking at the issue of affinity's dynamic nature, consider the case of Lloyd Bechakian, a gay Armenian from Idaho whose "type" with regard to AIDS has changed more than once. When he started high school, he was largely unaware of the issue at all, indicating that he was nonreferenced at that time.

> *I knew what the disease was basically, how it was transmitted. But I didn't know a hell of a lot about what it did to you. I didn't know a lot of details. I was just generally aware of the disease, what it did, how you got it. That was about it. I didn't really think about it much.*

However, during his sophomore year, Lloyd's outlook changed dramatically when a friend of his told him that she was HIV positive.

> *I asked her why she had been absent from school so much because she had been gone for quite a while—weeks at a time. She told me that she was dealing with some really big problems, and once you tell me that, I kind of tend to get on your case a little bit. Even if the person doesn't want to, I'll say, "Okay. You can talk to me. You can tell me." And it shocked the hell out of me because she pretty much just turned around and told me. "Whoa!" I thought. "Whoa! What am I supposed to do now?" And of course the thing that flashed through my mind very, very brightly was that, "Oh, my God! She's going to die! She's only 15 years old and she's going to die." That was the hardest part to deal with. That was the part that was not discussed when we talked about AIDS in class and which I did not expect to discuss.*

At this point, Lloyd moved from being nonreferenced toward the issue of AIDS to being relationally referenced. His degree of social affinity completely changed and his experience of the issue followed suit.

> *I was intellectualizing the disease before she told me. And then my emotions came into play and because emotions and feelings are just as real if not more real than thinking, the two came together and just pretty much exploded. I really felt it. It really affected me and it made me feel*

more for her and towards her. It made me a more educated person. But if I didn't feel that way, all the education in the world wasn't going to make a damn bit of difference.

This feeling toward his friend continued even after the shock of her revelation wore off. However, Lloyd's feelings and orientation toward the issue were not able to withstand separation from the young woman who elicited them in the first place, and again his type changed.

Once that singular experience was over and we lost touch when she moved, the issue pretty much died for me. My feelings and knowledge of her and what she must be going through just didn't follow through.

While his relationally referenced orientation toward the issue waned, he did not revert to his nonreferenced state. Instead, Lloyd became self-referenced toward AIDS. His consciousness had been raised because of his experience, and he learned a lot about how AIDS could affect him. In a sense, his innocence was lost. However, at the same time that Lloyd moved into and out of a relationally referenced position, there is a strong potential for him to change yet again. He anticipates becoming involved in the AIDS issue because now it interests him.

I want to know. I want to see. I want to experience. I want to have the stereotypes and whatever bullshit I have left in my mind and in my life broken down. I want to break off of the societal line into something completely different. Then I could live in society as a better person, better than I was before. This just entices me. I want to experience it because I think it will make me a better or more knowledgeable person. If you have an opportunity to experience and you're interested in it, I can find no reason why not to do it.

Lloyd's desire to become active focuses upon self-improvement rather than societal improvement, betraying his current self-referenced orientation, and yet the kind of involvement he looks forward to—AIDS activism within the gay and lesbian community—is community based. If he pursues this interest in AIDS within the context of community, Lloyd is likely to develop a socially referenced orientation toward the AIDS issue, in which case he will have moved through all four of the types presented in this chapter. It is also important to note that he did not "progress" through the types in a sequential fashion. This fact highlights the idea that these types are not to be thought of as steps even though they represent differing degrees of social affinity in the context of a particular issue.

It was the circumstances in which Lloyd found himself that had a major impact on the type that emerged at any given time and the degree of social affinity he experienced as a result. His intellectualized knowledge of AIDS, followed by his friend's revelation and eventual departure, shaped his consciousness, elicited a host of emotions, and prompted him to get seriously involved with the issue. Each of these elements—consciousness, sentiment, and action—in his experience of social affinity within the context of the AIDS issue played a central role in deciding into which of the four types Lloyd moved. As such, these three elements provide a useful heuristic device with which to proceed. With this in mind, we now turn to a consideration of each of these elements in the emergence of social affinity.[4]

Chapters 5, 6, and 7 treat each of these elements in turn. Thus far, we have painted a picture of social affinity in broad strokes. In contrast, the following three chapters focus on the minute details of the overall mosaic. While consciousness, sentiment, and action are the three fundamental elements of our view of social affinity, they will be further broken down into their constituent pieces, much like looking at each of the individual pieces of a large mosaic. Such close scrutiny of the details falls within the tradition of social psychology, and the reader is cautioned about getting overwhelmed by the details. Keep in mind that the many individual pieces are put back together again, and we are then be able to see the larger picture with new eyes and take a much more critical view of social affinity and its implications.

Oftentimes, the reader may be struck by the "obviousness" of some of what is presented. However, a major part of the distinctiveness of the sociological perspective is the penchant for looking at what is so easily taken for granted by most members of society and exposing the "unofficial story" lying underneath (see Berger 1963). Thus, while the details themselves may seem "obvious" to the reader, keep in mind that these very things that we so easily take for granted, when combined with one another, expose a rather complex story regarding the emergence of social affinity. As we see in the concluding chapter, the social and global implications of what so many people have taken for granted are enormous.

FIVE

The "Other Side of Silence"

The Construction of Social Consciousness

> If we had a keen vision and feeling of all ordinary
> human life, it would be like hearing the grass grow and
> the squirrel's heart beat, and we should die of that roar
> which lies on the other side of silence.
> —George Eliot, *Middlemarch*

Social consciousness is central to our understanding of the emergence of social affinity. Without being aware of the world outside of our individual selves, it would be impossible to feel any degree of connection with that world. With this in mind, it comes as no surprise that consciousness has been the subject of much philosophical, psychological, and sociological theorizing and research. The definition of this term includes "concern for some social or political cause"[1]—a definition that is highly relevant to our consideration of social affinity within the context of social issues. However, a broader definition of "consciousness" has to do with being mentally aware and perceptive, noticing the internal and external worlds that we inhabit. With this dual definition in mind, the major question addressed in this chapter is, "How do we go about noticing and making sense of the world around us, particularly with regard to social issues?"

Starbuck and Milliken, in their work on executives and perception (1988), focus on the processes of noticing and sense-making. Noticing is linked with the concept of *filtering*, and sense-making is tied to the concept of *framing*. We—together with our group, institutional, and cultural affiliations—determine the composition of our consciousness by selectively filtering most information out and allowing only some information in. That information that is allowed in becomes the basis for our view of the world—our consciousness. At the same time, individuals engage in framing: we build a mental construct of our social world and mold our consciousness accordingly.

However, Karl Weick, in his book *Sensemaking in Organizations*, notes that constructing our consciousness[2]—sense-making—involves not only filtering and framing, but also *facticity*—the need for individuals to feel as if we share the same factual world as those around us, that there is a single reality that exists outside our consciousness (Turner 1987: 19). In other words, we tend to assume others think as we do, that we are not alone in our view of the world. Sometimes, we even look to others to "confirm" the reality we see. It is almost as if we do not trust our own consciousness; and since our own consciousness is the only one of which we are fully aware, we seek to strengthen our view by finding others who share them. Without such confirmation from others, our view—and thus our consciousness—is likely to change. Through this process of constructing our consciousness, we make the highly subjective world around us "into something more tangible" (Weick 1995: 14).

Together, the concepts of filtering, framing, and facticity are analyzed with an eye toward understanding how we as individuals develop a social consciousness. Each of these concepts is further broken down into their most basic elements, much like the pieces of the larger mosaic described at the end of the previous chapter. By carefully scrutinizing these individual pieces, we attain a greater appreciation of the overall complexity of the construction of social consciousness and its role in social affinity.

Filtering

Individuals are bombarded with information at a rate that would overwhelm us if we tried to take it all in. The opening quote of this chapter eloquently reflects this notion of "stimulus overload" (see Milgram 1970). We cannot possibly attend to *everything*, even if we *wanted* to. Our attention begins to break down. In order to manage all the information available to us, we end up filtering it so that we only have to attend to that information that is *relevant* to us, to our individual *interests*, and our own worldview. This is the information that shapes our consciousness.

Herman and Chomsky, in their book *Manufacturing Consent* (1988), employ a propaganda model in discussing the process of filtering, focusing on the media for their analysis. They argue that before the news reaches the eyes and ears of consumers, it has been filtered in such a way that it supports the interests of the dominant elite in our country. The concentrated ownership of the media, the reliance on advertising and sponsorship for income, the reliance on government and business representatives as sources of information, "flak" or negative feedback to its statements and programs (such as boycotts, the withdrawal of advertising patronage, or political backlash by irate politicians), and cultural ideologies (such as anti-Communism, which was the example on which Herman and Chomsky focused) all serve to "cleanse" the raw material of news until it meets the approval of all five filters. Any dissident voices are marginalized (1988: 2, 3–31), or "filtered out."

Institutions such as the media have filtering tendencies in that not all of the available information outside of the institution is passed on to its members or consumers. What does get through to its members is any information that serves the interests of that institution. Unlike Herman and Chomsky's model, filtering does not have to be an intentional process. As we shall see later, it can be both conscious and unconscious. Moreover, Herman and Chomsky focus their analysis on the media; however, filtering is actually a process engaged in by all institutions. Individuals, groups, and—as they hint at by their attention to the cultural ideology filter—our culture and society also contribute to the filtering process. Regardless of the level at which filtering occurs—sociocultural, institutional, group, or individual—the process is the same: only information that is considered relevant or salient is consumed.

Sociocultural Filtering

As already hinted at, filtering at the societal level is carried out in large part by cultural ideologies, such as the notions of "rugged individualism" (Bellah et al. 1985) or "the American Dream" (Derber 1992). In our culture, we are expected to pull ourselves up by our own bootstraps, oftentimes forgetting that many do not have the bootstraps on which to pull. The many who do not accomplish this ideal end up overlooked and dismissed by those who do. This is why Silva, who was self-referenced with regard to the hunger issue, never discussed her experiences of hunger with anyone except her own mother. She notes that

We live in a society where we're supposed to be afraid if we were ever
hungry. That's our secret, mother and I. . . . We don't talk about that
because our society teaches us not to. We shun away the poor and
unwanted, so we don't talk about it.

Mary Tam concurs. Mary is a Chinese immigrant for whom hunger is a
part of her family's history; however, she too does not talk about it outside
of the family. She says that

Hunger is not something that my friends and I talk about, probably
because we live in this culture. . . . It's not a part of our lives, so we
don't talk about it; and the thought has never occurred to me either.

In essence, our society filters out the idea that its members can actually go
hungry. We know it exists "out there," but we prefer not to think about
it—especially within our society—and many times it does not even occur
to us to think in those terms. Our consciousness is not fully aware of all
the possibilities.

At the same time our culture filters out information, other information is filtered into our consciousness. For example, with regard to the
hunger issue, Sondra Arsenault recalls all of the fundraisers sponsored by
the performing arts industry.

Do you remember a few years ago everything was Ethiopia? It was
everywhere! Before that, I didn't even really think twice about it. But
then there was "Band Aid" and all these "Aids," you know what I
mean? "Live Aid" going for ten days at a time. Stuff like that. There
were all these different groups trying to sing for hunger and all these dif-
ferent people going to Ethiopia and everything else. People had a field
day with that. It was just everywhere. *Before that, I didn't think*
about it. After that, I was more aware of it.

In the mid to late 1980s, Ethiopia and fundraising for international hunger
became a fad that swept our society and suddenly the issue came to the
forefront of people's consciousness.

A similar thing happened with the AIDS issue. The red ribbons representing concern for the epidemic suddenly inundated our culture, to the
point where it was possible to buy red ribbon Christmas decorations, table-
ware, clothing, art, and so on. With this phenomenon came an increased
consciousness of the AIDS issue. The AIDS Memorial Quilt, sponsored by
the Names Project, is another example of a social issue infiltrating our cul-

ture and the consciousness of those who have seen it. Kesia Gorman's mother took her to see the quilt when she was younger and the experience made a lasting impression on her.

> *A family friend of my mother's had died from AIDS and it was their piece on the quilt that we saw. The quilt is a beautiful piece . . . as far as artwork goes, it's a beautiful thing just to see it. I cried. I still didn't really know what AIDS was or how it really affected people, but it still . . . I knew that all these people were dead from something and I just cried. I was kind of shocked. It has a tremendous impact on you. While it's not the individuals face-to-face, it is something representing an individual as opposed to just hearing the numbers. It's a tremendous impact to see how many pieces there are. I was just like "Damn!" I was just in awe. It was saying something with the eyes, which is probably more powerful than numbers.*

This cultural event played a pivotal role in the formation of Kesia's consciousness with regard to the AIDS issue. She signed up for the mailing list and read all of the literature about AIDS that was sent to her. In other words, her learning continued well beyond the event that inspired it in the first place. The quilt is a powerful cultural mechanism by which people's consciousness is broadened to include a new awareness.

At a more abstract level, our societal values also play a major role in filtering information. Because AIDS is often transmitted through sexual behavior and sharing needles, it piques our societal norms about licit and illicit behavior. For this reason, it has been sensationalized in ways that cancer, for instance, has not. Brad Wilson highlights this point.

> *I think that because AIDS is sexually transmitted, it's getting hyped more than other things. Thousands and thousands of people die every year from cancer than they do from AIDS, but cancer seems so much more "acceptable" almost. You're not constantly reading about how scary cancer is and how scared people are that it's sweeping the nation. But because AIDS is sexually transmitted and it's inhibiting a certain lifestyle it's getting a lot of attention.*

Because of the sensational nature of the AIDS issue, particular types of information are filtered in. In this instance, what is filtered in is the focus on illicit behavior and the often cited conclusion—even in the mid-1990s—that AIDS is associated with moral degeneracy.

Our societal values also have a role in the filtering of the hunger issue. Hunger has a long history of association with charity. In our society, such charitable behavior is encouraged, particularly within the context of church and during particular times of the year, such as Thanksgiving and Christmas. Our culture emphasizes giving to the poor and hungry during the holiday season and so we are much more likely to be aware of the issue at that time. Kesia has noticed this seasonal emphasis on charitable giving and is actually disturbed by it.

> I can see giving more around Thanksgiving because it's a time when people are going to eat hearty and people will be more aware and really think about it. Around Christmas time and other holidays, people are more sensitive . . . people can be more sensitive. But if it were me, I'd do it the opposite way because people have more money when it's not around the holidays.

In fact, Kesia has hit upon a major dilemma for organizations dealing with the hunger issue. These organizations are swamped with donations during the holiday season, but do not have enough to go around during the long summer months.[3] This illustrates how our societal values and cultural events have a tremendous impact on our consciousness through their ability to filter information in and out of our awareness. The major way in which this is accomplished is through institutional and group filtering processes.

Institutional Filtering

People respond to the holiday spirit conveyed in our culture, but it is almost as if the issue leaves our consciousness during other times of the year. The reason for this is that our cultural value of almsgiving is filtered in more heavily during the holiday season through institutions such as schools, churches, corporations, voluntary organizations, the media, and so on. Commercials and news stories focusing on the needy abound during that time of year. However, these commercials and stories do more than raise the viewer's awareness of the issue. They filter in a particular *view* of the issue. When I asked what the word "hunger" first brought to Michelle's mind, she demonstrated what she learned from the hunger commercials and news coverage she's seen.

When I first think of hunger, I think of Somalia—the people with really skinny legs and big, fat stomachs. Total hunger. You don't think of it as just going without a meal for a day. You think of the extreme hunger because you see it on the news, you see people starving in Rwanda, Somalia, whatever; but you don't see on the news the people in Boston who are starving. Even though it's right here next to you, it's not as visible as what you see on TV.

The commercials and news Michelle has seen has brought "Third World" hunger to the forefront of her consciousness, to the point where the hunger she sees on the streets before her very own eyes recedes into the background. When the media bombard viewers with images of children with skinny legs and fat stomachs from the other side of the globe,[4] that is what is most likely to stick in our consciousness.

In a similar way, the movie *Philadelphia* played a major role in filtering in information about AIDS. Twenty-two percent ($N = 36$) of those interviewed just happened to bring up the movie, indicating that it played a major role in shaping the consciousness of American viewers.[5] Colleen Meade tells of her experience seeing the movie.

I saw that movie—Philadelphia—and it made me think a lot. It's really frightening, especially to this generation, how it's just become so widespread. It's really scary to me. I just thought the movie was so well done. And then the discrimination issue made me so mad. I just thought it was such a depressing movie. And I think that did a lot because a lot of times people will shy away from AIDS cases. Philadelphia showed that the person who had AIDS is a person with feelings, emotions, which I think is necessary to be able to help the problem.

By showing the person behind the disease, *Philadelphia* contributed to a shift in consciousness—as in the character of the lawyer played by Denzel Washington who ends up representing the person with AIDS—from fear to acceptance, from blame to compassion. In this way, the institution of the media allowed information to filter in to viewers and changed the consciousness of many like Colleen.

On the other hand, because institutions are attuned to information that is directly relevant to their own interests, they also sensitize their members to information that may not be available to the general public. The information may be so specific that the majority of society finds it irrelevant while, for the institution, it may be highly relevant. For example, when Jesuit priests were murdered in El Salvador, Jesuit schools and universities focused on this information that was directly relevant to their identity and image. This event did not receive as much attention outside of these institutions. By filtering this information in, Jesuit schools made their members aware of a social problem—and the implications for U.S. foreign policy in El Salvador—which was actually quite distant from the average American citizen. In this way, institutions also have a unique ability to raise the social consciousness of their members, an ability that is particularly apparent when it is in their interests to do so.

But again, institutions contribute in large part to the filtering out of information. Prior to basketball star Magic Johnson's revelation that he was HIV positive, the media had done little to convey the fact that heterosexuals are just as susceptible to AIDS as are gay men. Another major institution engaged in this process of filtering are grade schools and junior and senior high schools. AIDS organizations have placed much emphasis on education as a means of preventing the spread of the disease. However, many of our nation's schools have balked at the idea of teaching anything about sexuality other than abstinence. Much of this fear is a result of "flak"—noted by Herman and Chomsky earlier—from outraged parents. Recall the story from the previous chapter in which Michelle tells of one such incident: a teacher caught much flak from parents for bringing a young adult who was HIV positive into class to speak because one student was "upset." As an organizer for AIDS education in her school, Michelle saw many instances in which the school, reacting to parental pressure such as this, hesitated and backpedaled. On another occassion, a major public speaker on the AIDS issue—Christine Getty, herself HIV positive—was scheduled to speak at Michelle's high school. Student representatives from all high schools in the area were invited to participate. However,

> there was a big thing in the paper about some groups that didn't want her to come, that she shouldn't be speaking to our children. Our Board of Education almost pulled the plug on it. Then the principal from Central High wouldn't let his kids out, including one who was supposed to speak at the presentation. He threatened them with suspension or something like that. It was just amazing the amount of publicity it got. Every news station was there and other groups protesting, and there were cops walking through the school in full uniform. And I was standing there in charge of all this thinking, "I'm going to jail!"

Michelle's story sounds like it occurred in the mid to late 1980s, but it actually happened in 1994—a time when more tolerance might have been expected. The story also illustrates the fact that there is often a struggle within social institutions such as schools over what information will be filtered out or filtered in, especially when the topic is as controversial as AIDS.

In effect, filtering out by institutions prevents the majority of their members from learning about the issue in question. Only those individuals who go out of their way to make themselves aware—such as those risking suspension in Michelle's story—discover the information that the institution finds dangerous. Filtering at the level of the group operates in much the same way.

Group Filtering

Time and again throughout the interview process, the research participants said that they did not really discuss social issues with their friends. Certainly, there were exceptions, such as after seeing the movie *Philadelphia* or in the context of an AIDS awareness club. However, left to their own devices, it was rare for interviewees to bring up social issues in discussions with those around them. The single greatest reason was that such topics were "depressing," or even scary, as in the case of AIDS. The result is a sort of group culture of avoidance and circumspection, which actually mirrors our societal culture.

Recall how conscious Silva is of this group culture and how she avoided speaking of her experiences with hunger in an effort to maintain her friendships. This group culture of silence is revealed when she says, "The kids are not going to like me if I tell them what's going on." Group norms reinforce the avoidance of hunger, and Silva is well aware of the peer pressure involved. Acceptance within a group is contingent upon adhering to its culture. More often than not, that culture is one of avoidance.

However, there are some exceptional instances in which group culture calls for active dialogue about issues in general or the embracing of a particular issue. Obvious examples are voluntary groups and clubs—such as AIDS or hunger awareness groups—formed with the specific purpose of addressing a particular issue. At the same time, there are examples of groups that are not set up around a social issue and that still enhance the member's awareness. Beth Reinhardt is a rather cosmopolitan 23-year-old Jewish woman who has worked on many theater productions.

> *At the theater where I worked, there were a couple of people who were HIV positive. They were still performing, and it was really wonderful to be around them. They were very optimistic and just wanted to keep performing until something happened. Everybody in the theater community dealt with it very well.*

Beth's involvement in the theater exposed her to the issue of AIDS in a way that our larger culture, the media, her school, and so on had not. Her theater group actually filtered in AIDS and conveyed a very specific message of openness and acceptance around the AIDS issue in its internal culture.

Lloyd also maintains a circle of friends with a group culture that goes against this norm of silence.

> *We always talk about social issues. We talk about it over coffee and cigarettes. Most students never talk about that kind of stuff. They talk about what they did over the weekend. Sometimes we just want to grab people and shake them, saying "Talk to me about something else!" We hardly ever talk about stuff that we did. Why do you need to? If you go through and you do it, it happened and it was wonderful; but it's over. So, we talk all the time, and not just about poverty and hunger— just all sorts of everything. And it's amazing how we'll just be talking about something such as hunger and all of a sudden it will completely fly off to another tangent. Someone else will bring something up or a personal experience and someone else will join in. You can learn so much from people. There is so much more in here [pointing to his head] than people usually give credit for, even if they're young. People like to think about things that are going on in their own lives. I don't think it's necessarily selfishness . . . I'm just as individualistic as anyone. But you don't lose anything of yourself when you talk about stuff other than yourself. You gain more because you're learning more about yourself from other people. It's great!*

Instead of focusing on the here and now of their own lives, Lloyd and his friends promote a group culture that is free of these constraints. By doing this, they are allowing a far more broad range of information to be filtered into their awareness. Experiences such as Silva's would not be shoved aside in this group. Instead, they would be embraced as a learning experience leading to personal growth and an expanding social consciousness. This is atypical of the experiences of those interviewed, however, and such a group dynamic is definitely countercultural. Individuals such as Lloyd show much more self-determination and self-awareness than the average American over how they construct their consciousness and allow it to be constructed by larger institutions and cultural values.

Individual Filtering

At the same time that society, institutions, and groups have the ability to raise and lower social consciousness by filtering information in and out of our awareness, the individuals within these contexts also engage in the filtering process—a point that is overlooked by Herman and Chomsky. Individuals have the ability to overcome the limited interests of societal values, institutions, and groups that block out particular information. At the same time, however, individuals are also able to desensitize themselves to the specialized interests that are filtered down to them from larger social contexts.

Just as our culture, institutions, and groups have specialized interests, so do individuals. Because, under normal circumstances, individuals are willing members of an institution (or group or culture), individual interests often overlap with those of the organizations and groups to which individuals belong. However, these interests may also be quite divergent, given that most institutions are not "total institutions," such as prisons or asylums (Goffman 1961), which specifically insulate their members from the outside world. Most individuals have lives outside of their institutional boundaries. At the point where those interests diverge, the individual becomes attuned to information that is irrelevant to the institution and vice versa: the individual filters out information that may be relevant to the institution but is irrelevant to him- or herself.

Garrett, whom we already met with regard to the AIDS issue, went out of his way to learn more about homelessness and hunger by stopping to talk to a street solicitor. Like most people, it was his habit to just walk by street people with a mind full of stereotypes handed down from our culture; but what Garrett learned from sitting down with one was quite different from the information given to him on television.

> I couldn't really tell if I should believe what he was saying. He said he used to have a job and have people working for him. He was making a lot of money and he lost it all. I'm not sure if that's true or if he's always been on the street. Before, when I would see someone asking for money or whatever, I would think, "He's just a bum." But now, after talking with him, I guess it was like humanizing him. It was a pretty wild experience. I

learned a lot and I enjoyed sitting with him. He told me how to collect
money the right way, just in case I was ever on the street. He was very
pleased that I sat with him. He probably would still be talking if I was
there right now. He just kept going and going! Wow! And about this time,
it was getting cold at night and I was getting chilly. So I said, "Well, I'm
going home because I'm getting cold." And then I thought, "Where's he
going?" Nowhere. It was like, "Whoah! I get to go home and be warm
and he gets to stay here and do what he's been doing."

Street solicitors were no longer quite the same for Garrett after this experience. They were real people rather than "bums." Because Garrett went
out of his way to learn more about this issue, his consciousness was
expanded in a way that most people never experience. At the same time,
what he learned was so directly at odds with what our culture had taught
him about the homeless—that they are somehow "subhuman"—that Garrett was still not sure if he could trust what he was hearing; but the bottom line was the same: this man did not have a warm home to return to
on a cold night, and this was something that Garrett learned with his own
eyes, ears, and open mind.

Leslie also relies on what she sees with her own eyes to inform her
about the world, and this is a characteristic of individual filtering: it is
oftentimes based on personal experience rather than just on what individuals hear. Information gleaned from other sources has already been filtered
by our society, institutions, and groups. So, when Leslie hears from the
media that there are people starving in other parts of the world, she has to
decide for herself whether or not to believe this. "I've just been told that
it's there. It's not like I saw it first hand or anything. It seems so abstract."
While Leslie questions what she has heard from the media, the fact that
world hunger is not really "there" for her is said in all seriousness. It is not
in her interest, she does not see it with her own eyes, and it is not a part
of her experience. For all intents and purposes, the issue does not exist for
her. She has further filtered out the already filtered information given to
her because it is irrelevant for her experiences and her life.

Selective and Subliminal Filtering

The act of filtering, whether at the sociocultural, institutional, group, or
individual level, has a significant impact on the consciousness of the indi-

vidual, as well as upon the collective conscience of the group or institution. Through this process of filtering, it is possible to raise and lower awareness of information and, in so doing, our consciousness of social issues. As already hinted at in the previous paragraph, it is as if there is a contest for dominance among the four levels of filtering. Our cultures, institutions, and groups have tremendous power to filter the information received by those lower on the organizational hierarchy, particularly individuals. However, individuals—as well as groups and institutions—have the power to circumvent the filtering processes above them by going out of their way to seek information not immediately available to them and to dismiss the information they deem irrelevant to their interests. Our culture, institutions, groups, and selves all engage in filtering simultaneously, making the construction of our consciousness a veritable battleground.

Just as the filtering process among the four levels occurs simultaneously, so does the process of filtering out and filtering in. Every act of filtering out some information allows other information into our consciousness. Every act of filtering in is simultaneously an act of filtering out. When the media devotes thirty seconds to world hunger, we remain uninformed about the hungry within our own communities. When we heard about a new "gay cancer," we were not informed that AIDS can strike heterosexuals as well. For every bit of information we take into our consciousness, another is left out. In fact, considering how much information is "out there," far more of it is filtered out than can possibly be filtered in, even among the most socially conscious. Thus, while we speak of "social consciousness," we must realize that, out of necessity, we walk through life conscious of very little information. Our consciousness is bounded by our experiences and interests.

Some of this filtering is intended—*selective filtering*—and some of it happens without being aware that it is occurring—*subliminal filtering*. For example, when Garrett stopped to talk with the homeless man, he made a conscious effort to filter in more information. He was engaged in selective filtering. By comparison, when Sondra—who noted the impact of "live aid" and "band aid" on her consciousness—passed the homeless on the street without really noticing them, much less the fact that they were homeless, she was engaged in subliminal filtering. In high school, Sondra worked in a soup kitchen in order to boost her community service hours and improve her transcript. While there, she suddenly realized that

> *there are homeless people in my home town. I really wasn't that concerned with the issue and mostly I thought, "Oh, these people kind of*

*smell!" I didn't really like it. But it was a good experience because it
really made me aware of what was going on. I realized, "These people
do kind of have it bad, and there are people there . . . I've just never
seen them before." And then I realized, "Oh yeah! I see you hanging
out at the train station all the time!" You really recognize these people and suddenly, "There are homeless people around here," even
though I've passed them every day and I really never knew, especially
how many. So, it kind of opened my eyes a little bit even though I
wasn't really concerned going in.*

It was only after volunteering in the soup kitchen that Sondra realized
what she had been missing because of her subliminal filtering.

When filtering happens unconsciously, it has a constraining effect on
the individuals, groups, institutions, and society. For instance, if individuals
are given only one option when making a decision and are unaware of all
other options, their "freedom" of choice is limited. It is only when we are
presented with multiple options that we truly have the freedom to choose.
When information is filtered without an individual's awareness of it, that
individual is not free to act and react in accordance with a "raised" consciousness—one that is aware of alternative information. The development
of consciousness is constrained. It did not even occur to Sondra that the
issues of homelessness and hunger would be relevant to her and her home
town. Because the unconscious filtering left her only with information
about the problems of homelessness in big cities and the Third World, she
could not "see" the homeless at her own feet. Sondra's view of reality was
constrained by her unconscious failure to notice the hunger around her.

On the other hand, in the case of selective filtering, the result can
either be constraining or enabling, depending on which agent is conducting the filtering. If a culture, institution, or group is accomplishing the filtering process, the consciousness of smaller groups and the individuals
within them is somewhat constrained. Again, this is due to the fact that the
decision making has been co-opted by the larger social context. The media
coverage that Sondra saw presented *one* option: hunger and homelessness
exist somewhere else. Hunger and homelessness were not presented by the
media as a part of her local environment. As a result, her social consciousness was limited by filtering mechanisms beyond her control. Yet, this con-
straint is not as complete as when filtering occurs subliminally because
there is always the potential for these smaller groups or individuals to circumvent the filtering process of the institution by engaging in some filter-

ing of their own. Thus, Sondra's volunteering in the soup kitchen, even though she did not like it, filtered in additional information that filled in the gaps left by the media. Only then did it occur to her that "there *are* homeless people around here."

This possibility for circumventing the filtering process also points out the enabling side of the coin. When individuals make themselves aware of particular pieces of information—such as Garrett talking to the homeless man, they are maximizing their potential for decision making because there is a greater awareness of the possible choices. At the same time, when individuals are selectively filtering out particular pieces of information and thus limiting the options with which they are confronted, they are exercising their ability to maximize their own interests and the perspectives that are congruent with those interests. In sum, the act of filtering has both enabling and constraining tendencies depending on how conscious the process is and at what level the filtering process occurs. With this in mind, we now turn to the flip side of the filtering process: framing.

Framing

The filtering process just described is also a means for framing the social issue within the consciousness of the individual. These two processes are inextricably linked. Alluding to the link between filtering and framing, sociologist and activist Charlotte Ryan notes that "frames are not consciously or deliberately constructed, but operate as underlying mind sets that prompt one to notice elements that are familiar and ignore those that, are different" (1991: 54). The information that is allowed into one individual's consciousness will give her or him quite a different view of the world than an individual who allows a different set of information in. There may be some overlapping tendencies where the information is the same or similar, but to the extent that the information filtered in is different, so will the frames be different.

The idea of framing stems from the work of Erving Goffman (1974), and has been particularly utilized within the field of media discourse analysis (Gamson 1992; Ryan 1991). Ryan defines framing as the process of "ordering information into a coherent story" (1991: 53). Moreover, "framing is more than a process of interpreting selected events; it is actually the process of *creating* events, of signifying, from the vast pool of daily occurrences, what is important. Struggles over framing decide which of the day's many happenings will be awarded significance" (1991: 53).

Ryan discusses the issue of framing in terms of how reporters and journalists present news to the public. Much like Herman and Chomsky's view, she discusses how the media filters information—facts—and then presents the selected facts within a given frame. Because these frames give the facts a particular slant, the "truth" of the event becomes distorted.

> "Truth" doesn't stand alone; rather, people engage in a selection process, actively making sense out of a confusing flood of experience. [Framing is] a value-laden process; ordering information into a story requires some pre-existing notion of the story. There is no such thing as the value-free ordering of experience. . . . Even when we are actual witnesses, we are not privileged with the truth. Who we are—our class, gender, race, past experience, values, and interests—all come into play when we try to make sense of what's happening. (1991: 53, 54)

These slanted, value-laden frames are then handed down to consumers of the media—the public—who presumably, at least for the most part, accept the frame as fact.

However, as with Herman and Chomsky, this focus on framing at the institutional level minimizes or even overlooks individual responses to these frames, as if individuals were merely repositories—like empty glasses waiting to be filled by whatever these institutions decide to pour out. Such emphasis strips individuals of the personal agency and choice already discussed. While it may be argued that many consumers uncritically accept the information they are presented and that the way in which individuals frame an issue largely mirrors the frames presented by the media and other institutions, such assertions can hardly be universal. As with the typology of orientations to social issues presented in chapters 3 and 4, individual responses evolve over time and vary with the issue and the circumstances.

Individuals are just as capable of framing an issue within their consciousness as an institution is. If individuals filter information into their consciousness, then they also frame it. Given that individuals must grapple with multiple, oftentimes contradictory information filters, the way in which they reconcile all this information through framing is important. Ryan briefly mentions the individual capacity for framing when she notes that "who we are"—in terms of our race, class, gender, and so on—plays a role in sense-making. However, her focus remains at the institutional level of the media. Instead, after a glimpse at institutional framing of issues, we will focus on framing at the individual unit of analysis, looking briefly at how the issues of hunger and AIDS themselves are framed and then moving to the more abstract level of frames for social issues in general.

Ryan and other media analysts focus on how single issues are framed by the media. She notes, for example, that the topic of United States intervention in Nicaragua in the early 1980s has been framed in a number of different ways. The issue was oftentimes framed in terms of an "east-west conflict" in which the focus was on whether the United States would "permit the establishment of a Soviet-oriented communist state in Central America" (1991: 62). The same issue, however, was framed by dissenters from the official U.S. position in terms of the "human cost of war," in which "the issue is will the United States continue an inhuman war that violates its own basic principles" (1991: 64). These are two very different frames of the same issue of U.S. intervention. The groups espousing each of these views have filtered different information into their consciousness in a way that is congruent with the interests of each group.

In a similar way, the issues of hunger and AIDS have been framed in various ways that are congruent with the interests of one group or another. Hunger is most frequently framed as an issue for the "Third World" and developing countries and is only secondarily seen as an issue for our country. Thirty-eight percent (38.5%) of the survey respondents listed Third World or developing countries as one of the top three populations affected by hunger, whereas only 4.7 percent listed Americans ($N = 426$). The issue is also much more likely to be framed in terms of the children who are affected by it. Adults are frequently overlooked. Twenty-five percent (25.4%) of the survey respondents listed children as one of the top three populations affected by hunger, whereas adults were listed by only 1.2 percent ($N = 426$).

Despite all the current evidence to the contrary, AIDS is still framed as a "homosexual disease" among a large part of the population. Thirty-four percent (34.7%) of the survey respondents listed gays, bisexuals, or lesbians as one of the top three populations affected by AIDS, whereas only 11.3 percent listed heterosexuals ($N = 426$). On the positive side, however, 38 percent listed "everyone" or "anyone" as *the* top population affected by AIDS while gays, bisexuals, and lesbians comprised 16.7 percent of the responses in the same category—the first and second highest categories respectively. AIDS is also framed as more of an issue for individuals than as an issue affecting our communities or nation as a whole. Only 8.7 percent of respondents ($N = 426$) listed community or nation as one of the top three populations affected by AIDS. All other categories represented individuals in terms of their group affiliation (i.e., adults, persons with AIDS, children, etc.) or their behavior (i.e., the sexually active, the promiscuous, IV drug users, etc.). Moreover, very few people saw it as an issue that affected themselves and/or those close to them. Only 3.1 percent of respondents ($N = 426$) listed themselves or those close to them as one of the top three populations affected by AIDS. However, when asked *directly* whether they are affected by AIDS, 75.7 percent responded "yes" (19.8% said "no" and 4.5% "don't know"—$N = 420$, 6 missing).

These frames, like the ones discussed by Ryan in her book, focus on a single issue. However, by looking across social issues, it is possible to determine more generic frames for looking at social issues *in general*. By looking at the frames underlying all social issues, it is possible to look into the *collective* consciousness of our culture as it is manifest within individual consciousness. While there are myriad possible frames imaginable to the social scientist, the six frames found in the data for this study are the *individual frame, bureaucratic frame, structural frame, universal frame, social ethics frame,* and *conspiracy frame*. While these frames are not necessarily mutually exclusive and may be employed at various times by the same individual, they are presented independently.[6]

The *individual frame* defines social issues as a matter of individual responsibility. When Reuben expressed his lack of sympathy for his aunt, who acquired AIDS through drug use, because she must bear the responsibility for her own actions, he was employing this frame. In other words, persons who utilize the individual frame believe that the issue arises out of the personal failings of individuals through such behaviors as promiscuous sex and illicit drug abuse. Only the irresponsible have to pay for their actions. This frame is symbolized by the image of the innocent child who is held up as a contrast with the irresponsible adult. Regardless of the issue, whether it be AIDS, hunger, or another issue, children cannot be blamed for their condition in life and are thus the object of much more sympathy than are adults, who are seen as having much more control over their situation. In other words, those employing the individual frame look at social issues in terms of the "guilt" versus "innocence" of those affected by the issue in question. Such a frame clearly resonates with our culture of individualism. If we have the "right to think for ourselves, judge for ourselves, [and] make our own decisions" (Bellah et al. 1985: 142), then we also are responsible for our own thoughts, judgments, and decisions. Based on this frame, the way to solve the social issue at hand includes helping those whom we deem "deserving" and allowing the undeserving to fend for themselves.

Social issues are defined by those employing the *bureaucratic frame* as a matter for "the experts" who are themselves responsible for addressing the issue. Recall the case of Chad, presented in chapter 4, whose uncle was HIV positive. He contributed money to the AIDS issue, but felt that he could not personally do anything about the issue because he was not a scientist and could not come up with a cure. For Chad and others adopting this frame, the issue is outside of the average individual's control. Without the experts with the appropriate knowledge, we would all be helpless in the face of the issue. Underlying this bureaucratic frame is the recognition that we live in a highly complex world where the division of labor is paramount. There is much faith in human progress and technological solutions hold much fascination. The way in which we must address the issue is by allowing the experts to do their job as they see fit, with a "little monetary support" from ourselves. Thus, we have come to rely on scientists, government agencies, charities, outreach programs, schools, and so on to do the work for us. Recall Milgram's discussion of how we deal with the stimulus overload which characterizes modernity. He refers to these "specialized" institutions that intercede on our behalf. However, the consequence is that these institutions serve to distance the individual from those institutions they serve (1970: 1462). As a result, our moral involvement in society is "restricted." We become satisfied with giving money to some organization that can handle it and, our responsibility having been met, we then wash our hands of the issue.

Those who utilize the *structural frame* define the issue as a result of structural breakdown or as a symptom of deeper problems in society. Brad, who volunteers in a "food bank"—a warehouse storing food for soup kitchens—frames the hunger issue in this way.

> *There's something structurally wrong because we have warehouses full of food. They say we have enough food to feed the world three times over or something like that, and yet some people can't afford to eat anything. There's something in the very structure, and if we tried it so long one way, why wouldn't we at least try it another way, because its NOT working this way. Just try something different; and if that doesn't work, at least you know you tried it. I don't think it's ever been tried.*

As is apparent in this passage, no individual or group in particular is held responsible. Instead, the system itself is to blame and this is especially pronounced in the tendency of those employing this frame, such as Brad, to speak in terms of "It"—The System. In its present form, the system is inappropriate for the current circumstances. The image here is of society as a broken or inefficient machine, so the goal is to optimize or change the system itself. Who is responsible for doing this? Everyone is. This frame falls back on our collective notions of social responsibility. As is true of an ambiguous term such as "everyone," the real outcome is "no one in particular." Instead, we rely on making changes through social policy, advocacy organizations, and social movements. In this respect, the structural frame is very similar to the bureaucratic frame in that we end up relying on these specialized institutions. However, the participation of the average individual is not discounted because of his or her "lack of expertise," as in the bureaucratic frame. Instead, these institutions rely on the participation of everyday individuals—the citizenship. "Grassroots" and "lay activists" become the principal actors here; their *lack* of expertise is at times a positive credential. Thus, this perspective resounds with our ideals of democratic participation for the greater good of all.

The *universal frame* also overlaps with the structural frame. Here individuals frame the issue as something that affects and should be of concern for everybody. However, this does not pose an imperative for personal responsiblity. For example, Joann Mansfield utilizes this frame in her understanding of AIDS.

> *I think everyone at some point in their life will have a stake in this issue. By this day and age, everyone at some point in their life will know someone. Even if it's a friend of a friend, it still affects you. Everyone who is born or alive now will know someone who has, or has died of, AIDS; and that will affect everyone.*

The image portrayed and that symbolizes the perspective taken by those employing this frame is that of ripples in a pond. A pebble breaks the stillness of the water much like a social issue directly affects the lives of a limited number of people. Everyone feels the effects to a greater or lesser extent, depending on how close they are to the point of impact. This frame found particular resonance in the "We Are the World" campaign—with the hit song by the same name—for hunger in Ethiopia sponsored by media celebrities in the mid-1980s. Taken alone, however, the universal frame has little depth. The causal roots of the issue are not explored, and it is not backed up with any method of finding a long-term solution. Those using this frame are at a loss as to where to start, or even if it is their responsibility at all. If everyone is affected by it, then everyone has the potential for addressing the issue; but again, "everyone" implies no one in particular.

The individual employing the *social ethics frame* defines the issue as a matter of ethics or morals. When Diane notes that homelessness and hunger are an integral part of our affluent society, she says "There's something morally and ethically wrong with that." Moreover, by framing the issue in these terms, she is assuming her *own* responsibility for it. This frame holds that the solution to the problem is for each of us to take personal responsibility for getting involved. Thus, the causal root of the problem is the fact that many individuals are not taking their fair share of responsibility. If we do not take our share of responsibility, we all lose. The social ethics frame, like the structural frame, resonates with our cultural ideal of social responsibility. However, this is taken a step further by couching this ideal in terms of moral obligation. Justice and equality are the catchphrases of those holding this frame. Like the structural and individual frames, there is again a focus on guilt versus innocence; but this time, it is the guilt or innocence of those witnessing the effects of the issue—the bystander who embraces or shirks his or her own responsibility.

Stepping outside of the hunger and AIDS examples presented thus far, it is possible to speculate about other frames, such as a *conspiracy frame*, in which the issue is seen as a result of an explicit attempt by the few to exploit and maintain control over the many. In other words, there is a focus on the guilt versus innocence of those in charge. Those utilizing this frame often speak in terms of "they" and "corruption." This frame appeals to our cultural concern for the underdog and the solution it poses is one of revolution: overthrowing those in power. Examples of this frame are presented in chapter 8 when we consider issues other than hunger and AIDS.

These six frames do not represent all of the possible frames available for thinking about social issues. However, they do represent the most central and influential frames found in the data. Again, these frames are not autonomous and mutually exclusive. In actual experience, individuals may utilize more than one frame, depending upon their circumstances. Media analysts focus on the struggle over frames presented to the public, but once a frame is presented we cannot assume it is the only frame that individuals take into account. Individuals are privy to multiple frames and, in a sense, there is also a struggle for dominance between the frames available within the individual's consciousness. While one frame may be prominent at one point in an individual's life, when her life circumstances change, she is likely to reshuffle the frames, choosing a different frame as primary because it better reflects her new situation. For example, it is widely believed that some of the radicals of the baby boom generation later became more conservative yuppies as they settled down, got married, and had children. As they assumed different responsibilities, the frames they utilized had to change. "Free love"—or "anarchy," or whatever slogan one might choose—might have been ideal when single, but when raising a family, it became much more problematic.

While these frames may be utilized in combination with one another, they do tend to correlate with the various types of affinity toward social issues. For instance, the individual frame is oftentimes found among those who are self-referenced and nonreferenced. Those employing the bureaucratic or universal frames can be found in all types except—usually—the socially referenced. The structural and social ethics frames are most often correlated with the socially referenced type. Again, however, these are not mutually exclusive frames. Some of those who are socially referenced may contain elements of the individual and/or bureaucratic frames. This scenario reflects the case of Beth, noted earlier. She says,

> *I feel like anybody can make a difference. I mean, I'm not a scientist and I can't come up with a cure for the virus, but if I can help somebody who does have the virus, if I can help prevent somebody from getting the virus by education, or if I can give $10 out of my weekly paycheck for the dance marathon and if that money can be used effectively to do one of those things—education, services, anything like that—it's definitely making a difference.*

While she realizes she is not a scientist and cannot cure AIDS (bureaucratic frame), she does recognize her own responsibility for getting involved with an issue that has such a dramatic impact on society (social ethics frame). She goes on to point out her responsibility for her own behavior (individual frame). However, it is the social ethical frame that is dominant within her consciousness. The fact that Beth has employed different frames simultaneously is a reflection of the types of information she has filtered into and out of her consciousness. This simultaneous use of multiple frames are further pursued in chapter 8.

Facticity

If reality were purely objective—if there were a single "Truth" in our experience of the world—we would have no need to "frame" it at all. Recalling that there are multiple frames for social issues at our disposal, that we typically embrace more than one simultaneously, and that there is a contest between frames for dominance, it is not surprising that the grasp of reality we have in our consciousness is actually quite tenuous and fluid. For this reason, we typically check our perception of reality with that of others. How many times have we heard someone ask, or have even done so ourselves, "Is it cold in this room, or is it just me?" Temperature is a property that can be objectively measured with a thermometer. However, our experience of being cold is largely subjective. So long as other people believe it is cold, the reality of our being cold is confirmed and we can say that the room is cold. If others do not agree that the room is cold, we either adjust our reality to match theirs or we come to the conclusion that "I must be sick." In other words, if our experience of reality does not match that of others, we are likely to determine that we are "abnormal" or "deviant" in some way. Popular opinion carries a lot of weight regardless of its accuracy.

This example illustrates what is meant by *facticity,* the need of actors "to feel—even if this is somewhat of an illusionary sense—that they share a common factual and obdurate world" (Turner 1987: 19). In other words, we seek to confirm the content of our consciousness by checking the "reality" of our experiences with that of others. We engage in "reality checking;" and when there is no one around with whom to confirm our reality, we make assumptions about what others believe to be true, oftentimes labeling these others as "everyone," as in "Everyone thinks that way" or "Everyone knows that. . . ." For example, recall that Garrett described how knowing a friend of a friend who was HIV positive brought the issue closer to home for him. He went on to say that

> *He's the only one that I know of who has AIDS, but I don't think it's too likely I know anyone else who does. Again, it's not that it's some-one else's disease, but* everyone *believes that it's not going to happen to them or someone they know. That's how everyone thinks. So, I just don't think that I would know too many people who would be HIV positive.*

Garrett uses his reference to "everyone" to substantiate his claim that AIDS probably has not affected anyone else within his circle. He does not feel "deviant" or outside of the average for his belief. If everyone believes that AIDS is not going to happen to them or someone they know, Garrett can feel better about believing in this same unrealistic "reality."

However, there are some individuals who are more certain of the reality of their experiences. They do not feel as much of a need to engage in reality checking. In fact, they may make it a point to set themselves apart from others while dismissing "everyone's" conclusion that they must be "deviant." In the language of poetry and pop psychology, they are moving "to the beat of a different drummer." Beth speaks more directly about the role of public opinion when she speaks of AIDS activism as more of a passing fad than as something that is taken seriously.

> *Everybody's very aware of the issue, but I don't think people are all that concerned about it. It was a real big trendy issue for a while and now people are bored with that. People aren't interested anymore. Wearing red ribbons was a real big thing in Hollywood and so on, but as time goes on you're starting to see less and less of that. You're starting to hear fewer and fewer people talking about the issue. The problem's only getting worse.*

In criticizing the attitude that concern for AIDS is more a fad than a commitment, Beth has set herself apart from public opinion. She does not rely on the perceptions of others to confirm her reality that AIDS is an issue to be taken seriously.

Based on this evidence, it becomes apparent that the need for facticity is not so universal and unwavering as some theorists might claim (see Turner 1987, for instance). While doubtlessly present among the majority who are nonreferenced, self-referenced, or relationally referenced, this need to confirm one's reality against that of others is something that varies from one person to another and from one context to another. Among those interviewed, those who were least likely to fall back on what "everybody" thinks and most likely to state their own opinions were also those who were socially referenced with regard to the issue that they were addressing. There is a notable exception, however. When speaking about AIDS, there was a tendency among all interviewees, regardless of type, to mention how poorly educated other people were with regard to this issue. For instance, Sherri Dreyfus, who is nonreferenced with regard to the AIDS issue, noted right up front that

> *People are kind of scared of people with AIDS or something because they aren't educated enough about AIDS to know they aren't going to get AIDS [from being around them]. People aren't aware enough about it, even though everyone thinks that they are educated about it. Everyone says, "Oh, yeah. AIDS. I know all about it. I know you can't get it just by sitting in the same room with someone." But at the same time, if they were sitting in the room with someone who had AIDS and they knew it, they might be like . . . you know.*

As seen here, even educational awareness does not always translate into appropriate behavior regarding the risks. For example, of those sampled for the survey who are sexually active ($N = 273$), only 33.3 percent use a condom every time they have sex. Those using a condom 50 percent or less of the time comprise 36.6 percent of the sexually active. Thus, the reality of being "better educated" is somewhat dubious at best. The fact that so many in the sample set themselves apart by claiming better awareness seems more reflective of a need for personal security—facticity—than it is an effort to set oneself apart from the majority.

Placing the Pieces into the Mosaic

Social consciousness forms the basis of the emergence of social affinity.[7] As already noted in the introduction to this chapter, consciousness includes not only an awareness of the world outside of the individual, but a "*concern* for some social or political cause." However, in order for such a concern to develop, the awareness must already be present. Thus, social consciousness is the first of the three major elements in the overall mosaic to be broken down into its smaller pieces and is logically followed by a consideration of the development of concern and sentiment.

In this chapter, we have learned that the construction of this social consciousness is a rather complex picture involving various levels of filtering and means of framing social issues. The view of the social world constructed through this process is then "confirmed" by checking it against the larger "truth" or reality shared by others: facticity. While it is important to understand and appreciate each of these individual pieces in the overall mosaic, the central point to remember is that the social context in which the individual finds himself or herself, as well as the degree to which he or she takes an active role in this process, is crucial to the subsequent emergence of social affinity.

Both society and the individual can play an active role in constructing one's consciousness. On the one hand, many of the filters and frames, such as those set up by our groups, institutions, and society itself, are already in place and outside of the control of individuals. Just as most television viewers sit back and absorb what is given to them on TV, most individuals are passive recipients of the reality handed down to them by their group affiliations. While such individuals can function quite well in the social world, they have become mere automatons, subject to the whims of our institutions and those who shape them.

However, the shaping of social consciousness is not unidirectional. Individuals do not have to be the passive recipients of information and "fact." Instead, it is possible to carve out a perspective on reality that deviates from the norm of passivity. By actively engaging in conscious, selective filtering—especially filtering in, by becoming aware of the frames one employs, and by being aware of one's reliance on public opinion to shape one's beliefs, it is possible to show much more self-determination in constructing one's social consciousness. In maximizing our awareness of the social world and the alternative information and choices available, it is also possible to play a more active role in our society and become a member of society who reflects the spirit of social affinity.

Consciousness of our social world is only one important element of this spirit. Between the development of one's consciousness and playing an active role within society, there is an emotive response to the reality perceived—the emergence of that concern for social issues captured by the broader definition of consciousness. Our emotions have the power to enhance our commitment to society and those within it, but they also have the power to shut down this commitment before it has a chance to be expressed. The role of emotions in this process—and of sentiment in general—is the subject of the next chapter.

SIX

A "Sentimental Journey"

Emotions, Role-taking, and Empathy

It is not enough for individuals to be conscious of the social world outside of themselves in order for social affinity to develop. We must also *feel* connected to that world, that our lives are an integral part of the larger society. In this way, we develop a *sense* of obligation to others and to society. Thus, sentiment is a key element in both linking the micro world of individuals with the macro world of groups, institutions, and society and in creating the social cohesion that holds society together at both levels. A discussion of this link forms the basis of the first section of this chapter. Then, we explore the notion of social sentiment and emotions in more detail, focusing particular attention on empathy. Such a consideration necessarily begins at the individual level, although the second half of the chapter moves on to the larger implications for developing social affinity in the context of social issues.

Sentiments and the Link Between
the Personal and the Societal

In the previous chapter, the process of the construction of social consciousness was discussed at the parallel levels of society/culture, institution, group, and individual. Each of these levels plays a vital role in that process. However, when it comes to emotions, the level of analysis must be brought down to that of the individual alone for the very reason that culture, institutions, and groups *themselves* do not *feel*. This is a central point to Milgram's notion of "specialized" institutions that intercede on the individual's behalf. Because these institutions come between the "concerned" individual and the people they serve, the social issue they address is distanced from the consciousness of the individual. This distance is made all the more poignant by the fact that the institution that takes the place of the "concerned" individual does not "feel" as that individual would if he or she were addressing the social issue directly. Organizations are not compassionate.

This lack of feeling by institutions and organizations is particularly apparent from the perspective of those on the "receiving end." In discussing the process of bureaucratization, Weber is highly aware of the depersonalization that occurs within these large institutions. Because of the emphasis on predictability and calculability, bureaucracies become "incapable of dealing with individual particularities" (Coser 1977: 231). Individual concerns become lost in a world of red tape, rules, and automated answering services. The cold, rational world of the bureaucracy has as its main end control of individuals and the variations of individuality (Ritzer 1996). All feeling is lost.

Thus, being able to "feel for" another is a uniquely individual phenomenon. Joy, sorrow, anger, and fear are individual experiences. However, individual emotion is, as we see in more detail later, dependent upon *relationships* (Clark 1987; Gordon 1990)—two or more individuals interacting with one another in a sustained way.[1] For this reason, one cannot divorce individual experiences of emotions from the collective nature of those same emotions. For example, David Karp, in his book *Speaking of Sadness* (1996), demonstrates how a feeling so personal and individually experienced as clinical depression is actually socially constructed and given meaning through interaction with others. Illness and depression are collectively defined in our society as a biological and psychological "problem" in need of medical attention—an assessment that is distinctly different from the interpretations of other cultures. In other words, even the most private feelings are shaped within a context of interaction with other individuals and with society itself.

It would appear, then, that emotions are not strictly the purview of individuals; and this is a central point in our consideration of social affinity: emotions are imbued with a collective nature that is inescapable for social beings such as ourselves. Our emotions arise out of our relations and have a significant impact upon them. Moreover, the notion of collective "sentiments"—a word closely tied with that of "emotion" (Gordon: 565)—has been central to social analysis since the birth of sociology.[2]

Emile Durkheim, one of the major figures in the early history of sociology, was highly concerned with the connectedness of society. He asked the question, "What is it which holds society together?" His answer was "solidarity," a phenomenon that is not an "intellectual agreement" so much as a "shared emotional feeling." These emotional attachments foster what Durkheim called our "collective consciousness"—a "sense of belonging to a community with others and hence feeling a moral obligation to live up to its demands" (Collins and Makowsky 1989: 105). In other words, at the same time that there are individual emotions, these sentiments serve the function of maintaining society.[3] While groups, organizations, and institutions themselves do not feel, the shared sentiments of the individuals within them make their emergence and continued existence possible.

Adam Smith, writing a century before Durkheim, made emotions and their collective dimension the focus of his first great book, *The Theory of Moral Sentiments* (1759; in Heilbroner 1986). For him, sympathy—what we today call "empathy"[4]—and the ability to identify with others—to see and experience the world as they do, to role-take—are central to the cohesiveness of society. His explanation for this assertion is rather ingenious. Smith was enamored of the capitalist economic system that was emerging during his lifetime because it maximized individual liberty. Yet, he saw this pursuit of individual interests as somewhat problematic in that it could lead to social chaos and anarchy. If everyone made their own rules based on their own interests, society would fall apart; and yet the capitalist world around Smith was anything but an anarchy. This realization led him to wonder how it was possible to maintain society while pursuing one's individual freedom.

If, for example, people who created and followed their own traffic laws got in our way, we would in all likelihood get angry with them, imposing sanctions such as honking our horn and becoming unsympathetic with their pursuit of freedom. Smith realized that we do not readily extend our sympathy to those whom we find reprehensible in some way. For this reason, individuals freely *choose* to avoid being perceived as "reprehensible." Because we desire the sympathy of others, and because there is a limit to our capacity for sympathy, we monitor our behavior so that it is socially acceptable. We make sure that we are "worthy of" the sympathy of others by imposing our own constraints on our behavior that might be perceived as "chaotic" or "reprehensible." Thus, the same self-interest that is the life-blood of capitalism also prompts us to act on behalf of others and in a way that respects their own interests. In this way, the anarchy that is one potential outcome of individual liberty is avoided. In Smith's argument, it is this exchange of sympathy that provides the basis for the moral order of society. Sympathy is the "moral sentiment" and virtue—the "embodiment of morality"—is "always mediated by the empathetic properties of human understanding" (Heilbroner 1986: 59).

It is important to keep Smith's *Theory of Moral Sentiments* in its larger context. Smith was a product of the Enlightenment—a period of heady optimism in the progress of humanity. He was also an economist, most known for his book *The Wealth of Nations*. His optimism was thus very apparent in his treatment of capitalism, leading him to this belief that self-interest could be the basis of the moral ordering of society. This is a belief that still predominates today as is apparent in the Reagan and Bush presidencies, which put so much emphasis on "trickle down" economics and the "thousand points of light." In fact, as we see later, modern exchange theory is highly reminiscent of this point of view. However, as we also see, such a basis of morality has received much criticism.

The work of Smith and his views on the centrality of human sentiment to the moral order of society provides a good backdrop for the consideration of emotions within the context of social affinity. With this in mind, we begin this chapter with an overview of the sentiments experienced by individuals when thinking of social issues such as hunger and AIDS, focusing particular attention on empathy and the crucial part played by role-taking. We will then look at those factors that serve to inhibit the empathetic response to social issues, endangering the social affinity that lies at the heart of our social fabric.

Sentiment and Affinity

When we allow social issues and their ramifications to enter our consciousness, this awareness is oftentimes accompanied by an emotional response. While this is by no means universal, even many of the nonreferenced admit, at the very least, to feelings of pity for those suffering. In other words, the sentiments elicited by one's consciousness of social issues are more varied than Smith's writings would indicate. While sadness and sympathy are certainly apparent and are the most typical responses, other sentiments include anger and frustration, guilt, fear, and the empathy that lies at the heart of Smith's *Theory of Moral Sentiments* and so much contemporary research on prosocial and moral behavior.

Anger and frustration are among the more rare responses to social issues. As Michelle's story illustrates, they are generally accompanied by an understanding of what the individual perceives as the root of the problem.

> *Hearing these personal stories of people with AIDS was really sad on the one hand; but it really, really angered me. In one of my health classes, we were talking about it and this guy was saying, "It would never happen to me!" And he's just the person you know it's going to happen to. He says, "No, I never wear a condom" and he talks about all these girls, then thinks, "No, it's not going to happen to me." You just want to kill him! I just want to smack him and ask, "What are you thinking?" It's people like that, that I just . . . it just gets me so mad.*

Michelle's frustration and anger at the "guy" in her health class were inseparable. For her, the problem of the continuation of the AIDS epidemic is due to people who do not take the issue seriously or play their part in preventing the spread of HIV. She is frustrated and angered by their attitudes.

In the context of social issues, guilt is an emotion most clearly associated with the awareness that others do not have what you yourself possess. For this reason, it was much more typical a response to the issue of hunger than to AIDS. Because AIDS is so frequently seen as a matter of personal responsibility, individuals do not tend to feel guilty for their own health. However, with regard to the hunger issue, and because it is so often associated with helpless children in other parts of the world, guilt is a prominent reaction. This is particularly true when one is confronted with a TV commercial like the one in Appendix B asking for seventy cents a day to help needy children. The commercial becomes even more poignant for Joann when she considers the money she and her husband spend on food for themselves and their child.

> *You just change the channel! I mean, it just makes me think, "Oh, my God!" You're sitting in your house with a can of soda, your dinner in front of you, your kitchen overflowing and you're just sitting there. . . . "Oh, my God!" It just makes you feel guilty. When you were little, your mom's always saying, "You have to eat your dinner because there are starving people in Africa." And now you just go to the store and buy groceries and . . . honestly, in two weeks Bob and I could probably spend two hundred dollars, including the baby stuff. That's so excessive. You think about it and if I saved the money from the little*

things, it would be my seventy cents a day. I spend that much in the soda machine every day. You don't even think about it. It just makes you feel guilty.

The juxtaposition of the utter poverty of those children pictured in the hunger commercial with the relative affluence of a young family with a baby is a disturbing experience for Joann. She would much rather change the channel and eat in peace. However, she realizes that this peace of mind is empty because of the gnawing awareness that even a brief glimpse of the commercial leaves behind. The result is guilt over all that she has and is unwilling to give up. Her emotion is also associated with the admonitions of her mother, who effectively used guilt to get her to eat and, presumably, to appreciate what she had.

Considering that the majority of individuals are self-referenced with regard to the AIDS issue, it comes as no surprise that the most typical emotional response to that issue is fear. These individuals are highly conscious of the potential for AIDS to enter their own lives. In fact, learning of people who are HIV positive heightens this fear, particularly when they are already known to the individual. The perception is that AIDS is a deadly disease that is coming closer and closer to them. Gevonne captures this "creeping up on you" feeling when she notes that first the brothers of her best friend were HIV positive and now one of her own friends is too.

I know it's close now! It makes me feel a little nervous. The two brothers are intravenous drug abusers, so that's not something that can threaten me; but it's a lot closer now. I can see it. It's not just on TV. And my own friend, he's this person who used to be vital and he's just slowly deteriorating. That's kind of hard to see. And know that that's it. That's what they've been talking about. That's AIDS. That's the big one. It's closer to home now.

While the fact that AIDS is coming closer to Gevonne only makes her "feel a little nervous," this is actually a source of great fear for many people. As we saw in the previous chapter, the reality behind AIDS that was portrayed in the movie *Philadelphia* proved rather scary for Colleen. Joann also expresses such fear.

I met this man and I had no idea he was HIV positive. I found out later. It just scares me because I see my friends—my peers—and how they act and how casually they take things. When I was graduating from high school, I always thought, "I wonder who it's going to be."

someone in my high school has to die of AIDS. Statistically, it's inevitable. It scares me to think that it could happen to somebody I know or . . . or me, or my sister, my brother . . . anything.

The fear expressed by Joann, Colleen, and even Gevonne is rather typical when discussing AIDS for the very reason that it is something they see as, in all likelihood, affecting them. Fear is not predominant with the hunger issue, however, unless the individual is also self-referenced toward the issue. Recall Silva's reaction to the issue of hunger—an issue toward which she is self-referenced. She has a paralyzing fear of hunger and even fear of having contact with the hungry because of the memories it would call to mind. Based on the common understanding of fear as an emotion strongly associated with self-preservation, the fear of the self-referenced comes as no surprise. These individuals are highly motivated to protect themselves, whether it be from AIDS or from hunger.

Sadness and sympathy—pity—are the most typical sentiments expressed within the context of social issues and are apparent among the nonreferenced, self-referenced, and relationally and socially referenced alike. Brad's reaction to AIDS falls within this category.

If I see someone dying of AIDS, I think of how sad it is. It's just sad and I wish that they would be able to relax and move on. If I see someone healthy, sometimes I can't convince myself that it's really true; but mostly I just think that is sad . . . sad that anyone has to live with that. It just doesn't seem fair almost.

Brad is someone who can sleep well at night even with the awareness of the death taking place throughout the world. In fact, it would be considered unhealthy if he or anyone lost sleep just because someone unknown to us is dying. Given that people are dying all the time, we have to "tune out" in order to keep on living ourselves—a point that is reminiscent of the filtering of irrelevant information in order to prevent "stimulus overload." Freud concurred with the necessity of such screening when he said that "protection against stimuli is an almost more important function for the living organism than reception of stimuli" (1920: 27).

On the other hand, such expressions of sadness can strike the one listening as somewhat hollow. Arlie Hochschild, in her classic study *The Managed Heart,* labeled this phenomenon "surface acting"—"pretending to feel what we do not"—and contrasted it with "deep acting"—in which the actor eventually comes to feel the sympathy he or she initially pretended to feel (1983: 33). Oftentimes, as Clark points out, such expressions of sympathy are said with the intent of impressing others and/or bolstering one's self-esteem.[5] However, for the recipient of sympathy, such hollow expressions are not valueless and are "more reassuring to the person with problems than no sympathy display whatsoever" (Clark 1987: 295–296). On the other hand, such shallow displays of sympathy do not lead to a compassionate outlook in the same way that empathy and role-taking have the potential to do.

Empathy and Role-taking

If such sentiments as sadness and sympathy are as easily expressed by the nonreferenced as by the relationally and socially referenced, what is it that sets the last two types apart from the others in terms of their sentiments? The classic answer to this question, from Adam Smith to contemporary social psychologists is empathy.[6] Just as the relationally and socially referenced have bridged the gap between themselves and others, empathy is the sentiment that creates a social bond between separate individuals: "Empathy is central to an understanding of that aspect of the self which involves we-ness, transcendence of the separate, disconnected self. It is, in fact, the process through which one's experienced sense of basic connection and similarity to other humans is established" (Jordan 1984: 2).

With anger and frustration, we are reacting against others and/or their circumstances; with guilt and fear, we focus on our own circumstances; and with sadness and sympathy, we feel for others—whether deeply or at a mere surface level. When it comes to empathy, we actually feel *with* others. In other words, sympathy—on the one hand—is an emotional reaction to an other's circumstances: we feel badly for them, but we do not feel what they themselves feel. We are not so much experiencing an emotion of our own so much as *responding* to that of another. With empathy, however, we not only understand an other's situation, we experience an emotion that is "congruent" with what they themselves are experiencing (Eisenberg and Miller 1987: 91–92). The person who empathizes with another experiences the same kind of emotion that the other feels, although not to the same degree since the emotions are "congruent," not "identical." Moreover, unlike sympathy, empathy is not just responding to another's emotion or situation. Instead, the individual empathizing genuinely feels an emotion in his or her own right.[7]

The definition of empathy implies that one has a full understanding of another's situation. To accomplish this, it is necessary to comprehend what they are experiencing from their own perspective. Empathizing requires that we see the world—as much as possible—as the other does. It requires role-taking. For example, Laura Kane expresses her empathy toward the hungry in terms of all of the similarities she shares with them.

> When you label someone as anything—whether it be "homeless" or "hungry" or "unemployed"—you see them through that lens . . . more so than just as a person. When I talked to these people at the shelter, I saw that they had the same dreams as I had and the same desires. They cared just as much about their kids as my parents care about me. I saw them, not as "homeless people," but as people who were in an unfortunate situation and circumstance. I lost a lot of those labels for people. When you just kind of lump all the people together and just say, "These are the hungry people," they lose their identity. Going to the shelter gave me the opportunity to meet these people who are lumped in this group and remember that they have a story and they have a personality; they just have a different type of baggage to carry than someone else.

The role-taking in which Laura has engaged highlights another point that is key to our understanding of empathy. She points out that we attach labels to these individuals, whether they be "homeless," "HIV positive," or, less flatteringly, "bums" and "moral degenerates." No matter what the label, the individuality of those bearing the label is lost. They are dehumanized (Keen 1991; Kohn 1990). In this way, it is possible to ignore their plight and the social issues lying underneath, much as those who, as discussed in the previous chapter, utilize the individual frame and disregard the "undeserving."

However, "empathy and perspective taking . . . can promote the sense of similarity" (Kohn 1990: 142). Laura came to see the similarities between herself and the homeless and hungry she met at the shelter. These previously nameless individuals were then imbued with their own stories and personalities. In effect, by appreciating their uniqueness, those Laura met at the shelter were "rehumanized." At the same time, Laura did not confuse her own identity with theirs—empathy did not result in merging with the other. Instead, she was conscious of the fact that they had "different baggage" to carry. Thus, "perspective taking and empathy allow us to appreciate that you are not me and that we can be connected in spite of that" (1990: 135).

Because empathy is a sentiment dependent on our role-taking ability, it is arguably the key to understanding the individual in a social context, for it is through role-taking that we establish links with the others in
society, and even with society itself. This is much the same point that Adam
Smith made in his *Theory of Moral Sentiments* noted in the introduction, and
that the sociologist George Herbert Mead makes. By stepping outside of
ourselves and taking the perspective of another, we are in a position to look
back at ourselves and evaluate our behavior. If we see that our behavior is
inappropriate from the perspective of those outside ourselves—from the
perspective of society—we change our own behavior (Cuzzort and King
1989). In other words, we regulate ourselves so that we do not take advantage of the individual liberty so prized by Smith. In this way, society is
maintained while individuals are "free" to follow their own desires.

However, to further our understanding of this connection with "others"—those who are unlike ourselves—it is first necessary to consider the
varieties of "other." When talking about the "other," most sociologists do
not distinguish between individual others and groups of others. Social psychologist Alfie Kohn, on the other hand, recognizes three different forms of
"other:" the *concrete other,* the *hypothetical other,* and the *collective other.*[8] The
distinctions among these three variations are highly informative in further
linking our present consideration of empathy and role-taking with the
typology of orientations toward social issues presented in chapters 3 and 4
(see Figure 6.1).

The case studies of the nonreferenced and the self-referenced types
made it apparent that role-taking and empathy are generally lacking
among those who fall into those types. While Leslie and Silva express
sympathy for those who are suffering from hunger and AIDS *and* who
are considered "deserving," they have not taken the next step of seeing
the world from the perspective of someone going hungry or who is
diagnosed as HIV positive. Leslie—representing the nonreferenced
view—does not really think about the issues much at all, much less from
someone else's perspective. When she does express her sympathy, it is
imbued with evidence of the "surface acting" discussed earlier. As an
example of the self-referenced type, Silva is so wrapped up in herself, so
focused on preventing hunger from entering her own life, that the
potential for role-taking and empathy is cut off before it can take root.
Silva explicitly points out that she does not want to feel as she did as a
hungry child again. The fact that empathy would necessitate her "feeling with" those currently experiencing hunger means that this is a sen-

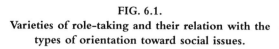

FIG. 6.1.
**Varieties of role-taking and their relation with the
types of orientation toward social issues.**

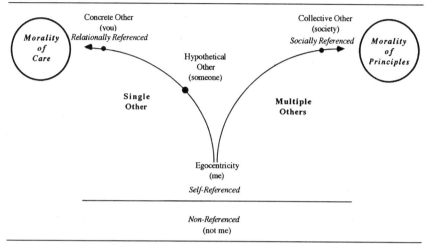

Adapted from Alfie Kohn's "Varieties of Perspective Taking" (1990: 107).

timent she actively avoids and prevents. As implied by Kohn, this is an essentially egocentric perspective.

In contrast, when we try to imagine what "someone else" actually goes through when they are hungry or HIV positive, we are attempting to take the perspective of the *hypothetical other.* The focus is on a single individual who may or may not exist and whom we call to our imaginations when considering a social issue. For example, and as evidenced by her reliance on the word "would" and the pauses in her response (denoted by "...."), Laura has a hypothetical other in mind when describing what she thinks about persons who are HIV positive or have AIDS.

> *Um ... I'm not ... I guess I'm not ... I wouldn't be scared of them. I don't think that ... I would reduce my contact with that person knowing that they had AIDS. I don't think that it would affect the friendship or the relationship that ... we've had. I would think that it would ... be very traumatic to have AIDS. .... I just think that that person and people with AIDS would need a lot of support and ... understanding because ... it's life threatening. When ... you know you're going to die, you have to face that and I think that's a very traumatic experience.*

Laura is a very thoughtful person overall, and the pauses emphasize this characteristic, indicating that she is taking a moment to try and think from another perspective—the perspective of a hypothetical other who is unknown to her. Moreover, when pressed, she admits the possibility that someone she knows *might* be HIV positive, but it is a purely hypothetical situation for her. Role-taking with a hypothetical other is not clearly linked with one of the four types of orientations toward social issues. Laura happens to be self-referenced with regard to AIDS, focusing primarily on how it affects her own life. However, the fact that she actively role-takes with a hypothetical other indicates that she has a strong potential to become relationally referenced. In other words, role-taking with the hypothetical other implies a transition between types. It is an exercise helping one to strengthen one's role-taking ability. If it turns out that someone close to Laura really is HIV positive, or if this occurs at a later point in her life, it is not hard to imagine her becoming focused on the issue in terms of its impact on her loved one. She is ready to make the leap from being self-referenced to being relationally referenced.

The *concrete other* refers to a single individual who is apparent to us—whether it is a stranger whom we see before us, a mere acquaintance, or someone with whom we have a deeper relationship—and who is affected by the social issue under consideration. It is with these concrete others that we most easily identify and empathize. This is because their circumstances are immediately available to us. However, the better we know this concrete other, the more fully we can identify with him or her. We may walk past an individual sitting at the edge of the sidewalk soliciting money and realize that she is probably homeless. Moreover, we can mentally put ourselves in her shoes and approximate the feelings she experiences. For example, when Michelle sees something or hears about something bad that happened, she immediately relates it to her own life. She puts herself in the position of the one affected and thinks about what it would be like if this happened to her. Her role-taking allowed her to come to the realization that homelessness and hunger could happen to "normal" people like herself who just happened to hit "hard times."

> *I just kind of assimilate everything to myself. I could see how, if something were to happen to my family or whatever, how we could very well become homeless. My cousin had a baby who was very sick and her husband lost his job. Now they are still climbing out of the hospital bills and so on. So, I see how it can be just one step away. You can be right*

on the edge there and if you don't have the family support, it's so easy to just fall over the edge. . . . I just always, if I hear a story about something bad happening to someone, I always think, "Oh, my God. It's going to happen to me."

Not only does Michelle role-take with the homeless she sees on the street, but she takes it to the point where she imagines what she calls the "worst case scenario." By taking the position of the concrete other, she is truly able to empathize with them in their situation.

However, this passage from Michelle's interview also highlights the fact that it is easier to role-take with those who are not only before our eyes, but who are actually known to us. For this reason, she jumps from the homeless she sees on the streets to the story of her cousin who was on the brink of economic disaster. The apparent reason for this is that more elements of the story were available to Michelle to incorporate into her role-taking. All she knows about those on the street—unless she takes the time to get to know them—is that they are homeless. However, given what she has heard about her cousin, she is aware of the fact that her cousin's baby was sick and needed expensive medical attention, the fact that the husband lost his job, the mounting bills, "and so on." The similarity between herself and her cousin was much more poignant than between herself and the stranger actually on the street, even if she was not continually in touch with her cousin.

Because of the importance of knowing someone affected by a social issue, taking the perspective of a concrete other is associated with being relationally referenced. The relationally referenced view a social issue in terms of how it affects someone they know. As with role-taking with the concrete other, viewing an issue in this way is much more likely when the relation is someone close. Recall that Mary focused on the hunger issue in terms of its impact on the lives of her parents who came to the United States from China. Her link with the hunger issue is through her relationship with her parents. As Chad describes in his narrative, the AIDS issue became more concrete for him because of the relationship he was attempting to rebuild with his HIV-positive uncle. Again, the relationship was central to establishing a link with the issue. Yet for Michelle, who is nonreferenced toward hunger, identifying with the homeless person on the street and even with her cousin were not sufficient for her because, as she says, "you could talk about any issue that's going on, but then once you drop it, it's over." As we see later, a close *and* sustained relationship is important in establishing an empathetic link between individuals.

When introducing his concept of the *collective other,* Kohn remarks that "to view an event or experience from a vantage point other than one's own is not necessarily to see it as another individual does" (1990: 106). In other words, it is possible to take the perspective of entire groups of people and even of society itself. Naturally, this is quite abstract, even when compared to the hypothetical other. It is this very abstract quality that Leslie notes in her narrative that prevents her from grasping the reality of mass hunger in other parts of the world. For her, it might as well not exist. On the other hand, role taking with groups of people and with society is central to Diane's narrative; and again, she is socially referenced in the context of the hunger issue.

However, Diane does not role take with the collective other before first grappling with that abstract quality, which is problematic for so many other people. In fact, as already noted, Diane immediately characterizes hunger and homelessness in her narrative not by its invisible, abstract quality, but by its visibility.

> *I suppose homelessness and hunger are so important to me because it's so visible. You can see a person on the street and know that they're homeless. You can see someone else on the street and not realize that they're illiterate and they need to learn to read or that they have AIDS. It's really . . . it's so . . . it's there. It's right in your face.*

While deeply concerned with the abstract social and moral dimension of the hunger issue, Diane focuses on its visible aspects in order to ground her compassion in her everyday experiences. When she sees a homeless person, she treats him as the individual he is, effectively humanizing him; but at the same time, within the face of this homeless and hungry individual, Diane sees herself—"There, but for the grace of God, go I," she sees her mother, and she sees all of the millions of "others" who go hungry just like the one with whom she happens to be conversing at the moment.

Beth has grappled with the abstract quality of the collective other in the context of the AIDS issue by linking it with her love of the arts and work in the theater.

> *I think it's just a shame. I start to think about all the work that's been lost, all the great things that people could have done. I'm the type of person who looks at people and thinks of all the positive things they can do; and then when their life is cut short by something like AIDS, I start to think of the things that they never got around to doing. For example, I've seen copies of works in progress that were never finished because the person died. It's a hard thing to deal with.*

Just like Diane, Beth is concerned first and foremost with the impact of AIDS on society itself. However, she too "concretizes" the issue and the collective other by relating them to her personal interests and focusing on the individuals who comprise this collective other. She leaves the authors of the "works in progress" anonymous in her narrative, but their identities are known to her insofar as they are expressed in these incomplete works. Beth does not lose sight of the faces representing the collective other, noting that what comes to mind when she hears the word "AIDS" is "a picture of a lot of the faces of people who have been lost. Some of them I knew, many I did not."

Empathy, Role-taking, and the Moral Society

By focusing on the concrete manifestations of the collective other, Diane and Beth have overcome its abstract and "invisible" nature. In this way, they are able to grasp the societal dimensions of these social issues, transcending the divide between themselves and others and, as idealized by Adam Smith, moving on to the moral and ethical ramifications of their individual roles in society. Past research has linked role-taking with the development of "higher" levels of morality (Eisenberg and Miller 1987; Kalliopuska 1983). In Lawrence Kohlberg's model of moral development, he saw stage four, which focuses on the maintenance of "law and order," as being oriented toward the maintenance of the social order. However, he later saw it as "an enlargement of horizons away from one's narrow group and toward a concern for the wider community" (Muson 1979: 340). This is where the affective dimension of empathy—the feeling *with*—comes into play. Conventional morality, which includes Kohlberg's stage four, is associated with higher levels of emotional empathy (Kalliopuska 1983: 578). In Kohlberg's model, conventional morality is followed by "postconventional" morality, in which "individuals *differentiate* between themselves and the rules of others, and define values for themselves in terms of rationally considered, self-chosen principles" (Vander Zanden 1987: 129). For example, when taking a position on the death penalty issue, choosing a moral principle requires that "a person . . . view the issue from the standpoint of one sentenced to death as well as from that of the murder victim" (Muson 1979: 340). With this in mind, Kalliopuska speculates that it is here that the cognitive dimension of empathy—our ability to role-take with others—becomes a key factor, indicating that role-taking seems to be conducive to the development of "higher" levels of morality. Kohn pursues a similar perspective noting that asking the question "How would I like it if somebody did that to me?" is "a solid basis for morality" (1990: 112).

When thinking of a single "somebody"—i.e., a hypothetical or concrete other—we are led to a position of morality of care (1990: 107), in which we take care of and are compassionate toward that other individual, as Chad grew compassionate toward his uncle with AIDS. On the other hand, when that "somebody" is actually a collective other, we are led toward "a morality based on abstract principles" (1990: 108). The reason is found in the link between Kohn's collective other and George Herbert Mead's "generalized other." Mead notes that "the attitude of the generalized other is the attitude of the whole community" (1934: 154). He goes on to say that

> the complex co-operative processes and activities and institutional functionings of organized human society are also possible only in so far as every individual involved in them or belonging to that society can take the general attitudes of all other such individuals with reference to these processes and activities and institutional functionings, and to the organized social whole of experiential relations and interactions thereby constituted—and can direct his own behavior accordingly. (1934: 155)

This is exactly the point that Adam Smith makes when he discusses the role of sentiments in the moral order: by taking the perspective of the collective or generalized other, we are able to coordinate our interests and activities in such a way that it preserves and enhances our collective well-being.

The principles that guide our behavior in the collective are highly abstract, but their influence is essential to the survival of society. As noted, the majority of individuals are not socially referenced and do not engage in role-taking and empathizing at the level of the collective other. This implies that the need for individuals to circumvent the abstract quality of the collective other—while obvious when examining cases like Diane's or Beth's—is not so apparent for the majority of individuals.[9] To the degree that individuals are unable to take the perspective of the collective other, society itself suffers. Ironically, the utilization of this framework regarding morality shows us that this lack of perspective-taking with the collective other that is so prevalent is actually the root of social problems and issues *and* the reason for their continued presence. Turning this deduction around, it is apparent that empathy and role-taking at the level of the collective other are essential to solving these social issues (regardless of the actual steps to be taken in accomplishing this task) and maintaining the health of society thereafter—a rather daunting prospect. Keeping in mind the societal implications of individual role-taking and empathy, we now turn to a consideration of those factors that serve to hinder the majority from developing this much needed sentiment of empathy toward social issues and their capacity for social affinity.

Hindrances to Sentiments in the Context of Social Issues

As noted in the introduction to this chapter, while emotions have significant societal implications, they are experienced at the individual level. For this reason, research begins at that level of analysis. Among sociologists, who recognize the social dimensions of sentiments, the level of analysis is raised to that of interpersonal relations between two people. For example, Steven Gordon (1990) focuses on making the case for a sociological interpretation of sentiments, distinguishing them from emotions, which he relegates to the level of individual experience. Candace Clark (1987) looks at emotions—particularly sympathy—in terms of their exchange value in the context of interactions between two people. However, by utilizing the process of theory elaboration, in which one changes the level of analysis (from micro to macro or from macro to micro), it is possible to reach new insights into the topic under consideration (Vaughan 1992). Thus, by focusing on our sentiments and how they apply when taking more than two people into account, it is possible to learn more about the role of emotions in larger societal processes.

By drawing upon key points discussed by Gordon and Clark and applying them to the larger context of social issues, it is possible to describe those processes that serve to hinder the emergence of individual sentiments toward not just other individuals, but toward entire groups of people who are affected by social issues, such as the hungry and persons with AIDS. There are six fundamental reasons why individuals have difficulty in creating a sentimental attachment to those affected by social issues: (1) a lack of close relationship, (2) a lack of sustained relationship, (3) an "overload" of sympathy claims, (4) "inherent" violations of sympathy "rules," (5) the interventions of emotional "specialists," and (6) the "deviantizing" of sympathy "overinvestors." In this section, each of these hindrances to sentiments will be considered in turn.

Lack of a Close and Sustained Relationship

Because our sentiments arise through interactions with others, it is no surprise that the nature of one's relationship with another is crucial to the depth of these sentiments, assuming they arise at all. Among most basic dimensions of a relationship are how "close" those in the relationship are and how long the relationship has lasted. Our emotions toward a stranger, such as a person we see at a bus stop, are very different than with regard to a loved one. In the latter case, a much fuller relationship has developed and we feel "close" to them. Moreover, that relationship had to develop over time. By acquiring a sense of shared history with memories to look back on together, the "closeness" of the relationship is strengthened. However, the length of time one comes into contact with another changes even the relationship between "strangers." For example, strangers who see each other at a bus stop on a regular basis become "familiar strangers," developing a rudimentary form of relationship. These individuals are more likely to help one another in times of need than are "total" strangers (Dovidio 1984; see also the influence of familiarity on relationships in Moreland and Zajonc 1982). Thus, the closeness and length of a relationship are central to our attitudes and commitment toward social issues.

Our sentiments actually mirror our relationships. If our relations are superficial, so are our sentiments in that context. If the relationship is deep, or fleeting, or prolonged, or abstract, or visceral, so are our sentiments in the context of that relationship. For example, if the "relationship" is very brief—as in watching a hunger commercial or listening to guest speakers on AIDS—so is the emotional response. At the same time, reminiscing about that fleeting relationship may call up the feelings again.[10] When Joann described from memory her reactions to the hunger commercial, quoted in the previous section, she actually *felt* much the same way she did as when she actually saw the commercial. Then, as we moved on in the interview, this emotional response quickly receded into the background, reflecting the short duration of her recollection.

With this mirroring quality in mind, it is possible to examine each of the four types of orientations toward social issues with regard to the length and depth of the relationship. The nonreferenced do not have any personal relations on which to base an emotive connection with an issue. They may have those fleeting "relationships" as Joann did with those portrayed in the commercial and reminisce over them on occasion, but without a sustained relationship or regular reminiscing, the nonreferenced are unable to maintain the emotive connection. This is particularly evident in the following passage in which Michelle compares her views toward hunger and AIDS. Her lack of relational ties with anyone suffering from hunger influences her feelings toward the issue.

> It's just that, in my state—where I am right now—I have a house, I have a mom, I have a dad, I have family, I have things . . . I don't have to worry about not having lunch or dinner or not eating for the next week. It's not something that I would worry about on a regular basis. You worry about the people out there who are hungry and you want to help them, but it's not me and it's not anyone around me; whereas AIDS affects me and the way I live my life. It affects friends and how they live their lives. It doesn't mean in any way that hunger is less important than AIDS. It's just me. If something happens to you or someone you know, if a friend or your sister is raped or something, then you're going to be more inclined toward women's issues because it affects you more.

Michelle discusses her sentiment of worry—a sentiment she does not always feel with regard to the hunger issue because it does not affect her or any of her relations. AIDS, on the other hand, does affect both her and her friends. Her worry is more pronounced in that context. In her last example regarding women's issues, Michelle implies that if an issue affects "a friend or a sister"—a close relation—then it "affects *you* more" (emphasis mine). Her sentiments toward issues mirrors her feelings for her loved ones and, since she does not know anyone affected by hunger, she has only minimal sentiments in that regard.

It is still possible that, without the relational tie, the nonreferenced may have a purely intellectual awareness of the issue, as Michelle does with the hunger issue. However, as we saw in chapter 4, Garrett was intellectually aware of the impact of AIDS on others and the fact that it should be taken seriously and yet he did not modify his sexual behavior. The survey that all those interviewed filled out included questions directly addressing sexual behavior, whereas the interview did not. Garrett indicated on the survey that he was sexually active. Yet, when describing his condom use, he indicated that it did not apply to him. While Garrett discusses the importance of sex education and condom use, and while he feels that those who "engage in dangerous activities" will "have to pay the consequences," he has not drawn the necessary connection with his own life. He is not committed to the issue of AIDS in terms of its impact on himself.

In other words, those with an intellectual rather than relational connection with an issue often fail to make a link between the issue and their own lives. Again, the major exception is when there is a fleeting "relational" connection with the issue. For example, in her narrative, Leslie mentions several occasions in which she offered food to a homeless person as she passed them on the street. When Leslie and the homeless person were in contact, they were engaged in a momentary relationship (Bergin, Coutsoukis, and Vela-McConnell 1994) and she could "feel for" the homeless person and respond in a way that is more characteristic of the relationally referenced; but as soon as she left the scene, she reassumed her distant, nonreferenced perspective. Without a sustained relationship, she is unable to maintain a sympathetic view.

The self-referenced also do not usually have a relational connection with the issue.[11] However, unlike the nonreferenced, they *have* made a connection between the issue and their own lives. In that sense, their emotive response is not based on a relationship with another individual or group *per se,* but on their perceived relationship with the issue itself. Recall Silva's fear surrounding hunger—a fear arising from her personal experiences. As Gordon (1990) suggests, there are some emotions—such as fear, anger, surprise, and lust—that do have a more internal basis because of their connection with the biological need for survival. The inward or internal focus of these emotions, together with the absence of any outward emotional response to another person, may account for the *self* part of being self-referenced. Silva was so focused on her internal fears of hunger that she automatically cut off any potential for a relationship with a hungry person. As a result, her focus on the hunger issue was in terms of its impact on herself.[12]

It is easiest to understand the relationally referenced in terms of their sentiments because their entire focus with regard to the issue is with the person whom they know is affected by that issue. Their sentimental response to the issue and its impact on their loved one is maintained along with the relationship itself. Garrett loves his estranged uncle and, so long as that uncle has to struggle with AIDS, Garrett will continue to concern himself with AIDS. This issue is a persistent presence in his uncle's life and therefore a consistent presence in their relationship and the sentiments arising out of that relationship. Moreover, the depth of the relationship promotes depth in his sentiment toward AIDS.

As noted, the socially referenced may be simultaneously relationally referenced. In these instances, however, they have generalized their emotive connection with that single individual beyond the confines of that spe-

cific relationship. They see the impact of the issue not only on their relation but on *all* those affected by the issue. At the same time, there are those
socially referenced—such as Beth—who do not rely on a prior relationship. What is the basis of their emotive connection? It is a variation of that
same reminiscing that occasionally motivates the nonreferenced and self-
referenced to reach out to others. While the nonreferenced and self-referenced may on occasion reminisce about someone or something they saw,
the socially referenced are *continually* "reminiscing." They keep the issue
and those it affects continually in mind; and if it is not in the forefront of
their minds, it is in the background. Recall the case of Diane. She experiences the same fleeting, face-to-face encounters with the homeless that the
nonreferenced, such as Leslie, do. The difference is that Diane *anticipates*
these encounters. In the midst of her preparations to go shopping, which
at that moment are at the forefront of her mind, she makes a mental note
to take one-dollar bills with her to give to the homeless. The homeless and
the hungry are continually at the back of her mind, which serves to sustain the "relationship" even when she is not in contact with them. In effect,
she experienced a combination of what Gordon calls "anticipatory
arousal" and "validative arousal" (1990: 576; see endnote 10): her repeated
emotional arousal when thinking of the homeless validated the continuity
of her sentiment for this issue and those it affects.

Beth had many fleeting encounters with persons with AIDS through
her work in the arts. At the same time, however, she reminisced about those
who had already died as a result of the disease. Not that she had a personal
relationship with them; instead, she related to the impact of their never-
completed works on her own love for the arts. She experienced regret
thinking about all the works that would never be created or completed due
to the losses from AIDS. The prominence of her work in the arts continually brought the issue to the forefront of her mind. Thus, her relationship
with her work was an adequate substitute for a close and sustained relationship with a particular individual. Only later—as we will see—did she
develop such a relationship, which served to strengthen her sentiments
toward the AIDS issue.

Overall, the presence or absence of a relationship and its duration are
important factors affecting the emergence of sentiments with regard to social
issues in the majority of individuals. Except for occasional reminiscing, the
nonreferenced and self-referenced do not generally have any relational contact with the issue and therefore do not express much sentiment for the issue
or those affected. The relationally referenced relate emotionally to those

affected by social issues by focusing on the one person they know and love who is affected by the issue. The socially referenced—even when not relating directly with someone affected by the issue—are able to maintain their sentiments by "continually reminiscing" and, as discussed in the previous section, "concretizing" the others the issue affects. In other words, they play an active role in keeping the issue within their consciousness. In this way, the socially referenced are able to overcome the hindrances to sentiments posed by a lack of a close and sustained relationship with those affected by the social issues.

Overload of Sympathy Claims

In her work on "sympathy margins," Candace Clark suggests that each individual has a certain number of "sympathy credits" for those with whom they interact (1987: 300). In other words, there is a limited amount of sympathy we can expect from other people, although these sympathy credits are "continually negotiated and may be increased, decreased, replenished, or used up entirely" (1987: 302). By turning the equation around, it is possible to posit a limited—and flexible—amount of sympathy available to oneself for extending toward others: "I have only so much sympathy I can give to you before you have reached your limit" (1987: 306). While Clark's analysis focuses on a relationship between only two individuals, much the same can be said when adding additional individuals to the pool under consideration. Susan may have two friends who are demanding her sympathy. John may have five friends and Carol eight friends. At one point or another, all of one's friends will look for sympathy and if they all happen to claim sympathy at practically the same time, our sympathy reserves may be overextended and empty. While these reserves fluctuate with our life circumstances—whether it be our mood on a particular day, the stresses we are experiencing, or even such variables as class, race, gender, and so on—the underlying message in Clark's work is that we have only so much sympathy we can expect from others or available to give to others.

Expanding our consideration of sympathy to include social issues, it is possible to see even greater strains on our reserves of sympathy or empathy. Not only do we have claims to sympathy from two or five friends, we also have claims to our sympathy from family members, coworkers, and even some acquaintances, not to mention all the people with whom we do not have a close or sustained relationship: the strangers on the street; "real life" and even fictional characters with whom we come in contact in the media; innumerable letters and phone calls asking for donations, time, feedback, and so on. Add on top of that the claims "made" by the social issues under consideration here: not only hunger and AIDS, but abortion, human rights, the environment, the economy, international relations, war, drugs, and the list goes on and on. All of these people, organizations, and so on are clamoring for not only our attention, as discussed in the previous chapter, but our sympathy.

In other words, in a modern world in which we are exposed to much more than local concerns, we experience a sort of "overload" of sympathy claims. In a global context, with ever increasing numbers of sympathy claims, it is simply not possible for an individual to attend to all the demands placed on his or her sympathy reserve. As a result, individuals engage in a filtering process with regard to their sentiments in much the same way as they engage in the filtering of information into and out of their consciousness. When we throw away our "junk mail," which includes a lot of literature on different causes, when we screen out telephone solicitors with our answering machines, when we—as Michelle does when she feels more sympathy regarding the AIDS issue than the hunger issue— focus on one social issue to the exclusion of others, we are filtering the sympathy claims that are placed upon us from a myriad different sources in an attempt to mitigate the "overload." This only further underscores the unsurprising fact that our closest relations—and those things, such as social issues, which are important to these relationships and their claims to sympathy—are the ones most likely to receive our sympathy.

"Inherent" Violations of Sympathy "Rules"

In order to manage our sympathy reserves, Clark argues that individuals follow sympathy "rules" for "owing, giving, claiming, and accepting sympathy" (1987: 303). Three of her rules include "do not make false claims to sympathy," "do not claim too much sympathy," and "reciprocate to others for the gift of sympathy."[13] Individuals follow these rules in their interactions involving sympathy in order to protect their "sympathy margin"— the amount of sympathy we can expect from others. If one violates one or more of these rules, one does so at the risk of losing sympathy or of "overdrawing" one's sympathy account with another.

Again, Clark's analysis focuses on relations between two people; but when extending the level of analysis to include social issues, a different picture emerges. Social issues cannot "manage" their sympathy accounts in the way that individuals can because they are not, in and of themselves, social actors. Social issues cannot "follow" any rules and, in fact, *in the eyes of* those to whom they pose sympathy claims, they often "violate" these sympathy rules. One can argue that social issues, by the fact of their nature, pose unavoidable and therefore "inherent" violations of these rules. Of course, since these issues are not social actors in the same sense that individuals are, any perceived violations of the rules are not the "responsibility" of the issue. Instead, any "violations" are in the eye of the beholders—the individuals to whom claims for sympathy are made. Violations reflect more on the person who identifies them as such than they do on the issue itself. In other words, violations of the rules of sympathy "by" social issues are defined and constructed by the individuals with the power to give their sympathy; they are a part of the mental framing of consciousness utilized by individuals.

The first rule violation has to do with the making of "false" claims. As we have already seen in earlier chapters, many individuals do not trust the solicitations put upon them in the context of social issues as being "valid." Clark notes that, "what is at issue here is a breach of public trust, a loss of faith that others will play by the rules" (1987: 304). For example, while taking part in hunger fundraising, Kesia also harbors this very distrust of homeless solicitors and, what is particularly interesting is that she bases this distrust on public accounts of past breaches.

> *I know where my money is going when I'm doing the Walk for Hunger. I know it's directly going to those who are hungry. The walk is well known. Granted, there could be someone in the office pocketing some of the money. You never know. Sometimes it's hard to tell when you're handing money to people on the street. They've shown stories on 20/20 about those things. Yeah, there are some people out there who are really doing it because they're hungry, but you have to. . . . One time they were asking for spare change and one guy asked, "Hey, can I take you out sometime?" And then he said, "I don't usually dress like this, you know. This is my job. I make $500 a week." And I was just standing there, "Well, damn, that's more money than I make in a damn week. How many hours a day do you stand out here?" "Maybe five hours a day." "Man, how many days?" "Three to four." And he's bringing home a hell of a lot more money than my paycheck is giving me. And he looked pretty bad. I'd believed he was homeless and hungry. So, you*

*might see someone who's really hungry asking, "Can you spare this so
I can get a burger because I haven't eaten in three days," and you're
thinking about the one you saw at the train station who had a bottle
in their hand, or about the person who looked pretty bad and who says
he's going to take me out and that he doesn't normally dress like that.*

While Kesia speaks of actual money here, her giving and not giving of
money is highly reflective of where her sympathies lie. Based on what she
has seen on television and what she has experienced in her own life, she
no longer trusts those soliciting on the street. Their "need" for sympathy
or money is not an innocent claim on her sympathy, but one that is tainted
with past breaches of public trust, both real and imagined. Moreover, while
she willingly donates money to the Walk for Hunger, she hints at a certain
degree of distrust there as well. Not only does she see individual solicitors
as likely violators of her trust, but organizations also have the potential to
make "false claims." Many other individuals—such as Leslie and Silva—are
so distrustful of organizations that they generally decline to donate money
even at that level. This distrust of those making sympathy claims on behalf
of social issues reflects on the issues themselves, making people like Kesia
less sympathetic to the hunger issue in general, for example.

Hunger organizations are not alone in this. The organizations representing other issues such as AIDS are also subject to this type of distrust.
For example, the AIDS organization that I studied in conjunction with this
project sponsors an AIDS Walk much like the walk described by Kesia.
Those who are walking gather pledges that are then donated to the parent
organization and many other AIDS organizations. Many of those gathering pledges will solicit them from strangers. However, several years ago,
there were one or two people who would stop people on the street to ask
for cash "pledges" in the name of the organization and then pocket the
money for themselves, effectively breaching the public trust in the organization. Rumors about these occurrences abounded. The following year, the
AIDS organization attempted to preempt such fraud by releasing a public
statement urging supporters of the AIDS walk *not* to give cash pledges to
anyone, especially those solicited by strangers on the street. In this way, the
organization meant to protect its public image and the legitimacy of its
claims to sympathy.

Another rule easily violated in the context of social issues is the claiming of "too much" sympathy. Clark explains that "one should not overdraw
one's sympathy accounts. The person who does so risks receiving sympathy

displays with less sentiment than would be forthcoming otherwise, displays without sentiment, or, worse, no displays at all" (1987: 304–305). When individuals hear "too much" about a social issue or feel that support for the issue has gone "too far," they are likely to withdraw their sympathy. For example, Gevonne has grown somewhat cynical with all the media attention given to hunger and other issues, feeling that people get stuck on whatever happens to be the "issue of the day." She blames the media for the overexposure.

> *The media has a big impact on everything. Whatever they want you to know about and care about, you'll care about. If they want you to "save" the mosquito tomorrow, all they have to do is make sure they have "Save the Mosquito" stories every single day for a month. And people will be out there saying "Save the Mosquito!" Whatever they say, you'll do. I think that's so true. Whatever they want. As soon as the media stops saying, "Save the Mosquito," people forget and then they'll go on to something else that they're trying to save or make you aware of. It's the story of the month, whichever one it is.*

While Gevonne blames the media for too much manipulative coverage, she also displays exasperation with the issues given so much attention, whether its as ludicrous as a "Save the Mosquito" campaign or as socially relevant as the hunger issue.

Martin Hayes is much more direct in his lack of sympathy for an issue that he sees as having claimed too much sympathy.

> *What has happened with AIDS is what happens to a lot of the issues. I hear it so much—I hear so many things about it and there are so many things being done for it—that after a while I just get fed up and I say, "Enough is done for that. I'll help with something else." I acknowledge that there is a problem, but I think that I just get sick of hearing it after a while, the same thing over and over and over again. And personally, I think AIDS is a big problem and it's the biggest growing problem for diseases, but I think money has to be given to cancer and other things, too. If you just keep focusing on AIDS, everybody forgets about everything else.*

As far as Martin is concerned, AIDS has overdrawn its sympathy account and he has moved on to the issue of cancer. In his mind, AIDS has garnered too much attention for too long.

In other words, among those who share Martin's point of view, the duration of the support extended to the AIDS issue has "overstayed" its "welcome." Clark points out that, the estimated duration of a problem is related to the size of one's sympathy accounts in a curvilinear fashion. Problems of either very short or very long duration will engender less, or less consistent, sympathy than intermediate-range problems. . . . Long-term problems, while they may be worth more sympathy, may call for greater emotional expenditures than others can or will put forth. (1987: 305)

Since social issues such as AIDS and hunger, by their very nature, are "long-term problems," individuals are less willing and able to invest a high and sustained degree of sympathy in them. That is why we are so easily led to the next "issue of the day." It is also a major reason for the prominence of the "seasonal charity" discussed in the previous chapter: our sympathy is not only lowered by long-term issues, but it is also less consistent, giving rise to an overabundance of food donations, for instance, during the Thanksgiving and Christmas seasons and little or no such donations during the critical summer months.

The third rule violation that is "inherent" in social issues is the lack of reciprocation to those who do show sympathy. Clark informs us that, "whether conscious of the fact or not, people usually expect returns when they give sympathy" (1987: 310). In a sympathy exchange between two individuals, they are typically "present" to one another, whether literally or merely emotionally. This copresence facilitates the reciprocation that is expected. An individual is fully capable of showing gratitude, deference, or some sympathy of his or her own (1987: 310). However, when it comes to broad social issues that affect large groups of people, unless an individual who is suffering under the weight of a social issue such as hunger is given *direct* assistance by the person upon whom a sympathy claim has been made, he or she is not usually able to reciprocate in such a direct fashion. There is usually an organization that mediates between those who get involved in social issues and those who receive their sympathy and assistance. For this reason, those on the receiving end of a sympathy exchange within the context of social issues are highly dependent on these organizations to act on their behalf not only in relieving their condition— whether it be hunger, disease, or prejudice—but also in reciprocating on their behalf.

For those on the giving end of the exchange, it is very difficult to recognize a return on their sympathy "investment." Unless they focus on a single individual affected by the social issue, such as the relationally referenced discussed earlier, or volunteer in a "hands-on" setting, such as a homeless shelter or a clinic, many do not come into contact with those whom they help. For instance, much of the help solicited for the hunger issue focuses on Third World hunger—something most people from the United States will never see face-to-face. If the hungry from other parts of the world are unable to show their appreciation, gratitude, or make a return offering of sympathy, they are in danger of losing support because of the apparent violation of the reciprocity rule.

For this reason, organizations dealing with social issues must give much attention to providing such reciprocation on behalf of the people they serve. These organizations make an effort to send thank you notes, provide token gifts, sponsor "volunteer appreciation" events, and so forth. Even a token thank you is important to maintain one's support and claim to sympathy with those who provide it. For example, the Christian Children's Fund, which runs the hunger commercial found in Appendix B, provides concrete reciprocation by sending their donors the name and photograph of a child they can help. In fact, many such organizations regularly forward letters written by these children to their sponsors. Not only do these names, pictures, and letters make the issue and the person being helped more concrete in the consciousness of the sponsor, they are also a form of reciprocation intended to ensure the continuation of all sympathy and support. Who can cut off funds to a child he or she has "gotten to know?"

In this way, organizations representing various social issues play a pivotal role in how individuals react to the issue in terms of sympathy. While, in a modern and global society, these organizations stand between the individual able to show sympathy and provide support and the individual who is in need, they also have the power to mitigate what might be considered the "inherent" sympathy rule violations posed by social issues. Since issues cannot "act" with intent and purpose—as individuals do—these organizations play a vital role in maintaining the public trust and in reciprocating donors' sympathy and assistance, all while attempting to walk the line between claiming what is perceived as "too much" sympathy and yet soliciting enough sympathy to meet the needs of the people they serve.

Interventions of Emotional "Specialists"

At the same time organizations representing social issues play an important role in mediating between the individuals they serve and the supporters they solicit, they also diminish the sense of social responsibility felt by those unaffected by the issue under consideration. Responsibility for addressing the issue is sloughed off the shoulders of the individual and placed on the organization and its members. In other words, as these organizations in one sense ease the overload of sympathy claims placed on the individual, they and their members also become substitutes in providing the sympathy that was directly provided by these individuals.

For example, in the past, elderly members of one's family lived and died in one's own household. In today's society in the United States, many of these elderly family members are placed in institutions—"old-folks homes"—and die in cold, impersonal hospitals. Their families no longer have the burden of providing sympathy and care. In effect, we have removed a very natural part of life so that it becomes "invisible." We choose to distance ourselves from death, filtering it out of our consciousness and out of any feeling of obligation for sympathy (Ariés 1981: 575–576, *passim;* see also Nuland 1994). Instead, we hire emotional "specialists" such as nurses to do the emotional work for us. What does the shirking of individual responsibility portend for society? Clark speculates as to the implications of this by saying that "postindustrial societies have also developed emotional specialists (counselors) and emotional agents and brokers (lawyers, charity organizers, and insurance agents), who have taken over sympathetic functions from intimates, leading to an overall decline in public sympathy" (1987: 319).

While relatively few individuals interviewed were relationally or socially referenced with regard to a social issue, many of these persons were actually considering converting their sympathetic outlook into a profession—or had already done so. They were or desired to become doctors, nurses, psychologists, and social workers. Diane presents a case in point. As briefly described in the introduction to her narrative, she works at a Planned Parenthood office and is in training to become a nurse. When she has completed her degree, she would like to work in a hospice caring for those dying from complications due to AIDS. In other words, she is taking what she considers her expertise in providing sympathy and assistance and turning it into a profession.

> *When I applied to the nursing program, it was because I finally figured out what I wanted to be when I grew up. I wanted to be a nurse and I wanted to help people die because I've always been interested in death and dying—the whole process and the grief. It just seemed like I would*

> *be a good person to do that because I'm not uncomfortable with it and*
> *I would want to help people try to get to a place where they're com-*
> *fortable with it before they actually have to go through it. I also want*
> *to deal with them on a medical level if they need that, but it seems like*
> *a nicer way of doing nursing, rather than hospital nursing. It has a psy-*
> *chological aspect and a spiritual aspect. Dealing with the family and*
> *being a support person for them, to me it's so holistic in some way. It*
> *just seemed perfect. I thought to myself, "Oh, good. It's about time I fig-*
> *ured this out." So, that's when I decided to go back to school.*

Diane's everyday sympathy has merged with her professional life. The fact that she plans to administer to the dying means that others have been relieved of some of the burden. She will become the sympathy specialist whose job it is not only to ease the dying process for those in the hospice, but also to mediate and "manage" the feelings of the family members.

Diane's is a valuable service, but one that nevertheless relieves others of much responsibility—an indication of the extent to which labor has been divided in our society (Durkheim 1984): not only do we divide up the work of survival—of putting food on the table—among a wide range of specialists, but we divide up our emotive work as well. However, instead of becoming more aware of our interdependence with one another, we have the impression that we as individuals are more autonomous. We think that the interventions of emotional specialists relieve us of the burden of sympathizing, of care-taking, of even managing our own emotions and we forget that by giving these responsibilities over to others, we have become dependent upon them to accomplish these tasks on our behalf. Moreover, unless an individual becomes an emotional specialist, we come to regard those who *do* take responsibility for the welfare of others as somehow "deviant."

The "Deviantizing" of Sympathy "Overinvestors"

Unless it is one's job, showing what is considered "too much" emotional investment in others has been defined in our society as deviant. As Clark explains, "sympathizing can enhance one's 'niceness,' but it can also increase one's 'softness'" (1987: 298).[14] Thus, in our society the term "bleeding heart liberal"—used to denote one who is moved "too easily" by the plight of others suffering from some form of injustice or social issue—has become a label of derision. In a world where "self-help" is the norm, those who reach out to others "too much" are seen as "unhealthy."

In keeping with this culture, David Karp, noted in the introduction to this chapter, speaks of the need to establish "clear sympathy boundaries in order to avoid becoming engulfed" (1996: 134). While Karp is focusing on care providers for the clinically depressed and speaks in terms of the somewhat "contagious" nature of depression, this "need" for sympathy boundaries is an integral part of our self-help culture, particularly with regard to what is termed "co-dependence." These programs send out the message that we are responsible solely for ourselves and that we should not attempt to assume responsibility for others, especially when it interferes with taking care of ourselves. In other words, too much empathy and role-taking is dangerous because one may lose one's own identity and merge with that of the other.

Within this philosophy, the very people who show the greatest degree of social consciousness, concern, and involvement with the moral and ethical implications of social issues—the relationally and socially refer-enced—are the same people who run the risk of being deviantized. Diane, because she is so involved with and concerned about the issues of hunger and AIDS, can easily be labeled as "co-dependent" and sanctioned for her behavior, despite the fact that she, in fact, does take care of herself as well. As evidenced in their narratives, they know "when to stop." For example, Diane does not give money to the homeless to the extent that her own account runs dry, even though she makes a point of carrying small change and one-dollar bills with her when she anticipates crossing their paths. Her own debts come first and, when she is low in money, she makes a point of providing emotional support by acknowledging the presence of solicitors and speaking with them when so many others look past the homeless and pretend they do not exist.

Later in her life, Beth developed a close relationship with Todd, a man who was HIV positive and who died about six months after Beth first met him. She met him through her role as a volunteer in an AIDS organization.

I was with Todd for about six and a half months before he passed away. I didn't realize it would be that short because when I first met him the only problem that he had was that he had gone blind from AIDS. He had never had any bouts with pneumonia or anything like that. And then, shortly after I started with him, he got his first bout with pneumonia and fought it. . . . His illnesses were hard, especially

later because he'd get the diagnosis and have to go to the hospital and
you'd just think in your head, "No, this is not happening." I went
through a lot of denial. . . . . After Todd died, I knew I couldn't get emo-
tionally involved again for a little while just because I needed a
break. . . . Eventually, I'd like to get back involved with a client, but
I needed some time.

After the death of Beth's friend Todd due to complications from AIDS, she
knew that she needed a break from such direct and personal care-giving.
She was aware of her limits and decided to "ease up a little." However, this
does not mean she gave up on the issue of AIDS entirely. Instead, she
decided to volunteer in a less emotionally "draining" position in which
there was no direct contact with the clients of the organization.

The philosophy that critiques co-dependency is beneficial for many
of those who espouse it, as in the mother of a depressed son described by
Karp who found "solace in 'seeing [others] who have been through [a
loved one's depression and are] still surviving.'" However, she also had trouble with the "group's collectively held view that caretakers of depressed
people need to maintain a healthy distance from those they care for and
about" (1996: 144). This woman experienced two conflicting "pulls" on
her psyche. On the one hand, she wanted to be there for her son and help
him as much as she could. She wanted to fulfill what she perceived as her
motherly obligation. On the other hand, the very same group that enabled
her to see that she could not actually "cure" her son also informed her that
getting "too close" to him in his illness was "unhealthy" for her as well. As
Landis points out, "in most discussion in the literature, firmer boundaries,
even extremely impermeable ones, are seen as positive and adaptive, and
'open,' 'weak' boundaries are usually viewed as indications of serious
defect" (1970: 17). How could she fulfill her obligation to nurture her son
and still be seen as "healthy" by society?

It is a narrow line to walk. As Karp notes, "it would be unfair to
minimize the real pain that pushes individuals to cure themselves of over-
involvement. It nevertheless seems clear that co-dependency can arise as
a pathological condition only in a society that fosters deep ambivalence
about the value of extensive [social] ties" (1996: 183). Karp, along with
many other social scientists (such as Derber 1992, and Bellah et al. 1985),
see a distinct link between our culture of capitalism and individualism
and the weakening of those social ties that are sustained by our sentiments and role-taking.

This link between the culture of capitalism and the culture of emotions is particularly evidenced by the applicability of "exchange" models to our understanding of emotional ties. Clark's entire article on sympathy is based on what is called "exchange theory." This perspective is evidenced by the use of such terms as "emotional economy," which she defines as "a method for dispersing throughout the group the feeling currency necessary for creating and maintaining connectedness in general—and valued social identities in particular" (1987: 296). The very fact that her analysis is so "on target" is indicative of the pervasiveness of capitalistic and individualistic principles in our culture. The idea of losing one's own identity by showing empathy for another is peculiar to such a culture. As mentioned by Jordan, "developmental and clinical theory have generally emphasized the growth of the autonomous, individuated self. . . . Likely this particular bias, if we can call it that, derives from [among other things] the emphasis in western, democratic countries on the sanctity and freedom of the individual" (1984: 1).

However, many social scientists see that exchange models are rather limited. Kohn notes that, "if empathy were a business transaction (which, thankfully, it is not), it would be a cooperative venture, a partnership, rather than a merger or an acquisition. . . . If they are worthy of their names, empathy and perspective taking . . . not only leave the self intact but also leave the self transformed" (1990: 154). In other words, the capitalistic model espoused by exchange theorists and our individualistic culture overlooks the *cooperative* nature of empathy. Kohn argues that, as in Diane's narrative, showing a high degree of empathy toward others does not endanger the autonomous self, but actually transforms it. Even classical theorists who saw the validity of exchange theories, such as Simmel who, as noted by Clark, saw exchange as an "original function of social life" (1987: 297), saw its limitations and dangers. In his treatise on "Faithfulness and Gratitude," Simmel says that "exchange is the objectification of human interaction . . . personal interaction recedes altogether into the background, while goods gain a life of their own. . . . [M]an himself [*sic*] is really irrelevant, although it goes without saying that he engages in the process for his own interest. The relation among men has become a relation among objects" (1971: 388). In light of the very applicability of exchange theory in our culture, it would appear that self-interest has gone too far—to the point where people themselves are "irrelevant." In our society, we have become so caught up with keeping mental "ledgers" (Clark 1987: 297) about who owes us how much sympathy and whom we owe that we have forgotten what it means to give first. Simmel argues that the one who gives first gives in the most selfless manner because of its voluntary character.

> Once we have received something good from another person, once he [sic] has preceded us with his action, we no longer can make up for it completely, no matter how much our own return gift or service may objectively or legally surpass his own. The reason is that his gift, because it was first, has a voluntary character which no return gift can have. (1971: 392ff)

From this perspective, the relationally and socially referenced, like Diane and Beth, are not "unhealthy" but are actually great benefactors of society—a point that is lost among those who, in keeping with the rules of exchange, would "deviantize" them. By "deviantizing" those who show a greater degree of the very sentiments that form the basis of the social ties holding society together, we discourage individuals who—like Diane and Beth—would otherwise be willing to "go that extra mile" and, in so doing, we jeopardize the very fabric of society.

Placing the Pieces into the Mosaic

In a modern world in which it is possible to communicate with even the furthest reaches of the globe within a matter of seconds, individuals are confronted with unprecedented claims upon their sympathy. Many factors, such as those addressed here—the lack of close and sustained relationships in the context of social issues, the high load of sympathy claims, the "inherent" violations of the sympathy rules when focusing on masses of people rather than on single individuals, the interventions of those who manage our emotive work, and the "deviantizing" of those who sympathize "too much"—actually hinder an individual's sentiments toward those others affected by whatever social issue is under consideration. As discussed, the "other" is not just the individual whom we know and with whom we interact. There are also those "collective others"—the masses of people we will never see, not even on a television commercial for an organization representing a particular cause.

If, in this "global village," we are to realize the promise of a moral society posited by social thinkers like Adam Smith, we must empathize with not only our immediate family and friends, but—like Diane and

Beth—we must empathize with the "collective other." To do this, it is necessary to circumvent the hindrances to our social sentiments described in this chapter—each of which is a function of our social location relative to the issue under consideration and those whom it affects. The most obvious and the easiest way to develop such a sentiment is to actually know someone affected by a social issue such as hunger or AIDS—to be socially, spatially, and temporally proximate to them. This is why, as described in chapter 4, the relationally referenced type is so pivotal in nature. Knowing a person with AIDS or who suffers from hunger is a means by which an individual can be propelled from the self-interest and individualism inherent in our culture to the concern for the moral dimensions of social issues that characterize the socially referenced. By knowing such a person, we go beyond mere feelings of pity or fear: we *exercise* our role-taking ability and deepen our capacity for empathy. The next step is to generalize these sentiments from the concrete other to the more abstract collective other.

Of course, not everyone is in a position to personally know someone who goes hungry or is HIV positive. However, there are many other forums for establishing such relationships. For example, noncommittal forms of action, such as visiting a soup kitchen with one's church or school, may oftentimes *precede* the emergence of social sentiments. Through such action, it is possible to come in contact with those affected by hunger and possibly develop a deeper relationship. As noted by Kohn, "prosocial behavior can cause empathy. Experience with helping others (for nonempathic reasons) might help to create an empathic connection that could, in turn, encourage further prosocial behavior" (1990: 127). Social theorist Georg Simmel believed in much the same: ". . . once the existence of the relationship has found its psychological correlate, faithfulness, then faithfulness is followed, eventually, also by the feelings, affective interests, and inner bonds that properly belong to the relationship" (1950: 382). Thus, these feelings are also central to the emergence of social affinity. Just as our sentiments have the power to increase our commitment to society, so does action have the power to enhance our sentiments. With this in mind, we now turn to the remainder of our overall mosaic: a consideration of the action component in the development of social affinity.

SEVEN

A Call to Action

Social Activism and Social Affinity

[H]uman beings are not machines, and however powerful the pressure to conform, they sometimes are so
moved by what they see as injustice that they dare to
declare their independence. In that historical possibility
lies hope.

—Howard Zinn

Taking part in our social world by getting involved in addressing the problems facing our society is among the most visible manifestations of fulfilling one's social responsibilities. Social activism represents the culmination
of the emergence of social affinity within an individual. However, as
numerous activists point out, many individuals fail to get involved, even
when recognizing the importance of playing one's part in society. For this
reason, inaction is just as important to study.

Action has been the subject of much sociological and social psychological research under a variety of labels: "altruism," "prosocial behavior,"
"helping behavior," "voluntarism," "activism," and so on. While the relevant
bodies of literature are highly informative and useful in and of themselves,
they have proven unsatisfactory insofar as they pursue a rather narrow
focus of research. For example, the social psychological literature on prosocial behavior has a long tradition of experiments on helping in emergency
situations in public settings—such as when an individual, who is a paid
actor, suddenly "collapses" for unknown reasons. These situations require
immediate and spontaneous responses from bystanders. Studies such as
these have been increasingly criticized for their exclusion of nonspontaneous forms of prosocial behavior (see Amato 1990; Benson et al. 1980;

Clary and Miller 1986; and Jackson et al. 1995). The findings obtained are affected as a result. Paul Amato, for instance, points out that "spontaneous measures of helping favor situational determinants at the expense of inter-personal ones; since subjects must make decisions quickly in ambiguous situations, they are forced to rely on situational cues (such as the presence of other bystanders) as guides to behavior" (1985: 234). By opening the research focus to what he calls "planned helping," other variables—such as those covered later—may be taken into account.

On the other hand, if one wants to move beyond such contrived events, one may look through the social movement literature (see, for example, Gamson 1990; McAdam 1982; Morris 1984). However, much of this literature focuses on the organizational dimensions of activism and can easily lose sight of the individual. There is also much literature on volun-tarism (see, for example, Wuthnow 1995); but formal volunteering within an organizational context is only one specific form of active participation in social issues. There is actually a wide variety of possibilities for involve-ment, from political activism to philanthropy to informal acts of charity between two people. This chapter focuses on the middle ground between the two extremes—"helping behavior" and social movements—effectively bridging the two by looking at the micro dimensions of social activism and including more than just voluntarism.

One study that focuses on individuals and activism broadly conceived is found in Paul Loeb's book *Generation at the Crossroads: Apathy and Action on the American Campus* (1994). His main concern when setting out on this project was with the perceived lack of involvement on the part of students during the 1980s and 1990s as compared to the students involved in the peace movement of the late 1960s and early 1970s. While traveling across the United States and speaking at a host of colleges and universities, Loeb had the opportunity to speak with students about their involvements and noninvolvements in the issues of the day. At first glance, the average person often breaks the field of activism into two groups: the apathetic and the activists. Loeb's research caters to this dichotomous view. Based on what he heard from the students he met, he distinguishes between those he calls the "adapters" and the "activists."

The adapters are those who are apolitical in their views and who "represent the dominant current" in our society (1994: 7). Contrary to popular belief, Loeb argues that noninvolvement does not necessarily imply conservatism (1994: 4, 33–34). Instead, these students are reacting to dim economic prospects, realizing that they will have to work harder than their parents did in order to maintain their standard of living. When coupled with the enormous costs of higher education and the debts incurred as a result, young people in our country are highly focused on their own personal survival. "Commitments of conscience 'would only get in the way'" (1994: 3). Students have also absorbed our culture's rereading of political involvement in the past, pointing out how former activists have "sold out" and become "yuppies"—which Loeb demonstrates is a myth (1994: 80–83). Given the individualism of our culture, there is a distrust of those who "take on causes that go beyond their personal lives" and of social activism in general (1994: 4). Loeb summarizes the views of the adapters by saying that "although they desire a world more humane, generous, and just, most hope the future will muddle along, whether or not they participate" (1994: 5).

Going against the "popular mythology" of student apathy are the activists. Loeb describes this group as

> the committed, the active citizens, by which I mean something different from media stereotypes of chanting marchers with signs in their hands. Instead, these terms denote a fundamental attitude through which students try to take responsibility for the moral implications of their choices, rather than pass off critical public issues to distant experts. (1994: 7)

These activists oftentimes have found role models for social involvement in their parents, teachers, and friends. A number of them are attracted to that very "dissident culture," which the adapters disdain and emulate, such as the ideals of "socially committed musicians like U2, REM, Public Enemy, Tracy Chapman, and Pearl Jam" (1994: 5). These students resent the fact that their generation is labeled the "silent" or "me generation" and refuse to accept the state of the world as "inevitable" (1994: 5–6).

While Loeb presents convincing evidence for these polar opposite positions and while the variables he describes—economic strain, cultural mores, role models and socialization, and so on—are undeniably important, a purely "black and white" understanding of activism is highly limited. A dichotomous view—activism versus nonactivism—is problematic in that it overlooks all of the gradations in between—the "gray areas." Moreover, such a view completely ignores the process—and sometimes even the possibility—of change. In fact, it is these very gray areas that prove to be highly important in our understanding of activism and nonactivism in general because, as we see later, it is here that the transition between the polar opposites occurs. Individuals rarely jump from nonactivism to activism overnight. An important, and sometimes very gradual, transition occurs.

With this in mind, this chapter breaks down the action dimension of social affinity into its component pieces in order to understand how they fit together into the overall mosaic. The first piece of the mosaic will focus on filling in the dichotomous distinction between nonactivism and activism by including an additional and intermediary point on the continuum: noncommitted participation. Moreover, upon examining the data, it became apparent that there was more than one form of activism: participatory activism and focused activism. Thus, I am proposing a four-point continuum ranging from nonactivism to noncommitted participation to participatory activism and, finally, focused activism.

However, distinguishing between degrees of activism is not enough to complete the picture of the action dimension of social affinity. The next step is to look at the conditions for the emergence of these different degrees, focusing specifically on the link between the social issues frames described in chapter 5 regarding social consciousness and their mobilizing potential. It will be shown how each of the frames can become mobilizing or demobilizing. Then we look at some of the factors that influence the mobilizing outcome of these frames. As the final piece of the mosaic, the impact of taking action on the individual's consciousness and sentiment is explored with an eye toward stepping outside of the linear models of prosocial behavior described in the past. In this way, the three elements of social affinity—consciousness, sentiment, and action—are integrated into a single model.

Degrees of Action

Going against the traditional assumptions that the students of the 1980s and 1990s are largely apathetic, Loeb notes that involvement is higher than stereotypes would suggest and actually seems to be increasing (1994: 264–265). Part of this is due to the fact that those who are in college today are frequently the offspring of parents who were themselves involved during the Vietnam War–era and who have impressed upon their children the values of caring and social commitment (1994: 280–283). My own data suggest that many individuals are indeed active with regard to social issues, although, as suggested at the end of chapter 4, such commitment varies widely with the issue under consideration. For example, with regard to the hunger issue, only 21 percent were found to be nonactive, 36 percent exhibited at least a low level of activity, and 43 percent were moderately or highly active. By comparison, 52 percent of respondents were nonactive toward the AIDS issue, 25 percent exhibited a low level of activity, and 23 percent were moderately or highly active when it comes to AIDS.[1]

As already stated in the introduction to this chapter and as reflected in the figures just cited, there is a full range of degrees of activism reflecting a gradual increase from being completely uninvolved in social issues to being fully committed and active in addressing a given social issue. Specifying particular points along this continuum is a way of simplifying the myriad possibilities lying between the polar opposites of nonactivism and activism. For this reason, while it is important to distinguish more than just two possibilities as Loeb did, it must be emphasized that the boundaries between these different degrees of activism are never so clear cut as their descriptions would indicate. Each one gradually melds with the next. Moreover, involvement at any level is very important and should not be criticized because, as we see later in the chapter, even the most superficial degree of participation has the potential to promote further involvement.

Nonactivism

In concordance with Loeb's description of the "adapters," *nonactivists* are those who are not committed to a particular issue and who are completely uninvolved with it. The stereotype of nonactivists is that they are cold-hearted and unsympathetic to the concerns of the needy. However, as Loeb notes, many "feel unable to challenge destructive actions by entrenched economic and political institutions. . . . [Therefore] they limit moral judgments to personal concerns" (1994: 25). As we see later in this chapter, values play a significant role in the tendency toward nonactivism, as do feelings of powerlessness, lack of opportunity, and personal priorities. The "lack of time" is a major theme among nonactivists, and this problem is not always "just an excuse." Loeb argues that, at least among students,

> America's economic crunch makes it hard for students to take responsibility for more than just personal survival. Compared to twenty years ago, they work more hours at outside jobs, graduate more in debt, and face a more uncertain economic future. They have fewer choices of what to take and fewer

resources to finance their learning. Economic pressures push them to seek careers with whatever institutions will hire them, whether or not these institutions play a constructive role in society. (1994: 44)

The individualism that characterizes our culture is especially apparent among nonactivists in that the self-interests of economic and job security receive higher priority than social interests. Given the need for economic survival, this is especially understandable.

Julius Gambarini exemplifies this individualism. He is the first in his family, brothers included, born in the United States, the rest of his family being from Italy. His immigrant family background had a strong influence on his ideals and political views. He strongly believes in self-determination and self-motivation (i.e., "those who really want to can accomplish pretty much whatever they seek"—the traditional ideal of the American Dream where, through hard work, anyone can pick themselves up by their own bootstraps). Julius saw his own family do this, and so it is easy to see why he thinks that it is possible for others to do it as well—at least those who are "truly motivated."

Not surprisingly, many of those who are nonactivists toward an issue are also nonreferenced toward that same problem. Thus, Julius's response to seeing a homeless person in the street is highly reminiscent of Leslie's viewpoint.

In New York City, or even sometimes in Boston, there are people that look like they could work who are saying, "I need some food" or "I need some money." Begging. I haven't seen those families that are in shelters because they're not out there on the streets begging for money. They're in the shelters with their children, so what you end up seeing is that person who looks like he is able to work and you know he's going to buy liquor with that money. Even if they have a sign that says, "I have two children in a shelter," you turn away and you honestly don't want to look at that. You think, "Oh, that can't be true." You don't want to be scammed, so you don't give anything at all. The people we see in the streets are those who can work or those who are alcoholics or drug addicts asking for money and not necessarily starving. But those who are starving are in the house—they're in an apartment and they're starving and they're struggling to get by and so you don't see them. They're the silent majority.

When I asked Julius how he had responded to the issue of hunger, he gave a response that typifies the nonactivist.

> *I don't know. To be honest with you, I don't think I've responded. I don't think I've done anything because—I don't know. I think to myself, "What am I going to do?" I don't know. I think it's partly because, like many other people, I'm so wrapped up in my own life. You're wrapped up in your own life, you're bombarded with your own problems, and then you're being bombarded with social issues—poverty, AIDS, et cetera, et cetera. You think, "Ah, how much can I deal with?" So, I don't know why I haven't gotten involved; but, who knows . . . I know I'll deal with it in the future as a teacher who may have students who are starving.*

Adherence to the individualist ethic—being "wrapped up" in his own life and the belief that people can and should take care of themselves—is a major reason why Julius has not become involved in the hunger issue. However, it is not the only one. Providing further evidence to the stimulus overload perspective of Stanley Milgram, which has been discussed several times in preceding chapters, Julius feels he is being "bombarded" with a multitude of issues competing for his attention. Moreover, he feels powerless to do anything effective in the face of an issue of such magnitude. These factors have a paralyzing effect, and the result is nonactivism.

Noncommitted Participation

The *noncommitted participant* is someone who gets involved in addressing a particular issue more by chance than by intent. These individuals are not committed to a particular issue nor to involvement *per se;* however, they may occasionally participate in addressing an issue merely because it is something that drops in their laps or that is expected of them because of some other role they play. For example, they may be committed to a group or organization that happens to be getting involved on occasion. In other words, this form of action occurs without necessarily being accompanied by any degree of social consciousness toward the issue itself or activism in general.

In the case of Ashleigh Livingston, her motivation to get involved in social issues derives from her commitment to her role in student government. When the student government got involved in an issue, she was right there at the forefront.

We had a blood drive at school for people who needed blood. I knew it had to do with AIDS. I guess if you have AIDS, sometimes you need blood donated. Our vice principal is lesbian, so she's involved in a lot of things to help people with AIDS and things like that, so we had a blood drive and I was the chairperson for that. But I don't person-ally . . . I just get involved with particular things and that's just not one of them. It's not like I'm avoiding it. It just hasn't been one of them.

We had the AIDS quilt come to our school, too, and I got involved with that because of my position in student government. I guess if your family member dies from AIDS, you can make a quilt for them. It's kind of interesting and sad to think that all these people had died. Ryan White's quilt was there and a lot of people from the area—not any per-sons whom I had known, but it just really made you think. It was kind of scary to think that all these people had died from AIDS and there was nothing that you could have done to prevent it after they got it. It's not something that I can identify with, but it was an eye opener.

If another opportunity to get involved comes up, I may do so—if it's around here. It's not something that—personally—I feel real strongly about. I know it's there and I accept it. It's not something . . . I get involved in things that I enjoy personally, and I'm not saying that it's not something that I enjoy getting involved in, but it's just not . . . I get involved in student government and things like that because it's something that I can express myself in better.

Without the responsibilities of her role in student government, Ashleigh is unlikely to have been involved with the AIDS issue in either the blood drive or the presentation of the AIDS quilt. Her commitment and strengths lie within student government.

Ashleigh's example clearly demonstrates that people can do some-thing about an issue without necessarily feeling an affinity toward it. And, at least for Ashleigh, such an affinity would require some sort of personal identification with the issue. For this reason, she does not consider herself to be a "true" activist. Thus, noncommitted participants get involved if an opportunity comes their way, but they are just as likely to discontinue their involvement with that particular issue once the "event" is over. However, it is also possible, as we see later, for an issue to capture the imagination of someone who "just happens" to be involved at that time. When this occurs, noncommitted participation can easily become a turning point to either participatory or focused activism.

Participatory Activism

Participatory activists are those who are committed to involvement in general without an equal commitment to one particular issue. They are likely to get involved in a wide variety of issues, jumping around from one to another and engaging themselves in several simultaneously. As seen in the case of Sherri, it is among participatory activists that the role of socialization is most evident.[2]

Sherri grew up in a family that she characterized as being oriented toward "Faith, Peace, and Justice."

> *My parents were very into Faith, Peace, and Justice. I think this has influenced everyone in my family. For example, my sister graduated from college with a minor in Faith, Peace, and Justice. We're all kind of into that. So, both of my parents are very involved in the community and church. My mom is involved in the migrant ministry—working with migrants in the area—and my dad is really involved in a lot of things with child care. He sits on something like the Pediatrics Board of America and they work on laws and stuff for children.*

Her parents are active in their parish. The parish itself is rather progressive compared to many insofar as the type of outreach it does. As Sherri noted, when she was younger, her mother volunteered to help with migrant workers in the area and sometimes Sherri went along herself. Her parents encouraged her to become involved on her own as well, so most of her friends were people whom she met in those contexts.

> *I got involved in the church youth group. We would do a lot of service projects in the area, like work with the elderly or build homes with Habitat for Humanity. And we'd take trips to places like North Carolina to work with the migrants. The youth group was a place where kids could come and hang out and be with other kids who had the same interests. A lot of my friends are interested in the same things. It's not weird for us to say, "Hey, you want to go work on a house this weekend at Habitat?" Most people would say, "What?," but I just think it's so fun. I don't see it as a chore. I just think that service work is so interesting because it provides a chance to meet so many different people and plus it's kind of exciting. If I have the resources and can help people, then why not?*

Based on this evidence, it is apparent that Sherri has been immersed in a culture of activism, so much so that she may actually take it a bit for granted. For example, she found it hard to describe the reasons for many aspects of her activism. It was just "what she does" and very much a part of her identity.

Sherri was not passionate about a particular issue. She was passionate about her involvement. The issue itself did not matter quite so much. When I asked her whether she chooses to get involved because of the issue it represents or just because the opportunity is there, she said, "I don't really know." When there is an opportunity to get involved with hunger or AIDS or the environment, she just takes it; and yet she is not really committed to the homeless or hungry or persons with AIDS themselves or even the issues they represent so much as organized involvement. For instance, when alone and confronting the hunger issue in terms of people asking for money on the streets, she is just as distrustful of the homeless as Leslie or Julius are, saying "you never know if it is someone who really needs the money or if it's just someone putting on an act to get money." Thus, participatory activists focus much more on involvement than on the issues they address. Not that the issues themselves are perceived as unimportant; it is just that no particular issue supplies the drive and motivation behind the commitment of participatory activists. Instead, it is the thrill of just being involved.

Focused Activism

Individuals who are committed to both involvement and to the issue itself represent *focused activists*. They often recognize the importance of a variety of issues, but have limited their commitment and involvement to just one social problem. In the case of Jason Kaufman, that one problem—injustice—was the root of a number of different issues, including hunger.

Growing up, Jason was active in addressing injustice in general and his involvement was with several different issues, such as censorship and the presence of Junior ROTC at his high school. Since then, as he decided to make activism his profession, specific manifestations of injustice have emerged into the foreground of his concern. Poverty and the issue of income distribution, which form the basis of hunger, have become central in his life, primarily because they were the focus of his internship when training for a social work degree. Activism is not just something in which he participates, but a way of life.

I wasn't involved with poverty and hunger a whole lot until I actually got into the social work program. At that point, I had more contact with the issue through my intern placement. I was doing interfaith work, but there was also this whole urban agenda and focus on urban social justice. So, I was active in that, and then, in this latest internship, I'm working with a program that deals with children's poverty. So, I got a lot of experience with that and I found it to be a winning issue as well as being something I was concerned about. It's an issue that a lot of people are concerned about, even conservatives so long as you reframe the issue as "poverty" rather than "welfare."

So, my interest in injustice has become my profession. What drew me to the social work program was the fact that it is an interdisciplinary field. I wanted to be an activist and, in the program, there was a community organizer concentration. So, the issues weren't as important as the process stuff, learning about communities, learning about organizing. And it's in good internships that I can learn these skills. They give you the practical experience that you then look at in light of the other stuff you learn in your classes.

Unlike those falling into the other categories of activism, Jason's focus on activism and the underlying issue of injustice has led him to a vision that goes beyond the actual work he does. As someone who is socially referenced with regard to injustice, poverty, and hunger, he sees the issue in terms of its societal implications. However, as a focused activist, he is also conscious of the part he is playing in a much larger effort at social change. In other words, he does not note that "I do this" or "I do that." Instead, he can say, "I *contribute* to this long-range solution." He speaks in terms of what "we" are doing, by which he means to include all activists like himself.

I feel like I'm an activist for the long haul. I grew up in the Reagan years, so this Clinton stuff was refreshing. Then he turned out to have no backbone and Congress went Republican and "Oh, God!" It just seems like I'm used to it and I can handle Reagan—it's all I know. I have no Roosevelt or Kennedy or any of that. All I know is Reagan— Reagan, Bush, and Newt.

But I kind of feel like we're getting ready for things to swing the other way. I think we're just making our stand right now and they're just plowing over it. Things are really going to hit the fan—maybe as soon as five years, maybe longer. There's just been people dying all over the place, and you can only starve people out so much. It's going to get really ugly.

Because Jason is committed to addressing injustice for the long term, he has been willing to make personal sacrifices in order to make change possible.

> *When going into the human services and social justice work, you have to make sacrifices in terms of money. I've thought to myself, "I could have been a lawyer. I could have been a damn good lawyer." All this stuff that I see that lawyers do, it's stuff that I'm good at—like twisting things around to my own purposes! I'm good at that and I think "damn, you know, it's something I could have done." And then there's the whole issue of a low income at the same time that I have such a large debt from going to school.*
>
> *But then I remember that activism and organizing are what I like doing. It's fun. I get to be myself. It's not like a form of prostitution which I think, if I was going to be the kind of lawyer that would make money, that's what I'd be doing. I'd be basically selling my services. Not in any big unethical way, but in a real boring kind of way. I think the day in and day out work of a lawyer—I wouldn't enjoy it.*

Jason has a clear set of priorities in his life. He would much rather be doing something he believes in and that taps into his enjoyment of activism than earning a lot of money in a line of work that is otherwise unfulfilling to him.

For many of those who get involved in social issues, there is almost a sense of shopping around for which issue will receive one's time and attention. For example, Lloyd, who could be considered a participatory activist, looked through all the postings by student organizations for opportunities to get involved: "When I wanted to find out what all my choices were, I would stop and take the time to go through every single posting to see what resources there were. Once I had a really good idea of everything that was offered, then I could just choose." In contrast, the process is much different for a focused activist such as Jason.

> *Well, you don't just choose an issue. It chooses you. You don't sit down and look at a book that has a little sheet on each issue and decide what I should work on. It doesn't work like that. It's more like what seizes you.*

In sum, focused activists such as Jason are committed to an activist lifestyle, as reflected in the willingness to make personal sacrifices and, while their focus may evolve over time, they have a strong commitment to the issue being addressed. They also have a vision that extends beyond their immediate tasks to encompass the cumulative contributions of all of those involved in the issue, at whatever level.

While it is important to define activism and distinguish its various degrees, one can still ask the question "Under what conditions does each of these degrees of action emerge?" Some social scientists, such as C. Daniel Batson, in his model of altruistic motivation (1987: 90–95), suggest that taking action is the end product of a linear progression from "perception of need" to "empathy and role-taking" to a "behavioral response." In other words, social consciousness and sentiment necessarily *precede* action. Loeb implies that he too subscribes to this model of motivation when he says that, "Students act based on what they know" (1994: 68). This perspective—in which consciousness and empathy precede action—has its merits in terms of explaining the emergence of action. As an example, we go back to the various social issues frames presented in the social consciousness chapter and discuss their mobilizing potential.[3] However, as we shall see later in the chapter, it is also possible for action to *precipitate* changes in our consciousness and sentiment.

Mobilizing Potential of the Social Issues Frames

After noting that "students act based on what they know," Loeb asks, "But what if their society shields them from its history, denies them the knowledge necessary to make informed judgments and choices? What if the understanding they need to accurately judge America's crises and their roots gets lost in misinformation and distraction" (1994: 68)? He is clearly alluding to the construction of social consciousness. Recall that our culture, institutions, group affiliations, and even our individual selves all filter information in and out of consciousness. At the same time, and just as Charlotte Ryan describes the media, we frame these issues in various ways. In chapter 5, we distinguished five primary ways of framing social issues without discussing their relationship with action. Now we relate social consciousness and action in a linear fashion.

Ryan distinguishes between "mobilizing" and "demobilizing" frames where the former "pushes audiences to see problems not as individual but as collective" and the latter make "problems ever more individual" (1991: 71). While her analysis focuses exclusively on the media and I have taken liberties when applying it to individual consciousness, her work does suggest that frames have a *mobilizing potential*. Although, while Ryan sees each frame as exclusively mobilizing or demobilizing, the social issues frames we utilize in constructing our consciousness have the potential for *both* alternatives, depending on how the individual interprets them. Thus, the individual frame, which Ryan would see as demobilizing, may also be mobilizing and the social ethics frame, which pushes a "collective" interpretation, may be just as demobilizing as it is mobilizing. Again, it depends on individual interpretation.[4]

The Individual Frame

Recall that those who employ the individual frame define social issues as a matter of individual responsibility. In other words, they pay close attention to what they perceive as the relative guilt or innocence of those affected by the issue. In the case of Julius, he distinguishes between what he views as the "silent majority" of the hungry who are the women and children he never sees because they are in their apartments struggling to survive and the apparently able-bodied men he sees on the street who "just want the money for alcohol or drugs."

As was apparent in the case of Julius, the individual frame is most often demobilizing since there is the belief that individuals are accountable only to themselves. Julius is "wrapped up" in his own life, fulfilling his end of the bargain by taking care of himself and seeing to his own needs. He implies that the men he sees on the street should be doing the same thing: pulling themselves up by their own bootstraps. Unless they are making an effort to take care of themselves, Julius has no sympathy for them and is not likely to offer any assistance. His framing of the issue in terms of individual responsibility has minimized the possibility of his taking action on behalf of these "undeserving" poor.

However, Julius has left the window open for future involvement by noting that, as a teacher, he may have to deal with "children who are starving." Moreover, he says that, "if I saw a family with children, I think I would give money." Those who espouse the individual frame can be mobilized if they focus on the *deserving* poor. As evidenced by what Julius has to say, their involvement is likely to be limited to charity. However, those holding the individual frame may also be mobilized toward education: first toward themselves, as in learning safer sex practices as a means of preventing the transmission of HIV, and second toward others—a form of involvement that can be seen as "helping others to help themselves." For instance, Laura believes this is the way to address the AIDS issue.

AIDS is something that can be slowed—maybe not stopped, but certainly slowed. I think that people's attitudes have to change about it too—before contracting it and after. It might be helpful to have people with AIDS go into high schools and talk to kids. I know they do that with drugs. I guess some high schools already do this, but I know my high school never did.

Again, the mobilization of those utilizing the individual frame focuses on the individual. In other words, any mobilization that does occur serves to further legitimate the frame being utilized by the person himself or herself.

The Bureaucratic Frame

Those employing the bureaucratic frame define issues as a matter for experts and so the general response, in terms of mobilizing potential, is to allow experts to do their job as they see fit. Thus, this frame can be demobilizing if individuals assume that only experts are capable of addressing the social issue in question. The most typical example of this reaction to an issue is the propensity to let scientists do their work in finding a cure for AIDS; but even if one is less ambitious than finding a cure, those employing the bureaucratic frame still rely on experts. For instance, Jodi Ferguson would not even feel comfortable involving herself in AIDS education. She says that, "I don't think I could ever be a speaker about it because I don't know that much about it, I guess. I know how to prevent it, but I guess I don't know statistics and things like that on it." Not only does she disqualify herself as an "expert" on the issue, she also does not consider the possibility of becoming an expert, effectively blocking what she perceives as all potential for getting involved in the AIDS issue.

However, the bureaucratic frame could also be mobilizing if the individual recognizes the need to provide support for the experts. Numerous individuals, realizing that they cannot cure AIDS themselves are willing to donate money to AIDS research. Elizabeth Taylor's AIDS organizing is founded on this premise. Moreover, a few individuals may become upset with the apparent ineptitude of the experts and become mobilized to do something about it. Such a response, while definitely occurring within the bureaucratic frame focusing on experts, also merges with the structural frame, although the "problem" is focused in one part of the system rather than being endemic to the entire system.

The Structural Frame

Within the structural frame, a social issue is defined as the result of structural problems and is merely a symptom of much deeper problems in society. The way to solve this problem is to change the system. However, this frame could be demobilizing if it is paired with feelings of powerlessness.[5] Laura describes just such a feeling of powerlessness and effectively bridges the structural and bureaucratic frames.

> *Hunger has historically been a problem; but—I think that I'm right in this—there is enough food to feed the world. It's not because we're having a food shortage. It's because of political and distribution problems. It's because of governments and things that we can't feed the world's people. I think sometimes people feel it's kind of out of their control and that it's not an arena that they can be directly involved in, whereas with something like the environment or pro-life, you can see the results, I think.*

Laura blames government and politics for the hunger issue, pointing out that there is, in fact, enough food to feed everyone. Such a view clearly reflects the structural frame. However, at the same time that she says it is beyond the control of individuals, she blends in the bureaucratic frame by implying that there are experts—at least government bureaucrats—who *can* address it.

The structural frame may also be mobilizing, especially among those who, like Jason, are empowered within a social movement or advocacy approach to the issue. He knows from his work, internships, and social work training that there many people out there who are concerned about injustice, poverty, and hunger. His focus is on community organizing—a key response of those who are mobilized in the structural frame—and he is optimistic that, by working together, "we're getting ready for things to swing the other way."

The Universal Frame

Like the individual frame, the universal frame is most often demobilizing. The issue is defined as something that affects everybody and, while "everyone" is seen as being responsible, no one person or group in particular bears the responsibility for addressing it. Those espousing this frame never really focus on solutions to the social issues. When it comes to getting involved in AIDS or hunger, Richard Louis believes that "everyone should," saying that "our society has an obligation to take care of people who are not as well off." However, he is generally uninvolved in the issues. The demobilizing tendency of the universal frame is especially noticeable in the language used by the person expressing this point of view as, for example, when individuals phrased their answers to questions about addressing social issues in terms of "you" and "they." In other words, a number of interviewees would say, "they could do such and such" rather than "we could. . . ." This is in stark contrast with Jason's use of the word "we" and serves to accentuate the idea that these individuals do not feel a personal responsibility toward the needy faced with a particular issue.

However, there are instances where the universal frame can be mobilizing. Just as in the individual frame, this involvement tends to be directed toward basic charity, although there is less a focus on the "deserving" than on the general popularity of the issue itself. If the issue is "in"—and if involvement is convenient—those taking a universal perspective may be mobilized to do something. In many instances, such involvement serves to alleviate any guilt the individual may feel as a result of the relative privilege he or she experiences as compared to those affected by the issue in question. For example, Richard has, on occasion, addressed hunger: "I won't walk by someone who's hungry and ignore them. I'll do what I can at that moment because it takes away the guilt and maybe makes me feel good about myself." By noting that he does what he can "at that moment" he is excusing himself for not giving to the hungry when it is inconvenient for himself. However, on another exceptional occasion, he got involved despite its inconvenience. Close to the Christmas holidays, his father saw an ad in the paper placed by a soup kitchen that needed volunteers. Richard hesitantly notes that

> It wasn't . . . "convenient" would be the best word. Not that being hungry is ever convenient. I needed a little arm twisting, not a whole lot. My dad said, "Oh, come on. Let's go do it." So, I said, "Okay." So, it's probably not something that I would have done on my own, but I was glad that I did it afterwards.

This passage also points out the popularity dimension of being mobilized within the universal frame. In the first place, the Christmas season was motivating because, as already discussed, attention is more likely to be drawn to the issue at that time. More importantly, Richard had direct pressure from his father—not in terms of direct coercion, but more like a friendly "you-won't-be-cool-if-you-don't" prompting.

The Social Ethics Frame

The social ethics frame focuses on the moral dimensions of social issues and on personal responsibility for getting involved. As we have repeatedly seen in the cases of Diane and Beth, this frame is most often mobilizing. The question is, "At what level will this involvement take place?" Beth's involvement in the AIDS issue focused on helping out a single individual suffering from the disease. Others, such as Diane, are active on a broader level, such as charitable outreach toward all those affected, contributing to entire organizations and a number of individuals simultaneously. Still others may move toward the structural activism where the focus is on changing the system through advocacy and social movements. Jason, while definitely falling within the structural frame, also shares many of the traits of the social ethics frame, especially in his focus on the language of "justice" and "equality." He, too, demonstrates a sense of personal responsibility.

There are a few instances in which the social ethics frame may be demobilizing. On the one hand, individuals may interpret their moral obligation to society as being seasonal in character. As already noted, many of those interviewed volunteered in soup kitchens during the holiday season and felt that this involvement fulfilled their obligation. At the same time, the social ethics frame can be demobilizing if the individual gives precedence toward his or her *own* moral behavior rather than social morality. However, in this instance, it can be reasonably argued that the individual frame is more central in the person's understanding of the issue than the social ethics frame, even though the framing utilizes moral language.

This discussion, showing how the construction of one's consciousness has an impact on one's potential for being mobilized to address a social issue, reveals that the various ways of framing the filtered information regarding social issues often overlaps in a variety of combinations. However, the bottom line is that they each have a mobilizing and a demobilizing tendency, depending on a variety of additional factors affecting the individual. As Loeb notes, "involvement requires more than having information." With this in mind, it is possible to ask, "What is it which directs an individual toward the demobilizing or the mobilizing outcomes?"[6]

Taking Action Depends On . . .

Whether an individual is mobilized to get involved in addressing a social issue depends on a variety of contingencies. A number of these contingencies were already hinted at in the preceding section: time and convenience, individual interests, values and priorities, activism's reflection on identity, perceived opportunity, and perceived effectiveness of one's contribution. We shall focus our attention on the last four, given their significance to the vast majority of those interviewed. However, as we see in the data presented later, all of these contingencies overlap with one another. It is also important to note that, in keeping with Robert Wuthnow's findings on voluntarism, these contingencies are typically presented as reasons or motives why each individual does or does not become active in addressing the issues.

> Motives are interesting, then, because they make volunteering meaningful, but they do so by making it ordinary. It is behavior we can make sense of, not some senseless or random activity. But it is meaningful, mainly because it becomes a part of our routine. (1995: 31)

... Setting Priorities

We have already discussed the influence of such values as individualism and the notion underlying the American Dream that individuals are responsible for their own fates. On the other hand, there is the apparently conflicting idealization of the moral dimension of social responsibility. As already seen, these values have a tremendous impact on our social activism in terms of the degree and the form it takes. Moving beyond these general values, it is also apparent that what individuals perceive as being important in their own lives has a tremendous impact on whether they will be mobilized to take action. Such values frequently are reflected in one's priorities. For many people, listing their priorities takes the form of an explanation for why they do not get involved. For example, Kesia justifies her inactivity toward the hunger issue by saying that she comes first.

> *Sometimes I help out in little ways, and oftentimes I want to do more; but I don't have the time and I do still come first. I'm not going to help my neighbor before helping myself because that's just not the reality of the situation. I have a lot of things in my life that I have to take care of and, at the same time, I'm still trying to make sure I [with emphasis] don't go hungry and to advance myself and get my education so that I can have some kind of job. The bottom line is that people are hungry and, when I can help them out, I will and when I can't, I don't. That's the bottom line.*

It is obvious that Kesia places priority on her own life. Even so, hunger has a special place in her priorities because of her experiences as a child—experiences that led to her self-referenced orientation toward the issue. Kesia came close to experiencing hunger herself when growing up in poverty, a situation that peaked when her home burned to the ground. After that event, she and her mother had to rely on the Red Cross for shelter and food until they could get back on their feet. Given these experiences, it is not surprising that her priorities include *preventing* hunger from entering her own life.

Other individuals discuss their priorities in terms of reasons for getting involved. Recall the case of Sherri, who regularly got involved in issues through her church youth group. Her attitude is that, "someone has to help them. And if I have a free Saturday afternoon or something, why not?" Clearly, her priorities are different than Kesia's. This became even more apparent when I asked her about those situations in which she did not have a "free" Saturday afternoon, such as when she had dance and piano lessons.

> *If I had to miss a lesson, I'd miss a lesson. Dancing and piano were every week, so if something new would come up, I'd do it because it was a chance to do it then. I could do dance or piano every week. . . . Why would I not help them?*

Taking part in addressing social issues is even more of a priority for Sherri than her dance or piano lessons, further underscoring the fact that she is a participatory activist.

Priorities not only play a role in whether or not an individual addresses a particular issue, but also in choosing *among* different issues. At present, Art Phillips focuses on care for the elderly. This concern has superseded his previous involvement with hunger. Moreover, he has never been involved with AIDS because of the priorities he has set. Art explains that,

> *there are just other issues that I feel more concerned about. It sounds harsh, but I'm not concerned about AIDS. I know it's a serious thing, but it's just that there's other areas I'd rather work. I don't really know how I go about setting up these priorities. Probably it's just that working with the elderly would be a community service that would also relate to my job aspirations. Also, people with AIDS are a minority in the society, but in the future, the elderly are going to be the majority, so I feel like doing volunteer work in that area reaches a broader spectrum of the population.*

While priorities have an impact on which issue Art will devote his time, they also figure into decisions regarding the type of activity individuals are willing to support. For example, some are very much against giving money to people on the street but are quite willing to volunteer in a soup kitchen on occasion. When it comes to the AIDS issue, Eddie Curtis is very much against the politicization of the issue as represented by activist groups such as ACT UP (AIDS Coalition to Unleash Power). He is even wary of the effectiveness of a fundraising event such as the local AIDS dance-a-thon. While this event raises money for a number of AIDS organizations, he is unsure of the educational effectiveness of such indirect participation in the issue, especially in terms of prevention. Instead, he says,

> *I want to see them educating the kids in schools because that's where it's needed. Kids aren't getting it on the street and the kids aren't getting it out of the AIDS dance-a-thon. The only place the kids can get it is where they spend most of their time and that is in the schools. It needs to be a part of their everyday lives.*

Eddie concludes by saying that, while he has given money to the cause, he would prefer to be a speaker who goes into the classroom and speaks to kids directly. While he has not pursued this option in the context of AIDS, he does plan to do so regarding gay and lesbian issues by becoming a member of a local Speakers Bureau.[7]

. . . How Action Reflects on Identity

An important consideration when it comes to setting one's priorities, especially among young people, is the perception that one's involvements will reflect on one's identity. In Wuthnow's study of young volunteers titled *What It Means to Volunteer,* he notes that "Volunteering contributed significantly . . . to one of their most important developmental tasks as young adults, namely, achieving a distinct personal identity" (1995: 38). Being recognized by others as someone who gets involved, or as an activist, has definite implications for one's self-perception and identity. We are highly motivated to regulate what sort of impression we make because we realize that we make assumptions about the identity of others based upon their involvements.

Recall Loeb's description of the "adapters." Coupled with the popular belief that the nation's activists of the sixties "sold out," [the adapters] learned to mistrust peers who take on causes that go beyond their personal lives. They learned to dismiss politically involved students of whatever style or stripe with an array of often contradictory stereotypes, explaining, "They all wear black," "They all dress like hippies," "They all just say the same thing." They demanded a perfect standard of political proof, as though people should not open their mouths unless they were eloquent enough to debate Henry Kissinger on *Nightline*. And when they *did* admire those who acted, they regarded them as a sort of different breed, explaining, apologetically, "I'm just not that kind of person." (1994: 4)

In the same vein, many of those interviewed explained their nonactivism or limited involvement in terms of the "kind of person" they are.

Veronica Sorensen is highly conscious of the way people perceive those who get involved, especially in terms of the type of involvement. On the one hand, she admires activists, saying, "Activists want to make a change so society is better. They want equal rights for people." At the same time, however, she sets herself apart from them in a manner that is simultaneously disdainful and apologetic.

> *I can't become some huge activist for AIDS and say "Well, I've got this rally. Screw my test." I don't think I'd want to get involved with it either because sometimes it gets violent and people get in trouble. I don't want to be part of that. I like to stay out of trouble. . . .*
>
> *Activists are more aggressive, obviously. They're probably a lot more knowledgeable than I am, too. And they have the guts, pretty much. They're willing to risk so much and I'm not at all. But I don't like change so much. I like everything to run exactly as I planned it and being an activist or something definitely includes change. Speaking out or something includes change.*

Sometimes it is not activism but the issue itself that makes individuals wary of getting involved. This is particularly true of the AIDS issue. There are still lingering beliefs that it is a "homosexual disease" and that anyone who is involved "must be homosexual." Even when stereotypes of homosexuality are no longer present, there are other fears that help to explain why the AIDS issue—even though "popularized" in our culture through such symbols as red ribbons—and those involved are still viewed with some suspicion. For example, while Martin is conscious of the fact that AIDS activists are not necessarily HIV positive themselves, he worries about what others think, and this has curbed his own response to the issue: "I think AIDS is almost taboo [laughs] where I come from. Even now, when they are having AIDS awareness dances, I'd always be hesitant to go because you have that idea, 'Oh, everybody there has AIDS or something.' And when you think about it, 'No, they don't.'"

While many avoid participating because of the implications for their identity, others like Brad have made it a central part of their own identity: "I'm not someone who says 'no.' I don't think as far as hunger and homelessness go, I *actively* search to participate in it, but it does come my way from other things that I've done and I will never say 'no' to it because it's important." Brad is actually well known for his willingness to help out, and so he is asked on a regular basis and people turn to him first.

In a similar vein, Patrick McGuire tells a story of his efforts at condom distribution among his friends, explaining that "It's just part of my character to do stuff like that all the time. It's the way I do things. It's just me. I can't explain it any other way than that:"

> I went to a Catholic school and the condom issue was extremely sensitive; but it's a reality I think the church has to face. People say that giving out condoms is like giving kids a license. Well, if they're driving anyway, you might as well make it legal for them. So, I got involved by handing out condoms. I'm just concerned about the guys and the girls that I'm close to—like my brother. I'll ask him and my friends point blank and I'll buy them condoms. I have no problems with that at all. If they're afraid to buy them or they don't think they need them, or if they "don't have the money" right then, if they give some lame ass excuse like that, I'll just go buy them because I don't want anyone I know running the risk. For example, my friend had a party for his graduation. His parents were away and we had a lot of drinking and there were guys there with girls and you figure something's going to happen. I just went out and spent thirty or forty bucks and bought boxes of them and passed them out to the crowd. "Okay, here they are!" I put them right next to the beer. Just put them in a candy dish on the coffee table or something just so they're there.

While Patrick was concerned for his friends and was generous enough to buy condoms for them, he also did not want to make a "big deal" about it as if he were a "real" activist. He rather modestly cloaked his generosity with yet another aspect of his identity: "I did it kind of to be a wise ass. I thought it would be pretty funny if this kid's parents came home and found the condoms. He'd have a tough time explaining that one."

. . . Perceived Opportunity

When it comes to having the opportunity to get involved in addressing a social issue, we have already seen two of the various mechanisms at work. In the first place, individuals like Sherri grow up with a culture of activism. Opportunities are regularly presented to her and her participation is encouraged by her family and friends. In the case of Jason, activism is closely tied with his career. As we saw in the previous chapter on social sentiment, integrating one's professional life with involvement in social issues is a way of legitimating a life devoted to helping others. Otherwise, these individuals are often perceived as "deviants" because they appear to be taking care of others more than themselves. In an individualistic culture such as our own, such "selflessness" is often viewed with suspicion. For this reason, among others, many of those in this study who are most active are also pursuing careers in social work, nursing, education, counseling, and so on.

But what about the many others who do not grow up in an activist culture or who chose career paths that do not focus on care for others? For these individuals, the opportunities to take action are much less consistent. In fact, many refer to the lack of opportunity as a major reason for not participating. While Sherri is a regular participant in activities addressing the poverty and hunger issues, AIDS is a different story. "I just haven't had the opportunity, what with the time and the fact that there really isn't anything . . . we have an AIDS group on campus, but I don't even know how to get involved with that." While Sherri is aware of an AIDS group, its presence is not enough to constitute an opportunity for her. Gevonne, on the other hand, is not even aware of such organizations. When I asked her why she had not participated in AIDS, she said "I just don't think I've had the chance. I've never seen. . . . For the hunger issue, the Walk for Hunger just happened; but I've never see a 'Walk for AIDS' or anything like that. I don't really know of any organizations to tell you the truth." Jodi, too, has not heard of volunteer opportunities regarding AIDS, and she thinks "there should be, especially on a college campus. All you hear about on my campus is activities like plays or sports or whatever. You never hear about AIDS involvement groups or anything like that. I don't know if it's just because this is a small campus or what, but. . . ." Both Jodi and Gevonne have hit upon an important principle regarding opportunities for involvement: just as in growing up in an activist environment, learning of such opportunities is highly dependent upon one's social environment.

When opportunities do "present themselves," they are usually presented by friends, family, or the institutions—such as schools and churches[8]—with which these individuals are already affiliated. Booth and Babchuck point out the importance of these connections by noting that, "in becoming affiliated [in a voluntary association], members usually rely on personal networks . . ." (1969: 179). In a sense, these opportunities are "filtered in" through a process very much like that discussed in chapter 5 on the construction of social consciousness. For example, Garrett had thought about the Walk for Hunger, but never really got motivated on his own.

> *The Walk for Hunger was actually a last-minute idea. I wanted to walk in it, but I never got around to getting an application and sponsors. Then my brother called me Saturday night because his girlfriend was sick and he wanted me to walk with him [laughing]. So, I walked with my brother, but I did think about doing it [laughs].*

Responding to the same event, Kesia was also drawn in by friends. "When I see the fliers, I think, 'Oh, and everybody else is going to do it. All my friends said they were going to do it. So, I'll do it with them.'" School and church-sponsored events are among the biggest draws to participating in one or more causes. As we saw with Ashleigh, she got involved with both a blood drive for those with AIDS and organizing the AIDS quilt exhibit when these events came to her school. Laura volunteered in a homeless shelter with her friends when it was announced in church that volunteers were needed. Brad also got involved with a shelter sponsored by his church, particularly because his mother was the shelter's director.

Since the opportunities presented to those who are not already immersed in a culture of activism or are pursuing careers that lend themselves to helping others are sporadic at best, responsibility for finding these opportunities generally lies with the individuals themselves. As Loeb notes, "Avenues for involvement do exist in most communities, but they aren't always visible. Young activists need to assertively seek them out if they want to do more . . ." (1994: 391). However, for those without an "activist" identity, seeking out opportunities rarely happens. Colleen exemplifies just such a person.

> *I've pledged for my local AIDS walk and stuff like that, but I've never really been active with AIDS. But where I am, there's no . . . I guess I'd have to go off. . . . The other opportunities for volunteer work kind of like came to me. I think for opportunities to help AIDS patients, I would have to* look *for them myself—I guess in hospitals and stuff like that. It's just that AIDS is not that widespread where I live, so I'd have to kind of look outside of that by* myself *to try to do something about it.*

Given the evidence presented here, it becomes clear that, to attract involvement, it is first necessary to make volunteering and other forms of participation and activism readily available and convenient. Institutions such as churches, schools, businesses, and clubs are primary targets of such advertising. Moreover, such appeals for involvement should encourage group participation. Once some individuals get involved, they are likely to draw others in as well.

. . . Perceived Effectiveness

As might be gleaned from our scrutiny of the mobilizing potential of the various social issues frames, feelings of powerlessness are a major reason for not getting involved, while being empowered is often quite motivating. Loeb notes that "students often grow up learning that it is impossible for them to affect history" (1994: 104–105). This is especially true of those who are apolitical because they "tend to believe that society cannot change. Global events seem out of their control" (1994: 119). When individuals focus on a problem of global proportion, such as hunger or AIDS, the effect can be overwhelming. The typical response in that situation is much like Garrett's response to AIDS: "I guess it never really occurred to me that I could do something that would make a difference." Veronica feels much the same way about hunger. When I asked her how one goes about addressing the issue, she replied, "I don't know. Individually? I couldn't. Sally Struthers does. She has a commercial." Veronica's idealization of the power someone like Sally Struthers has is actually quite typical and, as noted by Loeb, "The higher the pedestal on which America places its role models, the more those watching see no choice between leaping in totally and holding back, hesitant and wary" (1994: 105).

Among those who do not identify themselves as activists, the ability to see a middle ground between "leaping in totally" and "holding back" helps in recognizing that they can be effective. When Richard's father encouraged him to come along and volunteer at the soup kitchen, Richard enjoyed the hands-on quality of what he was doing and felt effective in his efforts.

> *Hunger was just something I felt I could really make a difference with at that moment. That's why I did it; whereas, if I was just going to be in a rally or a protest, I probably wouldn't have done it. But I was actually taking food and putting it on a plate for people, helping to cook it, prepare it. So, it was something that I could get immediate gratification from.*

Feeling effective is also important for Joann, who discusses why she became active with hunger rather than AIDS.

> *I think there's enough food in this country. While I couldn't go find all that food and give it to people myself, I could join forces with people and volunteer. Or I could be politically active in trying to get this food and medicine where it needs to go. Whereas with AIDS, you can't be a part of the solution. You just have to make sure you're not part of the problem. I can't go into a laboratory right now and find a solution for AIDS, but I can make sure I don't get it.*

Joann could see a means for addressing hunger. But AIDS was beyond her reach except insofar as she could prevent it in herself. Moreover, she hinted at the power of numbers—"joining forces" empowers the individual and increases the perception of effectiveness.

Many people feel that acting alone—as a single individual in a large, social world—is ineffectual, especially when the results are not immediate nor visible. Much social theory has corroborated this view, arguing that for social change to really occur, groups of individuals are much more effective (see, for example, Charon 1995). However, there are those who, while perhaps a minority, realize that individuals, acting *as individuals,* can still make a difference. Single acts have a capacity to accumulate to the point where some critical level is reached and social change occurs. Historian Howard Zinn calls these acts the "invisible roots of social change" (1994: 24) and, in his autobiographical history *You Can't Be Neutral on a Moving Train,* cites a number of examples. Many people can recall the figure of Rosa Parks refusing to sit at the back of the bus because she was black—a single act by a single individual that is frequently hailed as the beginning of the civil rights movement. While Parks's civil disobedience was planned in advance, Zinn demonstrates that the movement began long before with individual actions that were more spontaneous and just as brave, if not more so because of their spontaneity. There were even other instances of sitting in the "white section" of a bus. Rosa Parks's act was a small part of an "ongoing process" of social change (1994: 33).

Zinn's conclusion is that "No act, . . . however small, should be dismissed or ignored" (1994: 124). Even the smallest and most concrete activities, such as spooning food onto a plate for a hungry person, have enormous potential. Moreover, the evidence presented by the data in this study suggests that, even if acts such as these have no visible impact on society, individual actions do have a profound effect *on the individual* himself or herself.

The Impact of Taking Action

As was noted in the introduction to this chapter, action—or a "behavioral response"—often is seen as the end result after consciousness and an empathetic response. However, at this point, it will be seen that action can also *precede* the emergence of social consciousness. Many of those interviewed showed evidence that an internal transformation had occurred upon taking part in addressing a social issue. While this process is by no means universal, particularly among those for whom participation is a mere routine, becoming involved frequently leads to an increase in consciousness and compassion.

While Julius is a nonactivist toward the hunger issue, he has engaged in a few activities addressing AIDS, such as a benefit walk. When I asked him what he came away with from these experiences, he answered:

> *The personal tragedy behind every story that we don't see on TV. There's always a personal tragedy that's not shown. They can talk about it as much as they want and they can talk about all the statistics, but behind each statistic there's a tragedy. And there's a triumph—the courage, the work to bring it up and make it a social issue, the pushing, the struggling.*
>
> *When you see this, I think that you can go out and educate. You can present people with other ways of thinking or looking at an issue. If I'm speaking to someone and I tell them about my experience, maybe that person will change their mind or have a different view of it; and when that person speaks to someone else . . . it's a chain. Hopefully, it doesn't end. But "one by one" is how a problem is solved.*

Julius's involvement obviously made a big difference in his outlook regarding the issue. He became more aware of the personal dimension behind all of the factual information with which we are bombarded. By personalizing the issue, his initial activity has inspired him and he looks forward to more.

While the personal dimensions behind the issues are certainly very important, in some instances—such as with hunger—the facts are little known. When Brad spent time helping out in a homeless shelter, a topic that also came up in chapter 5, his consciousness of the personal *and* structural dimensions of the issue increased.

> *I've met a lot of homeless people and you just sit down and the one's I've met are just anxious to tell you their story. You learn what it's really like. You have people who lost their home for whatever reason and are hungry and are homeless with three kids. If they go out and get a job, then they lose their welfare check. It's a catch-22. It's so much harder after learning all this because you can't say to yourself, "Well, it's their fault." They're sitting there telling you that it's not.*
>
> *I just think that no one should have to live like that. No one should have to worry about where the next meal is going to come from, especially when other people are feasting somewhere else. There's something structurally wrong because we have warehouses full of food. They say we have enough food to feed the world three times over or something like that, and yet some people can't afford to eat anything. There's something in the very structure and if we tried it so long one way, why wouldn't we at least try it another way because its not working this way. It's just obvious it's not working this way, so just try something different.*

Working in the homeless shelter and in the food warehouse alerted Brad to aspects of hunger he had never thought of before he became involved. His reaction to this new information not only raised his consciousness, it prompted him to adopt the structural frame—the same frame that dominates Jason's consciousness. As a result, Brad has the potential to escalate his involvement and become a focused activist much like Jason.

At the same time, Brad notes that it's "harder after learning all this." He can never go back to the innocence of being unaware. In this sense, "ignorance" truly is "bliss." Loeb picks up on this same theme when he says that "apolitical students are right to assume that involvement may radically change them. The activists cite a new sense of responsibility that comes with knowing about issues of homelessness or Central America or the environment: the fears that you might 'see too much' and have to become 'too moral' aren't baseless" (1994: 104).

Thus, it is also possible for action to elicit greater levels of compassion. Patrick regularly passes the same homeless man on his way to work. He gives money to him almost every time he sees the man. At first, Patrick wondered where all this money was going; but the more he thought about it, the more he could role-take and empathize with the homeless man. Now, he does not mind so much if the money is used for alcohol.

> *I just think that, for the people who get themselves in those positions to survive, they turn to alcohol and things like that. It helps them forget what they are or where they are. He could be using the money for something else, but if he's addicted to something, the effects of him not having that are going to be far worse than the effects of him having it, just because of withdrawals and that kind of sickness. I've seen people who have been trying to get off drugs and it's just horrible what they go through. So, that coupled with the fact that you're homeless, I mean . . . I give them credit, because surviving like that is just . . . I don't think I could do it. I don't think I'm that tough. I don't think I could handle it.*

Again, Patrick started giving money to the homeless before his compassion displaced his initial distrust. The typical result, as Eddie notes, is the belief that one is a better person: "I feel that my involvement has really helped develop and shape me as a person, such as in being sensitive to other people."

A Dynamic Model of Social Affinity

In this chapter, we have seen how an individual's social consciousness leads to a particular form of mobilizing potential, implying that consciousness precedes action. There is much research that utilizes such a linear model. In an article on prosocial motivation (1987: 65–122), C. Daniel Batson brings together much of the literature on this topic into a model comparing both "egoistic" and "altruistic" sources of motivation in which the former focuses on how prosocial behavior is self-serving and the latter on how we are motivated out of empathy for others. Given the dimensions of social affinity described in these last three chapters, it is Batson's model of the hypothesized link between altruism and empathy that most concerns us here.[9]

While Batson's model is restricted to helping behavior—one of the limits of this line of research noted in the introduction—it is also the source of the heuristic device utilized in our analysis of social affinity.

Whereas the dimensions of social affinity are social consciousness, sentiment, and action, Batson refers to perception, empathy, and behavioral response.[10] What is more important is that he relates these elements of altruistic motivation in a linear fashion:

Perception → Empathy → Behavioral Response[11]

In other words, we perceive someone in need. This perception leads to empathy. Then we are motivated to respond. It is also possible to understand the dimensions of social affinity in much the same way, although the outcome is less definitive than in Batson's model.

Social Consciousness and Sentiment → (can lead to) → Action

However, in this chapter, we have determined that action can *precede* both social consciousness and sentiment. In other words, the process of reaching social affinity can be reversed:

Action → (can lead to) → Social Consciousness and Sentiment

In other words, there are two entry points at which social affinity may begin to emerge within an individual. He or she may develop a level of social consciousness regarding a particular issue that may eventually lead to taking action to address the issue. On the other hand, one may be drawn into addressing a social issue and, out of that experience, develop an increased social consciousness and sentiment toward those suffering from the effects of the issue—a response that may further strengthen one's commitment to social involvement and one's overall social affinity.[12] As Loeb notes, "involvement requires solidarity: an ethic that encourages people to act not only for themselves and their immediate families, but for others with whom they feel a basic human connection. . . . Yet solidarity is the fruit of involvement as much as its cause" (1994: 392). After one becomes involved, each of the dimensions of social affinity and social affinity itself is reinforced, suggesting a much more dynamic and circular model than the linear explanation of prosocial behavior presented by Batson (see Fig. 7.1).

While a seemingly minor modification to Batson's linear model, a cyclical understanding of the emergence of social affinity has significant implications such as in the realm of social policy. The fact that taking action—at whatever level—can lead to the development (or further maturation) of one's social consciousness makes efforts to institute a community service requirement—in public schools, for instance—quite understandable. Loeb argues that,

FIG. 7.1.
The cycle of social affinity.

FIRST CYCLE

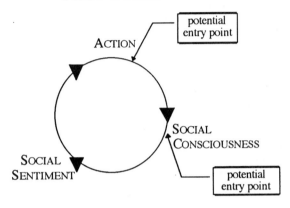

SUBSEQUENT CYCLES

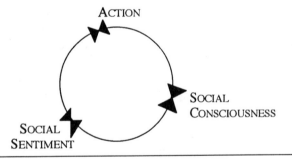

in a time when most students continue to treat politics as poison, the community service movement bypasses many of the obstacles that routinely hamper engagement. You don't need a perfect standard of knowledge to serve soup. You don't need to question the men who know best. You don't have to worry about being stigmatized. By breaking students out of insulated worlds, and by demanding that individuals take seriously those they seek to assist, such efforts introduce thousands of previously apolitical students to social concern. (1994: 233)

The National Service Program proposed by President Clinton is an attempt to institutionalize such a community service option. Many schools, especially private schools, have already initiated service requirements into their curriculum.

However, such requirements have been sharply criticized. In an article titled "Citizenship or Slavery?", Andrea Martin argues that mandatory service would create a backlash.

> In the long run, making volunteer work just one more demand imposed on students may create a backlash, prejudicing them against future volunteer work. Critics of education often point out that schools diminish the joy of learning. Now they run the risk of diminishing the joy of community service too. (1996: 16)

Robert Wuthnow's study on voluntarism supports such a position. He shows that many of those he interviewed are against such required service programs because they taint the "purity of motive" that draws individuals to get involved in the first place. Wuthnow notes that "requiring young people to do community service or offering them tangible incentives for doing so may detract from the voluntary spirit in which community service has been done in the past or from the humanitarian motives that many believe should be associated with caring" (1995: 72). Of course, such motivational purity is attractive. However, it assumes that individuals are motivated wholly by altruism. Given the importance of self-interest to a number of those interviewed, as evidenced in the data presented in this and earlier chapters, such an assumption represents more of an ideal than reality suggests.

Moreover, while Wuthnow's interviewees were reacting to the abstract idea of "required service," reactions of those who actually got involved because of such requirements were not included. A number of individuals I interviewed had a community service requirement to fulfill while in high school and, while required community service was not the focus of these interviews, no one ever brought up any negative reactions to the requirement. In fact, it was invariably labeled a "good experience."

Given the debate over the issue of required community service, a study comparing those who are involved in order to graduate with those who do so on a purely voluntary basis would be highly informative. Given that a U.S. president has proposed a form of community service, which, although not required, does provide significant incentives such as college tuition, the issue is decidedly political.[13] However, as research suggests, it is clear that alternative policies, such as those espoused by former President Reagan, are ineffective. Researcher Susan Chambré describes Reagan's policy:

> The Reagan administration continued the tradition of promoting volunteerism but differed in one significant way. In the five previous administrations, volunteer opportunities and federally sponsored human services were both expanded. There was a different strategy during the Reagan administration; relatively few new positions were created in government-sponsored [volunteer] programs. Instead, reduction of public services was expected to stimulate individual acts of altruism. The idea was that voluntarism would expand because people would become more charitable. (1989: 256)

The Reagan administration expected individual voluntarism to increase spontaneously and fill in the void left by the reduction of government-sponsored volunteer programs. The focus was on praising the contributions of volunteers, and numerous articles and even a book by Nancy Reagan—*To Love a Child*—were intended to inspire new volunteers. Not surprisingly, this policy failed: "Despite the rhetoric . . . the proportion of adults who volunteered declined during Reagan's time in office" (1989: 262).

As we have seen in this chapter, taking action does not develop in a vacuum and applauding such participation is not enough. Chambré's article lends support to this position by noting that one reason Reagan's policy failed was that "appeals to civic duty via the mass media are inconsistent with the process of becoming and being a volunteer" (1989: 265). Activism must be nurtured. Opportunities for taking action have to be actively brought to the attention of those who want to get involved and especially those who would get involved but who might not think about it in advance. Ideally, these opportunities should be conducive to group participation, convenient and easily accessible, and be able to show the effects of each individual's contribution. In other words, in order to attract new people to taking action—the nonactivists such as Julius—one needs to be able to appeal to their self-interest. Once they are involved—at any level, even the most superficial—it is possible for them to develop a more nuanced social consciousness and a more empathetic and other-oriented view of the social issues they address. While Julius pointed out that, "I am so wrapped up in my own life" when referring to his nonaction toward hunger, he is also the one who spoke so eloquently of the impact of taking part in addressing AIDS—an issue much closer to home for him than hunger—when he said he became aware of "the personal tragedy behind every story . . . and the triumph."

Placing the Pieces into the Mosaic

In this chapter, we have seen that involvement is not merely a dichotomy in which individuals are either active or nonactive. Social participation is not so "black and white." Instead, there is a full range of involvement falling between these two ends of the continuum. Secondly, we have seen that action is closely linked with social consciousness and sentiment—the other two dimensions of social affinity. We focused in particular on how an individual's framing of an issue and his or her interpretation of that frame can lead to the various degrees of action, depending on such factors as individual priorites, the implications of participation on identity, and perceived opportunity and effectiveness. Finally, we have seen that social involvement is not just the end result of a unidirectional development, representing the culmination of social consciousness and sentiment. It may also occur first in the overall unfolding of an individual's social affinity. Thus, a linear interpretation of prosocial behavior is misleading: the emergence of social affinity is not a step-by-step progression through stages as much as it is a circular process in which all three of its dimensions—social consciousness, sentiment, and action—are mutually reinforcing. Together, these pieces of the mosaic comprise the action component of social affinity.

At this point, our examination of each of the individual pieces in our overall mosaic is complete. We have broken down the three dimensions of social affinity into their smaller elements and now have available a complete "toolbox" to use in understanding personal biographies in the context of social issues in particular and social affinity in general. Again, this is not the only set of tools available. However, as is true of all sets of analytical tools, and as we shall see in the following chapter, it does provide unique insights for our understanding of social cohesion in a modern, globalizing world.

We are now ready to take a step back from our close examination of the individual pieces of the mosaic and look at the overall picture. In chapter 8, we utilize this set of tools in analyzing a new set of narratives regarding social issues *other than* hunger and AIDS. In this way, we will be able to see how each piece of the mosaic "fits in" with all of the others and complete our understanding of the emergence of social affinity. Then, in chapter 9, we take another step back and see how the mosaic itself fits into the larger social context of the modern world and U.S. culture in particular.

EIGHT

From "Compartmentalizing" to "Breaking the Boundaries"

Moving Along the Continuum of Social Affinity

In chapters 3 and 4, we took a close look at where individuals are on the continuum of social affinity in the context of hunger and AIDS. On that continuum, there are four types of orientation toward social issues: the nonreferenced and the self-referenced—who tend to "compartmentalize" their personal lives as being separate from the social world—and the relationally and socially referenced—who "break the boundaries" between their individual selves and the larger society. Then, in the last three chapters, we broke down the process of the emergence of social affinity by examining those factors that serve to shape it: our social consciousness; our sentiments, especially in the form of empathy and role-taking; and our degree of action. At the end of chapter 7, the circular relationship between these three dimensions of social affinity was described. In this chapter, all three of these elements will be used to analyze *how* individuals end up within a particular type on the continuum of social affinity.

With this goal in mind, two additional case studies will be presented—one for each extreme in the typology: the nonreferenced and the socially referenced. The focus will be on the issues regarded as most important by each of the respondents rather than on the issues of hunger and AIDS. The exclusive focus on the last two issues in the preceding chapters lent a certain degree of consistency and made it possible to draw comparisons between individuals. However, moving on to new issues will demonstrate the applicability of the theoretical analysis of the emergence of social affinity within the context of a wider range of social issues.

181

First, we shall consider the case of Chad Olson, whom we first met in chapter 4 and whose relationship with his HIV-positive uncle shaped his relationally referenced orientation toward the AIDS issue. Including a second narrative by Chad will underscore the point that individuals have different typological orientations toward different social issues and makes it possible for the reader to draw comparisons within the same individual. Health care is the issue of most concern to Chad. Although he is nonreferenced toward the issue, he displays much knowledge of it and so might be more appropriately labeled "intellectually" nonreferenced. On the other hand, Curtis Nascimento represents the socially referenced category. His top issue is racism—an issue that has greatly affected his life. However, he has broadened his definition of the issue to include *all* of those oppressed because they are considered "minorities" by others. Moreover, his focus on the issue and its solution is primarily at the level of the community. After each of these cases is presented, they are analyzed in terms of what we have learned about social consciousness, sentiments, and activism. Then we return to the underlying social location variables of social, spatial, and temporal proximity and distance. Each of these variables, and the self-interest they represent, has a direct impact on the dimensions of social affinity. An understanding of *how* these variables influence and interact with consciousness, sentiment, and action is crucial to understanding the emergence of affinity itself.

The Nonreferenced Type: The Case of Chad Olson

As the reader will recall from chapter 4, Chad is a highly introspective and reflective individual—rather philosophical in nature. He loves to keep abreast of current events and debates, immersing himself in the controversies that catch his attention. Given that the media is a major forum in which these topics are presented to the public, it is natural that Chad's interests would be influenced as a result. As is seen in his narrative, Chad happened to fill out the initial survey for this research project at a time when health care was the major issue of the day—at least insofar as the media was concerned. Not surprisingly, when he was asked to list what he saw as "the top three social issues we should be concerned about," health care topped the list.

In our interview, it was obvious that Chad was well versed in the many arguments surrounding the health care issue. He was highly informed, able to argue the nuances of his position, and could discuss its societal implications. At first glance, this gives the impression that he is socially referenced toward the issue. However, as soon as the public interest in health care waned and was supplanted by another issue, Chad's attention also shifted. At the time of the interview, which occurred approximately four months after he filled out the survey, he was no longer all that concerned about health care or its ramifications, indicating more of a nonreferenced perspective. In fact, it is possible to see that he was nonreferenced toward health care not only at the time of the interview but also at the time he filled out the survey and listed it as his top issue. His interest, even then, was purely intellectual in nature and reflected no personal commitment to the issue itself. For this reason, Chad can be characterized as *intellectually* nonreferenced and distinguished from those who are simply "nonreferenced"—those who do not even latch onto the issue at the admittedly superficial level of intellectual "concern."

I think the quality of our health care is incredible, but I think it discriminates too much and the reason that people get into health care nowadays is somewhat motivated by greed. You're almost guaranteed a job and you're guaranteed a good salary. It's interesting for me to hear people talk about how many people would drop out of pre-med if health care were nationalized. That just blows my mind. I guess capitalism works in that sense: if you have all the top doctors, you might as well pay them the most. So, this is an issue that affects everyone and the one that you hear about the most. I guess I have an opinion that it probably should go public, but that's more like my philosophy. I can't draw a conclusion about it. I don't really think about issues in general. I'm not really politically oriented.

Personally, it's not something that bothers me, but my roommates and I talk about it a lot. I think that the reason I think about it is because I'm kind of forced to. I wasn't really aware of it during Bush's administration. But then Clinton brought it up in his campaign promises and so forth. It's in Newsweek *and* Time—*magazines that are always around because my roommates get them.* Rolling Stone—*which is mine—is always around. Also, one of my roommates is into politics and a lot of his friends are around, so they're always talking about something. If we're not watching TV, we're talking about something which is interesting. And I certainly don't back out of those conversations. I'm kind of an instigator or whatever. So, when Clinton brought up health care, we debated the issue a lot. But we also talk a lot about refugees—Haitian and Cuban— and stuff like that, and a lot about immigration because my dorm is very multicultured. We have two Indians, an Iranian, a Mexican, and we used to have a Honduran, but he moved out. We have an Italian and an Irish guy and me, the mutt. So, we would talk about immigration and quotas and stuff. I've never believed in quotas because I think the country should be wide open. You shouldn't regulate who goes in and out of it. I don't think it's right to discriminate against one group and not discriminate against another. But we talk a lot about that kind of stuff. We still do. You can get people's fur flying that way. We're a room full of arguers. But now, since I filled out the survey, we're kind of off the topic of health care. We're more into what's going to happen now that Gingrich and everybody is in power. It's just that we fluctuate a lot, so I guess when I filled out that survey, that's what I was thinking about the most.*

When we did talk about health care, most of the debate was about "capitalism versus socialism." That's what the debate primarily focused on: "Why would you want to become a doctor if you're going to have to work for the state? You might as well get a government job. Besides, our health care system would plummet because of socializing it." So, it's like contrasting that kind of mentality with the idea that "Everybody should have the same kind of health care." On the other hand, it wouldn't be fair for everybody to have health care if they weren't receiving the best health care anyway. Again, I guess I think it should go public, and so I might have a personal problem with our health care system, but I don't really. And it's not something that's really affected me because our family . . . my grandfather—both sets of grand- parents—they're pretty well off. I don't really think it affects me like that because they can all afford it.

So, the only way I've responded to this issue is verbally, talking with other people. I'm not really a big activist, which is kind of sad. I wish I was, but I never had that particular drive to get out there and make a difference or whatever. I kind of envy people who make their mark and stuff, but I see myself more in the shadows, just observing. That's really all that I've done with it. I just don't think that I would sit down, say, "This is really bothering me," and write a letter about it to the President or something like that. That's just not me. I'd rather just think about it and believe, "Well maybe it will work itself out and maybe it won't." I don't think that my say will make that much dif-

ference. Maybe that's passivism or whatever, but I think that if someone important like Hillary Clinton actually called me and said, "I need you to do this"—which is kind of unrealistic—I think that, yeah, I would do that. I think when you're given a grand opportunity, you take it instead of doing something minor. Or maybe if a family member had a problem or something like that, I would write a letter because I kind of see my family as my bond. If a family member had problems with the health care system or maybe a really close friend of mine who withstood the test of time—with whom I've actually kept in touch—then maybe I would. Yeah, most likely I would; but that's what would motivate me to do something.

I think my sister would do something. She's more social than I am, a more conscious type of person. They spend less time looking in on themselves than looking out at society. I think this is kind of a generalization, but someone who's kind of shallow and who doesn't reflect that often, that kind of introspection is kind of like "my thing." I think that someone who's more concerned with what's going on outside their mind rather than inside of it would be more apt to get involved. I wrestle with things too often and too much to actually decide, "Well, I'm going to be conclusive finally and say, 'I'll write a letter and get my opinion published.'" My opinion is always battling in on itself. What if my opinion changed? I think, "What happens if this? And what happens if that?" For example, before I went to college, I was kind of adamantly pro-life. Since I've been here, I started thinking about it more and more. Now, I'm not as vocal as I was before. I try to listen to every side.

So, as far as doing something about health care, I think that's for politicians. That's their ball game. I think that there's so much bureaucracy right now that it blows my mind and I really get pissed off at it every once in a while because people say they're going to do all this stuff and they don't do it. Do something! Even if it's wrong, at least you're doing something about it. I hate stagnancy. But it's their ball game. I think that if anything's going to be done, then they're the ones who are going to implement it.

Also, I don't know how effective the average person can be. I don't know how much attention is paid to us anymore. Back in the sixties, college students were very influential, but I think we've kind of lost our thing. I don't know what it was. Maybe we're more introverted now and now we're like me—not socially conscious. I don't know why we would lose that. Maybe it's just a different generation and maybe it was the *drugs back then [laughter]. I don't know what made that generation so active as compared to our generation, which doesn't seem active. You don't really see demonstrations out here, even with the atrocities that I see going on. I guess that's kind of a weird comparison between these two generations because those in the sixties were directly affected by Vietnam. I guess if the issue directly affected us, like all of a sudden the federal government said, "Everybody at school: all your financial aid is cut," then we'd have motivation. I think we are more apt to do something about problems that affect us.*

The reader will recall that those who are nonreferenced have not developed a personal commitment to the social issue in question or those affected by that issue (see chapter 3). This is certainly the case with Chad regarding the health care issue. However, unlike "pure" nonreferenced individuals, he has seriously thought about the issue—even to the extent of linking it with broader social concerns, such as the debate between capitalism and socialism. Even so, his intellectual attention to the issue does not translate into actual concern or commitment. Why is it the case that Chad has not moved beyond being intellectually nonreferenced toward the health care issue?

By utilizing what we have learned in the previous three chapters on social consciousness, sentiment, and action, it is possible to reconstruct the path that Chad took in developing his nonreferenced outlook. As such, these elements provide a useful analytical tool for understanding the development of social affinity, how it emerges in those instances where it does and why it fails to emerge in those instances where it does not. Of course, these three dimensions are intertwined with one another, so considering each in turn presents a somewhat artificial view of Chad's development. However, it also proves rather illuminating.

In terms of the emergence of an individual's social consciousness, we learned that filtering, framing, and facticity each play an important role (see chapter 5). Again, filtering occurs at four levels, all of which are evident in Chad's narrative. At the cultural level, Chad is quite conscious of the fact that capitalism and socialism are in tension within our society. While he does not describe from where this awareness comes, it does provide a backdrop to the more concrete forms of filtering in his narrative. The most obvious institutional filter to which he refers is the media. Chad notes that he thinks about health care basically because he was "kind of forced to" by the media. Beginning with President Clinton's election campaign, the issue received much attention in the media—attention that he could not avoid. Magazines such as *Newsweek, Time,* and even *Rolling Stone*—not to mention television—made the issue an ever-present part of Chad's reality.

While he could have filtered all of this information out by ignoring the media, Chad and his friends actually thrive on debating whatever the current headline happens to be, indicating that filtering at the group and individual levels play a significant role in developing his consciousness. He describes one of his roommates as being "into politics" and, together with additional friends, they "talk a lot about that kind of stuff. . . . You can get people's fur flying that way. We're a room full of arguers." Chad is immersed in a group culture of discussion and debate, a culture on which he thrives. His individual role in this culture is quite clear: "I'm kind of an instigator. . . ." Thus, Chad does what he can to "filter in" as much information about the topic under debate.

However, these individual and group actions to filter in such information are subject to the filtering occurring at the institutional level of the media. As soon as the media moves on to another topic, so do Chad and his roommates. He describes this tendency by saying that, "it's just that we fluctuate a lot. . . ." That is why, between the time he filled out the survey and when he was interviewed, Chad had lost much of his interest in the health care issue. Instead, he and his roommates had moved on to "what's going to happen now that Gingrich and everybody is in power." Thus, while the individual and group levels of filtering play an important role for Chad, his consciousness is still largely shaped by filtering, which occurs at the larger level of the institution.

Based on the information that Chad has filtered in and out of his consciousness—which is largely political in nature—he has framed the health care issue in a particular way. On the one hand, he does show some evidence for the universal frame: "this is an issue that affects everyone. . . ." However, the frame that is most prominent in his narrative is the bureaucratic frame that defines an issue as "a matter for experts" (see Appendix C for a quick summary of the various frames). In this case, Chad defines the experts as politicians: "as far as doing something about health care, I think that's for politicians. That's their ball game. I think that there's so much bureaucracy right now that it blows my mind. . . ." As we see later, his framing of the health care issue is closely linked with his nonactivism.

Chad also bolsters his social consciousness—his position toward the issue—by establishing a certain amount of facticity supporting his reality.

This is particularly apparent when explaining his nonactivism. A major component of this explanation has to do with what he describes as the culture of his generation: "Back in the sixties, college students were very influential, but I think we've kind of lost our thing. I don't know what it was. Maybe we're more introverted now and now we're like me—not socially conscious." In effect, Chad has used himself as the prime example characterizing his entire generation, as if he were the epitome of apathy. By doing this, he has backed up his own reality by asserting that it is the same reality for "everyone" in his generation. In other words, he can feel safe that he is not alone in his beliefs.

Moving on to the sentimental dimension of social affinity, recall that (in chapter 6) we focused on the emotional responses individuals have toward social issues and the central role of empathy and role-taking in creating a bond between the individual and others. Chad's narrative is notable for the distinct *absence* of references to sentiments in general and of empathy in particular. Chad does feel "pissed off" toward those politicians who refuse to do anything regarding health care; however, this feeling is not directed toward the issue itself or those affected by it. The one time he does mention sentiment toward the issue, Chad actually highlights its absence: "Personally, it's not something that bothers me." Thus, there is no empathy and no evidence of role-taking. By failing to take the perspectives of those actually affected by the health care issue—the hypothetical other, the concrete other, and the collective other—Chad, in effect, cannot move beyond being nonreferenced toward the issue (see Fig. 6.1). It is at this critical point that the potential for full social affinity breaks down. The circle of the development of social affinity (see Fig. 7.1) breaks down with the absence of sentiment, leaving only the connection between social consciousness and action.

Given Chad's framing of the health care issue and his lack of sentiment, the fact that he is a nonactivist is not surprising. He is quite aware of his inactivity and its implications: "I'm not really a big activist, which is kind of sad." Recall that frames can be both mobilizing and demobilizing. In the case of the universal frame, which is one variation in Chad's overall framing of the issue, it is most often demobilizing. The bureaucratic frame can go either way, depending upon how upset the individual is with the experts and whether the individual assumes that the experts are the only ones capable of addressing the issue. It is apparent that Chad is upset with the experts: "I really get pissed off at it every once in a while because people say they're going to do all this stuff and they don't do it. Do something! Even if it's wrong, at least you're doing something about it. I hate stagnancy." However, he then immediately asserts, "But it's their ball game. I think that if anything's going to be done, then they're the ones who are going to implement it." This statement points out that Chad believes it is the job of politicians to address health care. However, does he believe that they are the only ones capable of "doing something?" The answer is "yes." Chad does not believe that the average person can do much, if anything, to effectively address the issue: "I don't know how effective the average person can be. I don't know how much attention is paid to us anymore."

Moreover, Chad does not feel that *he* can be effective in addressing the issue: "I don't think that my say will make that much difference." As described in chapter 7, the individual's perception of how effective they can be in taking action plays a key role in whether or not they decide to do something. In Chad's case, he feels incapable of doing anything and so he does not bother.

An individual's perception of his or her self-identity is another important factor influencing the decision of whether to take action or not. Conscious of the fact that one's actions reflect on one's identity, individuals ask themselves whether they are the "kind of person" who gets involved. For Chad, the answer is "no." The statement that he uses to describe himself as a nonactivist—quoted earlier—is also closely tied with his identity, which becomes even more apparent when including his subsequent thoughts: "I'm not really a big activist. . . . I wish I was, but I never had that particular drive to get out there and make a difference or whatever. . . . I see myself more in the shadows, just observing." Being an activist is just not a part of "who" Chad "is," even though he is well aware of its possibility for others, such as his sister: "She's more social than I am, a more conscious type of person. They spend less time looking in on themselves than looking out at society." Thus, it appears that Chad's reflective nature, in which his "opinion is always battling in on itself," is also defined by him as his "downfall" when it comes to activism. Being *intellectually* nonreferenced—being, as it were, *too* aware of the nuances of the issue—has had a paralyzing effect on Chad: "I wrestle with things too often and too much to actually decide [that I'm going to be conclusive and] write a letter. . . ."

Another factor influencing his nonactivism is the lack of opportunity to do something. When I pursued this topic in his interview, it was apparent that he was not aware of any opportunities. In fact, we had to fall back on the hypothetical opportunity of Hillary Clinton personally asking him to do something. Under those circumstances, Chad said that he would: "I think when you're given a grand opportunity, you take it instead of doing something minor." However, when speaking hypothetically, Chad admitted that such a "grand opportunity" was not actually required to get him involved. In fact, it was a rather mundane situation that would call him to action: "maybe if a family member had a problem or something like that, I would write a letter because I kind of see my family as my bond. If a family member had problems with the health care system or maybe a really close friend of mine . . . most likely I would; but that's what it would have [to take]." Without health care having a direct impact on his family, the issue is rather distant for Chad, despite the fact that he debated it so much with his roommates. As a result, he says, "I don't really think it affects me. . . ."

The fact that this issue is so distant is key to our understanding of why social affinity has not emerged within Chad. In fact, the relative distance or proximity of an issue to the individual provides an important backdrop to the development of his or her social consciousness, sentiment, and action. It is here that self-interest colors our picture of social affinity. This self-interest is epitomized by the need for an issue to "affect me." Chad most clearly describes this process when he compares the "apathy" of his generation with the "activism" of the sixties. He concludes by saying, "I guess that's kind of a weird comparison between these generations because those in the sixties were directly affected by Vietnam. I guess if the issue directly affected us, like all of a sudden the federal government said, 'Everybody at school: all of your financial aid is cut,' then we'd have motivation. I think we are more apt to do something about problems that affect us." Chad links self-interest with his nonactivism. However, as we see in more detail later, self-interest, in terms of the necessity for an issue to be "proximate," has an impact on all three elements of social affinity—social consciousness, sentiment, and action. It is for this reason that Batson's focus on separating self-interest as a source of motivation toward prosocial behavior that is separate and distinct from empathic motivation is so misleading (1987; also refer to chapter 7, footnote 9): self-interest is inseparable from even the deepest, and apparently "selfless" commitments to society and concerns for its members—something, as described in chapter 6, which Adam Smith already firmly acknowledged.

The Socially Referenced Type: The Case of Curtis Nascimento

Curtis is an academic scholar in college and looks forward to going to law school. Given his eloquence during the interview, I am confident he will be most effective in that profession. He grew up in the South Bronx of New York City as a Puerto Rican who can "pass" for black. His father left the family sometime after he and his three younger brothers were born— a topic that he did not want to discuss in much detail. His mother had worked before the children were born but stopped working in order to raise them full-time. Currently, she is on welfare and has gone back to college to complete her degree. She is also working again in order to put her children through private school. However, in order to keep her welfare benefits, she does not work for money. Instead, she exchanges her labor at the school for tuition. Curtis feels that this arrangement is highly exploitative given that, even if she worked for only five dollars an hour, she would still make more money than the amount of tuition. In other words, she is getting less out of her labor than should be the case.

Curtis himself went to public schools when in grade school. However, when it became apparent to his mother that he was beginning to hang out with kids who were a bad influence, she put him in a private school. This, he maintains, "turned him around" completely. While there, he met a Jesuit who would become his mentor and guide him into college. Otherwise, he thinks he would be a "little hoodlum" on the streets of the Bronx. While Curtis made it out of his childhood community, he has decided he will not turn his back on that community and it is here that his number one issue of racism enters in. His hope for addressing racism is by "reinvesting" in one's community: buying property there, hiring those who live there, spending money in local establishments, utilizing for the common good the skills people have learned on the streets and outside the classrooms, and so on. Curtis feels a communal bond with minorities like himself, and this bond extends beyond the realm of Puerto Ricans, or even of race in general. Instead, he defines racism in such broad terms that it includes all of the marginalized, such as women and sexual minorities. Given his focus on the communal dimensions of both racism and its solution, Curtis exhibits a socially referenced orientation toward the issue while he is simultaneously self-referenced and relationally referenced.

———————

Racism is an issue I grew up with. You don't know about it from day one, but you know about racial differences as soon as you can perceive things. When you go to school—and my schools were predominantly black and Hispanic, maybe 1 percent white and that's very, very rare—you notice that everyone looks the same. But then your teacher looks different. You walk up the hallway and everybody looks the same, but then your principal looks different. At that young age, you don't really think about it that much; but then you go home and you watch shows. Everybody on that show is different from you and the only way you're going to find someone who's the same as you is if there's some kind of maid, butler, or janitor on those shows. When you're little, you just notice that people are different, but you really don't care because you're little. It's something that doesn't really hit you. It hasn't hit you, but it's in there. You know all that and you know your teacher's different, but it doesn't matter yet. It's something that seeps in and sticks to the back of your head and stays there. By the time you're in fourth and fifth grade, you see the news. You never really noticed what was going on in the news, but you did notice that those "different people" were on TV and that people who were at fire scenes and these dangerous scenes were people similar to you. But the newsperson isn't. That's when you start noticing. You say, "Hey, he's different. How come somebody like me isn't there? How come my teacher isn't the same as me? How come my principal isn't the same as me? How come when I go to the doctor's office, the doctor isn't the same as me? How come when I go into any store and ask for the manager, the manager isn't the same as me but all the employees are?" By that time, you check this out with your friends, or maybe your friend has a big brother who tells you what's going on. And that's when things start hitting you. It just hits you and it hits you hard. Then you either handle it—do what you gotta do—or you just succumb to it like many have done.

So, awareness of race and of racism kind of grow together. When you start wondering, "How come people like me—of my race—aren't in that position?," that's when you know that something is going on. Something's suppressing you. Something is there. There's a factor there that's preventing you from seeing people of your own race in these positions. When you start looking up and investigating that factor, then you're told, "Hey, it's something called 'racism.' And it's up to you to just accept it or deal with it." So, it starts out with race and then the racial factor builds into racism and then they just go side by side.

Since I came to college, I've matured even more. I've become aware of even more issues. The only issue that I was really aware of when I was back in the inner city was being a person of color and knowing I was discriminated against. Here, I see that I'm not the only person who's being discriminated against. There are other people who are discriminated against, and I've come to respect these people for what they go through. I think a lot of people go through worse things than I've been through. For example, the gays. I don't like saying "the gays" because they're just like us. That's like saying "the blacks." I don't like saying stuff like that, but just to classify it real quick so you know what I'm talking about. I've grown and now have tremendous respect for them, and I remember being totally homophobic in New York, partly because of my Catholic upbringing. I was a good Catholic kid. I remember walking down the street and going through the Village in New York. The so-called Pink Panthers[1] were there and I was thinking, "Man, they're going to try and rape me and stuff. And if they look at me, I'll punch them in the face." You walk by and you think these people are different. "Oh, my gosh! They're different. Oh, no. They're not human. No way!"

But coming to college has just totally revealed the ignorance I had. It started with some dorm meetings where they actually brought people who were gay to speak. I remember coming out of those meetings and still being kind of homophobic, thinking "Whoah! I can't believe he's gay." But I was already opening myself a little bit. Then I went back home for the summer and I actually worked in the Village with men who were gay. I saw that they are human just like me. They want the same things in life. It's just that they have a different sexual preference. And that's personal, you know? My sexual preference is my personal life. That's their personal life, so why should I get involved with that? So, realizing that they're just like me helped me change. Now I have the utmost respect and admiration for them because they're going through so much trouble; but they continue fighting. Although I can't know the exact discrimination they're going through, I can relate to their situation. I know that it's kind of similar to the discrimination that I go through and, even if it's not similar, the point is we're both going through discrimination and we're both fighting it. And it's like, "Wow." And so it's not even the whole racial thing anymore because when you deal with that issue, everybody's multicultural.

So, what I mean by racism actually deals with a lot of things, not just with race. This can be problematic: when I say "racism" now, I particularly mean the ignorance shown and dealt out to people who, in other people's minds, are so-called "minorities." And actually, they're not in the "minority" at all. It's just ignorance towards those people. So, racism deals with race. Racism deals with sexual preference. It deals with that. It deals with gender. It deals with so much. I mean, racism is so broad. There's no way of really defining racism. And the reason it's most important to me is because I know it's my race that makes people look at me when I walk down the street. I know that's what keeps my people mentally and physically deprived. And this racism, it brings them right down. It doesn't let them achieve. If you're not mentally strong, you can't deal with it. So, I know racism definitely helps deprive my people. I mean, and if there's one thing I can't stand for, it is ignorance—and I know racism is ignorance. It's so unfortunate and ironic because half the people who fall underneath the category of being racist are otherwise smart people. So, that's an oxymoron: "How can you be smart and ignorant at the same time?"

It's sad. And it hurts just to see that because you know you're not accepted for who you are. You know you're not given the chance, and every single time, everywhere you go, you have to prove yourself. I can't be myself. I can't say what I want to say. If I want to dress in baggy clothes and real "bummy," being a person of color, I'm classified as a hoodlum. And that's stereotyping. Stereotyping falls underneath racism. But if a Caucasian comes up dressed in baggies, they say he wants to be black. So, you can't be who you want to be, okay? Racism is just sad. And people think it only affects people of color, but it doesn't. People of color are always saying, "Yeah, racism affects us." It affects everybody because that Caucasian was also stereotyped. Why can't he wear baggies? Why can't he just wear those and be comfortable? Why does he supposedly have to think he's black? It affects everybody and it's really sad to see that.

I have responded to racism in many different ways. First, I vocalize myself and I explain it to them. "Hey, that's wrong. You shouldn't have stereotyped me like that, okay? You should not judge me like that." So, the best way—right now—for me to deal with it is to vocalize myself. One thing I'll never be able to do is let it go by. I can never let that happen. I vocalize it. I try my best to educate the ignorant. That's one of the best ways to handle it because—again—racism comes from ignorance. If you can educate the ignorant, you might not change their mind frame, but you could give them a little push down the slide to change it. Also, I try not to be ignorant myself. I try to stay away from that—from stereotyping and racism—because I myself was very racist. Everybody has that in them. I thought a lot of things about Caucasians, about the music, about the whole culture. So, I try to stay away from that by educating myself, by establishing friendships and acquain-

tances with *people who are Caucasian so that I learn about their culture. Then, I can stop being the racist pig that people are being towards
me. So, I've got to educate people and I've got to educate myself.*

*Basically, my theory is to get your education. Go to school. Get
your diploma. In my case, go to law school. Make it. Make it big. Don't
just make it. I'm not satisfied with that. I want to make it big and then
come back to my community—help my community. That's the only way
I'm going to stop racism: showing people that, no matter what they did
to me, "I can make it. I can make it, okay? So, don't think you can suppress me. You can try another technique, but the problem is I've already
made it. So, don't even try it. Just accept it. And if you can't accept, I'm
going to have to force you to accept it, because when I go back to my community, those people are going to rise up also. That's more of my people
coming up, okay?" So, educating myself, establishing myself, going back
and bringing the whole community up. Malcolm X said, "If you want
to make it, if you want to stop racism, if you want to do all this, what
you need to do is"—like I just said—"you need to educate yourself. You
need to get somewhere. You need to establish yourself. Get the money you
deserve, come back to your community. Don't sell out your community.
Come back to them and what you do is help your community." In terms
of Malcolm X, the best way of addressing racism is by helping your community. Unfortunately, it has not been done yet; but it will be done. Go
back to your community. Build some industries in your community.
Own the property in your community. That's what the Jews and Asians
have done within their own communities—buying things in it, buying
industries, hiring their own people, circulating the money within their
communities. They're not giving it to the capitalist, racist pigs who are
suppressing them. No, they're keeping it within themselves and, by doing
that, they're rising up. They're doing what Malcolm X said. They've
proven his theory works.*

*Some people get their education and move to New Hampshire or
Maine—an all-Caucasian setting. They have their own house, are living in luxury, and are forgetting about their community. That's not doing
anything. You're not even 1 percent of the population. You need a critical
mass to educate the ignorant. What you have to do is come back to your
community. I strongly believe that with my generation, that will be done
because many of my generation are very into this. Up to this time, I
think people haven't been accomplishing this partly because of the government. No matter how much you want to deny it, the government does*

try to suppress us. They know they have to. They want to, they need to. And I know that most of the people who are my people—who are people of color, and are in positions of power—are falling for it. That's something that's becoming obvious. Even those who are ignorant notice it. You have to be strong-minded. In this world, money is everything. Money is power. Money talks. And when people do come into power—and there's a lot of blacks and Hispanics who have some of this power—they're falling for it. They're not strong-minded enough to see, "Hey, I've still got to help out my community." They try, but they fail because they've become a part of white society.

My interest in my community came about just because of my experiences there. I was never allowed downstairs, but I always stood on the windowsill and looked out. All you have to do is stay on that block for a week and observe. You'll think the same thing. It's not fair. It's just not fair, you know? You see so many kids who go through their life on that city block and who never get anywhere. They have so much potential. For example, all these drug dealers have great managerial skills. It's unbelievable. You have accountants in the making downstairs because when you're dealing with drugs, you're dealing with money and business. There's so many skills that you see, and yet they're not being used properly. Those skills could help raise up our community. But no, they're helping degrade our community. And those are my people. They're my people. That's one thing that got me. I said, "That has to be changed." These people have to see that they do have skills. But they also need the means to go to college. I know that, in establishing fundraisers and doing things for the community, you can let them see from early on that they're worth something, that they don't have to grow up to be drug dealers in order to make it. By going back to the community and showing them your hard work, they can see you can do something without being a drug dealer and getting shot. They have to see that they have somewhere to go. And I know that by doing that, they will get somewhere. So, I do have a love for the community. Not for the community as it is now, but for the community it could be.

So, I've come to college in order to be able to help myself and my community. Since I've been here, I've gotten involved with groups addressing race, but not always. For instance, there was one person in student government who sparked this whole race situation by a poor campaign slogan. He lit the fuse, but the bomb has been made over many years. I've been on this earth nineteen years. The bomb has been with me, developing for nineteen years. Someone just lit the fuse with that slogan. So, I got involved in the initial movement addressing the problem. But then I saw that there were a lot of ignorant views and there was no way of even dealing with it, because they became militaristic. So, I went my own way and I did my own thing. Most of them noticed I did my own thing. They saw my theory and where I'm coming from. And they changed their ways a little; but it was something. So, I personally always get involved with this movement. I might not be in an organization, but my organization is called "myself." That's my organization, okay? And my organization is open twenty-four hours a day, seven days a week because, no matter how much I don't want to, I am representing my people. At a school where there are only a few people of color, I'm always being looked at. So, my organization is always open and the way I defeat racism is by showing people their stereotypes and that their perceptions of my people are wrong. I don't walk around with my pants hanging off my butt and stuff like that. I always dress in my nice corduroys and my slacks just to show people that what they think of my people is wrong. In the classroom, my organization is in effect because when I open my mouth, everybody's eyes are on me. Yes, I have joined broader organizations, but I'm also an organization. Each and every one of my people is an organization. I'm always at work. Even now, I'm at work. You might know about a lot of the things I've said. You might not. But no matter what, I know I said at least one thing today that maybe you didn't know or you failed to realize. And therefore my organization has succeeded for today and not even for today.

Of all the issues out there, racism is the one that affects me the most, so I have to do something and I can't go about helping others if I can't help myself. That's even in the Bible. It says, "God will not help you unless you help yourself." So, if I can't help myself, how can I help others? That's why I'm working on how I present myself and my education: If the ground I am walking on is not strong and has the capability of just collapsing right underneath me, I can't be of use to others. Before walking on to other issues, I have to make sure this ground is strong. And it has to be strong enough for me to walk across before I can bring you along. If I construct it properly, we can both cross it. Three of us could cross it. All of us could cross it. So, you've got to establish yourself and you've got to make sure everything's on the right path before you can move on to an issue that doesn't directly hit you first. It's just like your priorities. Who comes first? It has to be you and your family. Blood is thicker than water. In this case, racism is thicker for me than other issues, such as feminism. I can't throw myself into the shoes of a feminist because I'm not a woman and I can't see everything about it. They have to educate me about it. I strongly agree with a lot of the things they say, but I don't know everything because I'm not a woman. But they can't give me their knowledge if I don't have knowledge of myself. And when I sought that knowledge, I found that—like I said before—racism is bigger than race. It deals with women's issues, too. And gay issues. So, If I jump into your bandwagon and I help you and your fight and we both get killed, there's nobody dealing with the racism I feel so strongly about. But, if I deal with my issue, I become even more powerful from conquering that issue. Then, I'm more powerful helping this person who also has increased in strength. But you've got to start with your issue first. That's why I chose racism before anything else. That's the issue that affects me the most.

So, that's why racism interests me a lot. But, it doesn't interest me just because it affects me. While I know it affects me tremendously, racism isn't going to stop me. I'm not going to get mad just because someone called me a name. I don't give a damn because I know where I'm at and I know where they're at. I know the level they're at for calling me a name and I know the level I'm at for ignoring it. So, it's not just because it affects me. I just know that the more that discussions are held on it, the more people realize it, the more people speak about it, you could have some tremendous and totally astonishing solutions. When you get all these smart individuals putting their heads together trying to stop being ignorant, you'd be surprised at the solutions and ways of getting around racism that can come about. And you never know—hey, maybe all these smart intellectuals can come up with a solution that would totally abolish racism. You never know. It seems really impossible, but you never know. You "never say never." So, it really interests me, not just because it affects me, but also because I know that there can be a change and I know that there's means of changing it. Racism is something that has to be discussed, but it cannot only be discussed. And I have to be interested for those changes to come about. Have to be.

Unlike those who are relationally referenced and who refer to friends and/or family members when describing their experiences with a particular issue, Curtis makes frequent references to his community, highlighting the fact that he is socially referenced toward the issue of racism. This is also an issue that affects him directly and intimately—accounting for his simultaneous self-referenced orientation—he has moved beyond the boundaries of his own life experiences and has concerned himself with his "people." His interest in the issue, while obviously stemming from his own experiences, is no longer dependent on those same experiences. He has generalized the racism affecting his own life to include all those who are considered "minorities" in our society. And not only has he broken these boundaries between the individual and society, he has effectively bridged the individual and the social realms. But again, we can ask the question, "How did Curtis develop his socially referenced orientation toward racism?"

Curtis did not start out as socially referenced. As a child, he started out as nonreferenced, not recognizing that race was an issue at all. However, as he grew up, the cultural, institutional, group, and individual filters created an awareness of racism that he could not avoid. The opening paragraphs of his narrative tell the story of his budding social consciousness toward this issue. In the first place, the racial history of our country created a backdrop in which race matters (see Cornel West 1994). This cultural background was particularly evident in the institutions with which the young Curtis came into contact. Within education, the media, the economy, and so forth, some roles were occupied by people who were similar to himself and other roles were occupied by those who were different. At first it did not really matter for him: "[Y]ou really don't care because you're little. It's something that doesn't really hit you." At this point, he was still nonreferenced.

However, as he got older, he began to question *why* the roles of privilege and power were occupied primarily by those who were different. He wanted to know more and took an active part in the filtering process by going to others and asking questions: "Hey, he's different. How come somebody like me isn't there? . . . By that time, you check this out with your friends, or maybe your friend has a big brother who tells you what's going on." By checking with his friends, group filters come into play. The lived experience of his "people" was conveyed through the informal network of his group of friends and the answer to his questions was summed up by the word "racism:" "[T]hat's when things start hitting you. It just hits you and it hits you *hard.*" Thus, for Curtis, "awareness of race and of racism kind of grow together."

At this point, Curtis is self-referenced. His top issue of race is something that affects him directly and in every aspect of his life. Unlike the case of Chad, the issue is not something so distant he has to work to comprehend it. Curtis does not have to empathize with others in order to "know what it's like." His everyday experiences are fundamentally shaped by this issue: "[Y]ou know you're not accepted for who you are. You know you're not given the chance, and every single time, everywhere you go, you have to prove yourself. I can't be myself. I can't say what I want to say." Thus, it is quite understandable how Curtis moved from being nonreferenced to self-referenced; but how did he move to the socially referenced position? Again, the answer lies in an examination of the construction of social consciousness, sentiment, and action.

While this process resulted in his thinking of his community as well as himself, it is particularly evident in how he broadened his definition of "racism." In college, Curtis has realized that he is not alone in his experiences with this issue: "Here, I see that I'm not the only person who's being discriminated against." Again, the process begins with filtering. His college filtered in additional information about discrimination: "It started with some dorm meetings where they actually brought people who were gay to speak. I remember coming out of those meetings and still being kind of homophobic, thinking 'Whoah! I can't believe he's gay.' But I was already opening myself a little bit." His exposure to the discrimination faced by another population—gays and lesbians—placed him face-to-face with his own prejudices—prejudices that were also filtered down to him through his prior "Catholic upbringing." Later, Curtis "worked . . . with men who were gay." Thus, the discrimination faced by others became increasingly proximate to his own experiences; and then he realized they were essentially the same, prompting him to engage in his own filtering by expanding the definition of racism: "So, what I mean by racism actually deals with a lot of things, not just with race. . . . [W]hen I say 'racism' now, I particularly mean the ignorance shown and dealt out to people who, in other people's minds, are so-called 'minorities.'" Thus, racism was no longer an issue that concerned only himself or even "his people." As we see later, each of these successive filters was also closely tied with empathy and roletaking.

The way in which Curtis frames the issue of racism is also central to understanding his social consciousness. He utilizes multiple frames when thinking about racism. In the first place, his redefinition of the term "racism" led him to the universal frame, in which the issue is defined as something that affects everybody: "[P]eople think it only affects people of color, but it doesn't. . . . It affects everybody. . . ." However, he does not espouse that part of the universal frame that says that no one person in particular bears any responsibility in addressing the issue. This is because of the primacy of the other frames he has adopted: the structural frame and the social ethics frame.[2]

The structural frame defines issues as a symptom of deeper problems in society. Moreover, no one particular individual is to blame. The "system" itself is to blame. His entire description of his budding awareness of race and racism indicates that the issue is a part of the very fabric of society. Curtis realized that, "something's suppressing you. Something is there. There's a factor there that's preventing you from seeing people of your own race in these positions [of power]." Racism is embedded in our schools, our media, our economy, and our very history. In his structural understanding of the issue, there is even a hint of the conspiracy frame, in which those who hold positions of power within the structure of society attempt to exploit and maintain power over others. This view is particularly evident when he describes the role of the government: "No matter how much you want to deny it, the government does try to suppress us. They know they have to. They want to, they need to. And I know that most of the people who are my people—who are people of color, and are in positions of power—are falling for it." Together, the conspiracy frame and the structural frame indicate that Curtis sees the individual as constrained by his or her social environment.

However, Curtis also utilizes the social ethics frame in which individuals take personal responsibility for getting involved in addressing an issue that is defined in moral terms. While the issue is societal in its dimensions, Curtis sees its solution as beginning with the individual—himself: "Basically, my theory is to get your education. Go to school. Get your diploma. In my case, go to law school. Make it. Make it big. Don't just make it. I'm not satisfied with that. I want to make it big and then come back to my community—help my community. That's the only way I'm going to stop racism: showing people that, no matter what they did to me, 'I can make it. . . .'" At this point, Curtis's view of the issue and its solution assumes a philosophical undertone and the moral view that is the hallmark of the social ethics frame. Moreover, he grounds his proposed solution by referring back to its sources: Malcolm X, a black leader who also sought to address the structural problem of racism by starting with the oppressed individual. As seen later, this combination of the structural frame, which focuses on the larger dimensions of the issue within society, and the social ethics frame, which emphasizes personal responsibility for getting involved, provides an ideal means for maximizing one's feelings of effectiveness when addressing an issue that is viewed by many as being of "overwhelming" proportions.

Like the previous cases, Curtis also seeks to back up the "truth" of his social consciousness by falling back on the support of others—by creating facticity. The most obvious example is his reference to Malcolm X—a prominent, historical figure who is apparently the source of many of Curtis's views. However, he also supports his viewpoint by claiming that many of his generation support it: "What you have to do is come back to your community. I strongly believe that with *my* generation, that will be done because *many* of my generation are very into this." However, and at the same time, he contrasts his view, which is shared by many, with the road taken by the minority—those he views as "sellouts:" "[W]hen people do come into power—and there's a lot of blacks and Hispanics who *have* some of this power—they're falling for it. They're not strong-minded enough to see, 'Hey, I've still got to help out my community.' They *try,* but they fail because they've become a part of white society." In other words, while maintaining the reality of his position—by falling back on the majority— he also sets himself apart from the minority. In effect, he takes a stand.

It is apparent in his narrative that Curtis is upset by this issue, a point that is underscored by his repeated referrals to "ignorance"—the ignorance of others as well as himself. However, his sentiment goes well beyond his personal feelings. Curtis's typological orientation toward racism is heavily influenced by his role-taking. Moreover, and in contrast with the previous cases, he role-takes with all three forms of other—hypothetical, concrete, and collective. As discussed in chapter 6, role-taking with the hypothetical other allows one to transition beyond being self-referenced toward an issue. Curtis utilizes such a hypothetical situation to show how he came to realize that racism is an issue that affects everybody, not just himself and other people of color: "[I]f a Caucasian comes up dressed in baggies, they say he wants to be black. . . . [So racism] affects everybody because that Caucasian was also stereotyped. Why can't he wear baggies? Why can't he just wear those and be comfortable? Why does he supposedly have to think he's black? It affects everybody and it's really sad to see that." By role-taking in this way, Curtis breaks the boundary between himself and others.

However, he does not stop with a single, hypothetical other. Returning to the story of how Curtis gave up his prejudices toward gay men, role-taking—in conjunction with the filtering discussed earlier—played a central role. When he had never met gay men, but heard about the Pink Panthers in the Village in New York, Curtis not only did not engage in role-taking, he actually dehumanized gay men: "You walk by and you think these people are different. 'Oh, my gosh! They're different. Oh, no. They're not human. No way!" By dehumanizing this population of individuals, Curtis was, in effect, distancing himself from them and their experience of prejudice. In other words, they were not "like" him at all. He denied the "proximity"—the similarity—of their experiences.

Later, Curtis was exposed to gay speakers in his residence hall. While he still could not identify with them, he no longer dehumanized them. In other words, the distance between their experiences and his own was beginning to collapse: "I was already opening myself a little bit." Then, he worked with gay men—concrete others. At that point, Curtis "saw that they are human just like me. They want the same things in life." By role-taking with these individuals known to him, he realized that they actually had many things in common, including discrimination: "I can relate to their situation. I know that it's kind of similar to the discrimination that I go through and, even if it's not similar, the point is we're both going through discrimination and we're both fighting it."

Finally, Curtis has generalized his roletaking beyond these concrete others to the collective other. He speaks in terms of "people" without specifying individuals: "I see that I'm not the only person who's being discriminated against. There are other people who are discriminated against and I've come to respect these people for what they go through. I think a lot of people go through worse things than I've been through. For example the gays . . . I've grown and now have tremendous respect for them." Curtis no longer has to refer to concrete or even hypothetical others. Instead, he refers to entire groups of individuals, whether they be "gays," "women," or simply—and most compellingly—"my people:" "And those are *my* people. They're *my people*. That's one thing that got me."

Based on his own personal experiences, his empathic concern for his people and all others who endure similar discrimination, and his commitment to his community, Curtis feels compelled to get involved in addressing racism. Given his moral view of the issue, he knows it is incumbent upon him to do something. Thus, while the frames he utilizes in understanding racism—the structural frame and the social ethics frame—can be demobilizing, Curtis has not chosen that path. In the first place, the social ethics frame is most often mobilizing in its outcome. The question is, "at what level?" For Curtis, who draws upon Malcolm X, taking action begins with himself. At the most personal level, he directs his action inward, toward himself, by making sure he does not contribute to racism: "I try not to be ignorant myself. I try to stay away from that—from stereotyping and racism—because I myself was very racist. Everybody has that in them." The result is an attempt to educate himself in order to overcome his own prejudices and, in the long run, to be better able to help his own community when he returns.

At the same time that he educates himself, Curtis makes sure to educate others. When he sees racism in others, he points it out: "I vocalize myself. 'Hey, that was wrong. You shouldn't have stereotyped me like that, okay? You *should* not judge me like that.' So, the best way—right *now*—for me to deal with it is to vocalize myself. One thing I'll never be able to do is let it go by." Not only does he directly address it when he sees it, but he is also highly conscious of the educational value of the fact that he is observed by others. He describes himself as his own "organization"—one that is always at work managing the impression he gives to others—an impression that is generalized to all people of his race: "At a school where there are only a few people of color, I'm always being looked at. So, my organization is always open and the way I defeat racism is by showing people their stereotypes and that their perceptions of my people are wrong. . . . Each and every one of my people is an organization. I'm always at work. Even now, I'm at work." He also makes a special effort to assist people of color: "By going back to the community and showing them your hard work, they can see you can do something without being a drug dealer and getting shot. They have to see that they have somewhere to go. And I *know* that by doing that, they will get somewhere."

The structural frame can be demobilizing if it is paired with feelings of powerlessness. However, Curtis realizes that racism can be changed: "I know that there can be a change and I know that there's means of changing it." And unlike the previous three cases, Curtis feels that he, himself is able to make a difference, particularly when it comes to educating others: "You might know about a lot of the things I've said. You might not. But no matter what, I know I said at least one thing today that maybe you didn't know or you failed to realize. And therefore my organization has succeeded for today." He recognizes that his individual efforts are effective in addressing the issue of racism. Moreover, Curtis realizes that his past successes in addressing racism further empower him to accomplish more: "If I deal with my issue, I become even more powerful from conquering that issue." He also has prior, successful examples of addressing racism to fall back on, particularly with regard to his vision of raising up his community: "Build some industries in your community. Own property in your community. That's what the Jews and Asians have done within their own communities—buying things in it, buying industries, hiring their own people, circulating the money within their communities. . . . [T]hey're keeping it [the money] within themselves and, by doing that, they're rising up." Thus, while it is clear that Curtis still understands the issue of racism in terms of its societal dimensions, the fact that he can still focus on its individual dimensions—a result of his combining the structural frame with the social ethics frame—means that he is not overwhelmed by the magnitude of the issue—or its "abstract," distant qualities—as Chad is.

It is also clear that Curtis is a focused activist. While he recognizes the importance of a variety of issues, he has focused his attention on the one issue of racism, saying that he "can't go about helping others if I can't help myself." Moreover, he sees himself as an integral part of a larger effort. If he takes care of the ground beneath his feet—his metaphor for the racism issue that affects him so directly—making sure that it is stable, and if others do the same with their respective issues, then they all have stable ground on which they can walk together. Each person must play her or his part. Thus, as characteristic of focused activists, Curtis also has a long-term vision for his activism. In the first place, he extols the benefits of returning to his community to reinvest in it and raise it up, saying that he does "have a love for the community. Not for the community as it is *now,* but for the community it could be." His vision also contains a strong element of hope: "I just know that the more that discussions are held on it, the more people realize it, the more people speak about it, you could have some tremendous and totally astonishing solutions." Thus, Curtis is involved in addressing racism for "the long haul." He is not thwarted by the lack of short-term returns. Instead, he recognizes the value of his own contributions: "Racism is something that *has* to be discussed, but it cannot *only* be discussed. And I *have* to be interested for those changes to come about. Have to be."

While, as already described, the impact of the proximity of the racism issue—how "close to home" it is for Curtis—has had an impact on his social consciousness and sentiment, it is also apparent in his activism. Curtis has focused his involvement on this issue in part because, "of all the issues out there, racism is the one that affects me the most, so I have to do something. . . ." In other words, he has set his priorities so that he first addresses this issue: "[Y]ou've got to establish yourself and you've got to make sure everything's on the right path before you can move on to an issue that doesn't directly hit you first. It's just like your priorities. Who comes first? It has to be you and your family. Blood is thicker than water. In this case, racism is thicker for me than other issues. . . ." This passage, while conveying the fact that racism is socially the most proximate issue for Curtis, also implies that his need to address it first is based on self-interest. Thus, the question of one's social location—of how "close to home" an issue is—and its centrality in the emergence of social affinity informs us that self-interest plays a major role throughout the process of moving from one point in the typology of social affinity to another. In the concluding section of this chapter, we focus our attention on this topic of self-interest as it is represented by the relative "proximity" or "distance" of an issue.

"Out of Sight, Out of Mind:" Traversing the Social Epicenter

The analysis of each of the preceding cases has demonstrated how an individual progresses to a particular point on the continuum of social affinity—a point represented by one of the four types of orientation toward social issues. As demonstrated in the analyses, the heuristic device of social consciousness, sentiment, and action provides a useful tool for understanding the emergence of social affinity. However, by conducting these analyses, it also became apparent that it is important to take an individual's social location into account.

In other words, a certain degree of self-interest is involved in each of the elements of social affinity, a point that is underscored by the repeated occurrence—throughout the vast majority of the interviews—of the idea that an issue is more compelling for an individual the "closer to home" it is and the more readily available are the solutions for addressing the issue. Those issues that "hit closer to home" and that are more readily and easily addressed by the individual are seen as more proximate and are more likely to elicit a higher degree of social affinity. Those issues that do not directly affect an individual and that are perceived as more complex in terms of addressing them are seen as more distant and abstract and are more likely to elicit a lower degree of social affinity. Thus, as was apparent when the typology was initially presented with regard to the hunger and AIDS issues, the same issue may be perceived differently by different individuals.

The reason for these variations between individuals is that, as seen in the previous four analyses, the proximity and distance of the issue varies depending on the individual's life circumstances and experiences. We also saw—as initially described in chapters 1 and 2—that these social location variables are of three kinds: social, spatial, and temporal proximity and distance. In other words, we give higher priority to those things that are socially, spatially, and temporally proximate to ourselves than to those things that are more distant in terms of the same three variables. In *The Limits to Growth,* a book published in 1974 that created quite a "stir" among economists and policy makers around the world, the authors are well aware of this interaction between our priorities and proximity: "Every person in the world faces a series of pressures and problems that require his [or her] attention and action. These problems affect him [or her] at many different levels" (Meadows et al. 1974: 17). The authors then go on to describe the impact of spatial and temporal proximity (which they represent in a two-dimensional graph), and, while they overlook the social proximity dimension, their description is highly informative regarding the effect of these proximity and distance variables.

> The graph has two dimensions, space and time. Every human concern can be located at some point on the graph, depending on how much geographical space it includes and how far it extends in time. Most people's worries are concentrated [on their immediate and personal problems]. Life for these people is difficult, and they must devote nearly all of their efforts to providing for themselves and their families, day by day [reminiscent of the nonreferenced]. Other people think about and act on problems farther out on the space or time axes. The pressures they perceive involve not only themselves, but the community with which they identify. The actions they take extend not only days, but weeks or years into the future [reminiscent of the socially referenced].
>
> A person's time and space perspectives depend on his culture, his past experience, and the immediacy of the problems confronting him on each level. Most people must have successfully solved the problems in a smaller area before they move their concerns to a larger one. In general, the larger the space and the longer the time associated with a problem, the smaller the number of people who are actually concerned with its solution. (1974: 18)

In their explanation of the two-dimensional graph, Meadows et al. hint at the importance of the social proximity dimension that they otherwise overlook when they say that "the majority of the world's people are concerned with matters that affect only family or friends." Notice the similarity of this comment with that made by Curtis when referring to why the racism issue receives priority in his life: "It's just like your priorities. Who comes first? It has to be you and your family. Blood is thicker than water." Chad said much the same with regard to health care: "[M]aybe if a family member had a problem or something like that, I would write a letter because I kind of see my family as my bond. If a family member had problems with the health care system or maybe a really close friend of mine . . . most likely I would; but that's what it would have [to take]." In fact, in a modern world where we are able to "see" live broadcasts of major world events even when they occur on other parts of the globe, the dimension of social proximity is potentially more important than the dimension of spatial proximity. For this reason, the two-dimensional graph presented by Meadows et al. would be much more accurate if it included this third dimension, as suggested in Figure 8.1.

FIG. 8.1.
The three dimensions of social location.

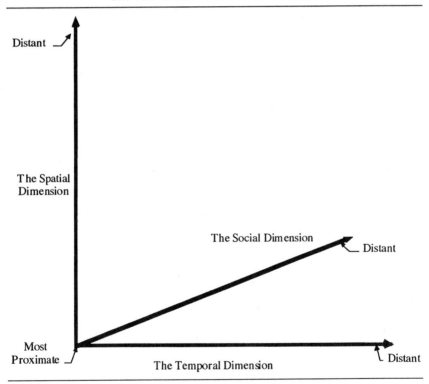

As discussed in chapter 2, these social location variables interact with *each* of the three elements of social affinity, affecting the emergence of our social consciousness, sentiment, and action. For example, the quotes from Chad's and Curtis's narratives in the preceding paragraph illustrate how the proximity variables—particularly the social dimension—have affected their decisions regarding the action component of social affinity. Curtis has taken action addressing racism *in part* (the other parts being the dynamics involved in the construction of social consciousness, sentiment, and action already discussed in his case analysis) because of its proximity to his own life and family. The issue affects him and those close to him. Chad, on the other hand, has not taken action regarding the health care issue *in part* because of its distance from his life and the lives of his family and close friends. It does not affect him or those most proximate to himself.

Erica Pierce also struggles with the impact of spatial distance. Her top issue is human rights violations. Most of the abuses she recounts in her interview happened in other parts of the world, such as Vietnam and Bosnia. Given the global nature of the human rights issue, she feels quite small by comparison: "I think I'm one of those people who's overwhelmed by it. The problem is so big and it usually involves governments. There's an old saying, 'You can't fight city hall.' Well, when you try to fight the government of a foreign country, I think you feel even smaller." The distant (spatial and social) and overwhelming quality of the issue implies that the proximity variables have had an impact on her framing of the issue. Thus, she espouses some elements of the bureaucratic frame, especially the idea that the issue is better addressed by the "experts"—in this case, governmental leaders.

We also saw that Curtis initially had difficulty overcoming the social distance between himself and gay men. This distance had a negative effect on his role-taking ability, to the point where he dehumanized gay men: "I remember being totally homophobic in New York, partly because of my Catholic upbringing. . . . You walk by [these gay men] and you think these people are different." It was not until Curtis worked with and developed relations with gay men that the social distance between himself and this "outgroup" was broken down.

While the proximity and distance variables can easily affect the development of our social consciousness, sentiment, and action, these same elements of affinity can be utilized to manipulate the proximity and distance variables. For example, the information that is filtered out of our consciousness can serve to distance ourselves from social issues just as easily as it can make a social issue more proximate. The same is true of our emotions: the role-taking and identification associated with empathy can variously distance or make more proximate the social issue under consideration. As we saw in chapter 7, by taking action toward an issue, we are quite likely to raise our consciousness and role-taking ability. Getting "in touch with" an issue by taking action can serve to make the issue and those it affects more proximate to ourselves. Thus, there is a dynamic relationship between the three elements of social affinity and the proximity variables that represent our self-interest.

For example, the fact that the social distance between Curtis and gay men was "broken down" demonstrates that it is possible for individuals to manipulate the proximity and distance variables. The gay men that Curtis describes never changed their own identities in an effort to make him like them. Instead, it is Curtis's *perception* of gay men that has changed. The fact that Curtis could not readily identify with gay men—people whom he admits are "just like me," who are human and who suffer from the same kinds of discrimination that he does—shows that he first had to *distance* himself from them as much as possible. He accomplished this by dehumanizing them—thinking of them as "less than human" (see Keen 1991). In other words, his consciousness changed the proximity of gay men and their experiences—making them more distant. And that increase in distance then acted back on Curtis, making it difficult for him to role-take with them. It was not until he worked with gay men—a situation that forced spatial proximity despite the social distance he had created—that he was able to role-take and empathize with them and later change his definition of "racism" in order to include more variables, such as sexual orientation and gender.

In effect, Curtis was able to transcend the social distance he had created, an act that eventually prompted him toward a socially referenced rather than a self-referenced orientation toward the issue. This ability to transcend the distance variables is highly characteristic of those who are able to "break the boundaries" between self and other, as represented by Curtis and all the relationally and socially referenced individuals. Conversely, exercising one's ability to distance oneself from an issue and those it affects is much more characteristic of those who "compartmentalize" the self and society—those who, like Chad and even Curtis in an earlier stage of development, are nonreferenced or self-referenced.

Thus, when examining the interaction between the social location variables and the elements of social affinity, we can speak of the *span of social consciousness,* the *span of sentiment,* and the *span of action:* how *far* does our

FIG. 8.2.
The continuum of social affinity.

Non-Referenced	Self-Referenced	Relationally Referenced	Socially Referenced

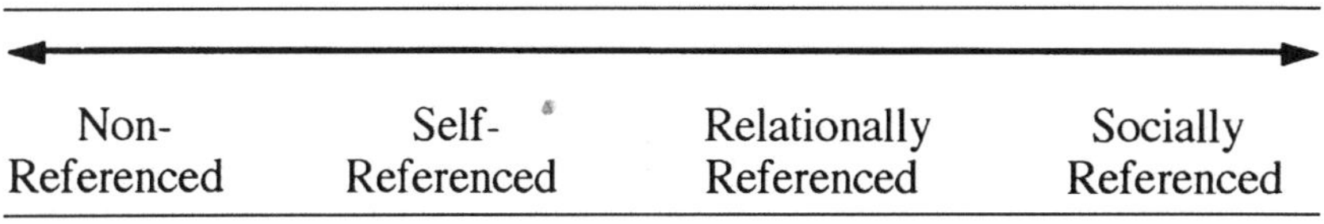

consciousness, sentiment, and action extend beyond ourselves toward others affected by a given social issue? Those who are nonreferenced occur at one end of the continuum, representing those whose *span* of these three elements of affinity is quite limited. The socially referenced fall at the opposite end of the continuum because their *span* extends well beyond themselves and encompasses whole communities and even society itself. The self-referenced and relationally referenced fall at intermediate points on the continuum of social affinity (see Fig. 8.2).

Based on this discussion of the proximity and distance of social issues in relation to a particular individual, it is possible to conceive of what might be termed the *social epicenter* of an issue: That point in society, geography, and time that an issue has its greatest impact (see Fig. 8.3). (While it is also possible to describe a "spatial epicenter" and a "temporal epicenter" as separate and distinct from the social epicenter, the later term is here used to denote the intersection of society, geography, *and* time even though its name only refers to the social dimension.) The farther one moves away from the social epicenter of an issue (or even a specific event concerning an issue), the wider its impact and the larger the number of people who are aware of it. However, at the same time, the farther from the epicenter one moves, the less complete the knowledge of the issue or event is. For example, the AIDS issue first affects those who are HIV positive, then their loved ones and friends, their acquaintances, and so on. At the outer rim of the social epicenter of AIDS, there are those who do not know anyone who is HIV positive. In addition, those who volunteer or work for the AIDS issue fall at different points extending from the social epicenter outward, depending on how direct their contact is with the disease itself.

Let us consider a more concrete example. At the midpoint of the interviewing/data collection process, an adamantly pro-life individual walked into a Planned Parenthood clinic and shot two employees, killing them both. Because it was a local event, the topic was brought up in several subsequent interviews, usually in connection with the abortion issue.

FIG. 8.3.
The social epicenter.

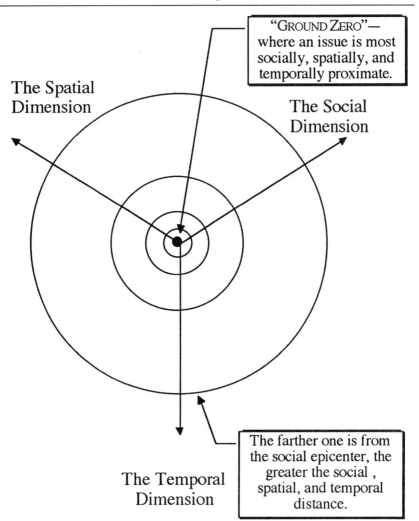

The interviewees who brought up the topic fall at different points within the social epicenter, making this event an interesting case study for examining the impact of social location on the individual.

Recall that Diane Bellieveau, whose case regarding the hunger issue was presented in chapter 4, worked at Planned Parenthood—the same clinic at which the shooting occurred.[3] While she happened to be on her way to work when the shooting occurred and thus did not witness the actual event, as a member of that institution, Diane was at "ground zero" and thus highly attuned to all of the information regarding that incident and the issues—pro-life and pro-choice—surrounding it.

> *I showed up about ten or fifteen minutes after it happened—I was working 11 to 7 that day—and I saw the media and the police. At first, I just thought, "I wonder what's going on around here?" I didn't even connect all of that commotion to Planned Parenthood. So, I walked up the steps and there was a cop standing there and he said, "You can't go in there. Two people have been shot." And it was just numbness. It was just shock. It wasn't until twenty or thirty minutes had passed that I actually began to cry and comprehend what had happened. I was listening to news radio and they're saying the story over and over again. I almost needed to have it repeated to make it real. That entire weekend, I was addicted to the television news and I would drive over to Planned Parenthood and see people putting out candles and flowers. It was good for me to go there and to see the other people I worked with. I just wanted to see them and hold them. All of these people were calling and giving me all this support. It almost felt fraudulent. "I don't deserve this. I wasn't there. It didn't happen to me." And they kept saying, "Of course, it happened to you. You worked there." I had thought it wouldn't—or even couldn't—happen here. "This isn't Florida. This isn't Kansas. It's never going to happen up here. Are you kidding? These tight-ass Yankees? Forget about it!" I think that the reason it took me so long to make it real was because I was in so much denial that it would really ever happen here.*

Diane was so close to the issue that, at first, she "couldn't believe it," indicating that those at ground zero may actually distance themselves from the event or issue—deny its occurrence—as a means of coping. The event was too traumatic—too close—to comprehend all at once. Only gradually did the reality of the event sink into her consciousness, settling in "like a weight"—to the point she felt guilty for all the attention she received. Diane describes her consciousness prior to that event as "naiveté." Afterwards, her consciousness was forever altered and she will not return to that state of innocence. Now she is quite aware of the event and the abortion issue it represents. Thus, the incident was a major event in her life and in the lives of the other surviving coworkers.

Obviously, given the nature of this case, many people outside of that institution were also highly aware of what had happened. Slightly more removed are Diane's friends and family who, while highly exposed to the shooting by the media, were also exposed to the impact it had on the Diane. Others—including myself—only had the information made available on television—at least until I interviewed her, at which point I was brought a little closer to the epicenter. But I was still comparatively removed.

However, those who worked at Planned Parenthood were not the only ones to be affected by the shooting. There were also the clients. Kathy Thompson, the last individual I interviewed, was one such client. While she was not at the clinic when the shooting occurred, it did have a direct effect on her: "It was really hard for me. It was just terrible. Horrifying. I just feel really bad for everyone involved. I feel really sympathetic because I do see the pro-life side of it, but they don't need to be harassing people. I think that sometimes they take it too far. You can't talk to them either." Kathy's response to this event was immediately to relate it to her own experiences (she herself was harassed by pro-life protesters while approaching the clinic), thereby drawing herself closer to the social epicenter.

At a slightly greater remove from the social epicenter is Erica. Her reaction was one of anger—a reaction that was quite strong. She, too, draws as many personal connections as she can, relating the event to her own interests. In the first place, she points out that the event occurred down the street from her own office. Moreover, she highlights the fact that, several years earlier, she had "interviewed people at that clinic, both inside and outside. I was right there." However, what is most interesting about her account of the event is how she compares it to similar events that had occurred in other parts of the country.

> I know there have been attacks at other clinics in this country, but I didn't react as strongly because it wasn't right down the street. It was something that happened somewhere else. Yes, I was upset and I didn't understand it and I thought those women should have access to health care, but it wasn't a clinic that I go to, a clinic that I walk by, a clinic that's on the street where I work like the one here. When those clinics were bombed, or when the doctor was shot in Florida, I didn't think of it as being a violation of my rights. In a larger sense, yes, it was a violation of the rights of all women in this country, but not . . . it wasn't a place I would go to because I don't live in

Florida. So, it wasn't as strong or as personal a reaction as when it happened here. This shooting is more personal. It hit me harder. It made me more angry.

Clearly, the proximity of an event such as a shooting or a bombing has had a significant impact on Erica's perception and reaction toward the event. While all three of the events she mentions were a violation of human rights "in a larger sense," it was only the one that was most proximate to herself—and thus most in keeping with her self-interests—that elicited her moral outrage.

Chad also refers to the shooting. While this event occurred in the same city in which he lives, he has no personal connections with the clinic. His only exposure to the event and the issues it represents was through the news media. Thus, he is relatively removed from the social epicenter of that event. His reference to the shooting was merely an offhand comment while discussing another topic—how media coverage draws attention to an issue: "The guy who was gunned down in the abortion clinic in Florida—the first person, the first doctor—drew a lot of attention. But that didn't prevent this latest killer from going to another abortion clinic and shooting some more people." Chad clearly does not express any personal feelings regarding the shooting at Planned Parenthood. It was just another shooting—another example to use—one among many.

However, Chad is still more proximate than many people. There are those individuals who live in other parts of the country. While the story made national news, national coverage was given much less detail than local coverage because of the fact that the media had so much other competing information to convey to their viewers. So, viewers from other parts of the country are yet another step removed from the impact of this event. Then there are millions of other people throughout the world who never even heard the story because its relevance was so minimal to their life spaces. Their consciousness about this incident is nonexistent. Thus, the impact of this event is like the ripples in a pond after a pebble has been tossed in: the closer one is to the epicenter—to ground zero, the more highly the social, political, personal, and emotional impact of that event is felt. And the more removed one is, the more gentle the shock waves, until at some point, there is no longer any impact felt at all.

As already discussed regarding the social location variables, the ramifications of one's position relative to the social epicenter on the development of one's social consciousness, sentiment, and action—one's degree of social affinity—are very important. Figure 8.4 represents a composite

FIG. 8.4.
A composite view showing the relationship between the dimensions of social affinity, social location, and the social epicenter.

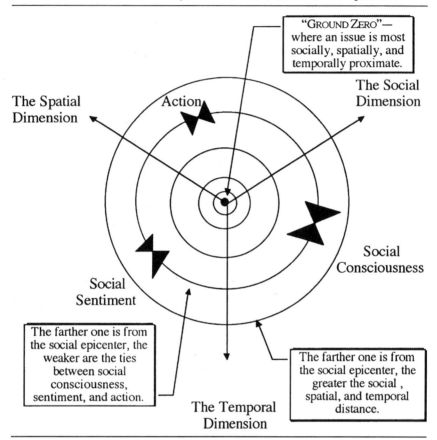

"GROUND ZERO"— where an issue is most socially, spatially, and temporally proximate.

The Social Dimension

The Spatial Dimension

Action

Social Consciousness

Social Sentiment

The farther one is from the social epicenter, the weaker are the ties between social consciousness, sentiment, and action.

The farther one is from the social epicenter, the greater the social , spatial, and temporal distance.

The Temporal Dimension

showing the relationship between one's social location, the three dimensions of social affinity, and the social epicenter. The farther one is from the social epicenter of an issue's impact in terms of social, spatial, and temporal proximity and distance, the more tenuous the development of social affinity given the difficulty in constructing one's social consciousness, in role-taking and empathizing with those directly affected, and in taking action to effectively address the issue.

From this, it is possible to conclude that, in contrast to Batson's effort—discussed in the preceding chapters—to separate egoistic motivation (represented by self-interest) and altruistic motivation (represented by empathy), self-interest actually permeates all aspects of prosocial behavior, not just the decision as to whether or not to take action. Self-interest—as represented by social, spatial, and temporal proximity—shapes our social consciousness, our sentiment, and our action. As seen here and throughout this chapter, self-interest affects the processes of filtering, framing, and creating facticity. It effects the arousal of our emotions, our empathy, and our role-taking ability. It affects our perception of the opportunities for getting involved and our perceptions of the effectiveness of our actions.

In an individualistic culture such as our own, the role of self-interest is understandable and arguably more pronounced than in cultures in which social interests take precedence over individual interests. And in a world that is characterized as a "global village," in which the proximity and distance between individuals, groups, organizations, issues, and even cultures is easily changed by modern technology—for better and for worse—the topic of social affinity, its development, and how it is shaped by self-interest is of paramount importance. With this in mind, we now turn our attention to the larger implications of the development and experience of social affinity.

NINE

Becoming "Fully Human"

Social Affinity in a Modern World

> The adolescent who insists upon a critical reexamination of conventional wisdom is making himself [or herself] into an adult. And the adult whose concerns extend beyond family and beyond nation to mankind has become fully human.
>
> —Leon Eisenberg

The notion that what is "out of sight" is also "out of mind" is highly problematic in a global context. Much of the world is "invisible" to us in that we cannot see it with our own eyes. At the same time, the communications technology that makes it possible to connect all corners of the world—to bring the world into one's living room—is seen as an adequate substitute for direct, personal contact. However, the preceding chapters have indicated that the vicarious experiences offered by the media and technology are an inadequate approximation for actual experience—"Ain't nothing like the real thing, baby." The "realities" portrayed by news coverage, when juxtaposed with all the fiction in the media assumes an unreal quality. For many media consumers, the boundary between fantasy and reality is quite ambiguous.

Recall the cases of Leslie and Diane. In their case studies, they both responded to the hunger issue. However, Leslie characterized hunger by its abstract quality. Even though she saw what was happening in Ethiopia on the television, hunger was still considered by her to be "unreal." She had difficulty grasping the reality of the problem. Diane, on the other hand, characterized hunger by its visibility. For her, it was a reality that could not be avoided or ignored. Unlike Leslie, she did not rely on television coverage of hunger—whether on the news or in commercials—to provide her with information because she saw it on the streets *with her own eyes.* At the same time, though, she did not regulate the reality of hunger only to what she herself saw; instead, she had a definite appreciation for the global magnitude of the hunger issue. Just because hunger in other parts of the world was not visible to her, does not mean that it did not exist. Just because it was "out of" her "sight," does not mean that it was also "out of" her "mind."

The difference between Leslie's reliance on what she learns from television and stereotypes of people on the street and Diane's ability to step outside of her own direct experiences implies a difference in their development of social affinity. Diane's degree of social affinity, represented by her socially referenced orientation to the issue, demonstrates a greater degree of maturation on her part than Leslie's low degree of social affinity, represented by her non-referenced orientation. Interestingly, this difference in "levels of maturity" has an analogy in the field of developmental psychology. Jean Piaget, an eminent psychologist, describes the development of what he calls "object permanence" in infants. Only with time and maturation do children come to realize that objects—and I would add people—actually continue to exist even though the infant cannot see them for himself or herself. Prior to this development, " 'out of sight' is literally 'out of mind' " (Berger 1988: 125). Psychologist Kathleen Stassen Berger gives the following example:

> [I]f a 5-month-old drops a rattle out of the crib, for example, the baby will not look down to search for it. It is as though the rattle has completely passed from the infant's awareness. However, [as the baby continues to develop], babies show tentative signs of realizing that when objects disappear, they have not vanished forever. When a toy falls from the crib, the 7–month-old might look for it for a moment rather than immediately lose interest in it. [Finally], the momentary impulse to look for an object that has disappeared becomes an active effort to search for it. . . . Piaget interpreted the search for objects as the emergence of the concept of object permanence. It signals the beginning of "goal-directed behavior." (Berger: 125)

Moreover, Berger asserts, "as [infants] gain an understanding of object permanence and act on it, infants become less malleable, more self-assertive, and, consequently, much more characteristically human" (Berger: 126).

Given this perspective—and while keeping in mind the importance of each of the types on the continuum of social affinity—the idea that individuals can be "blind" to what happens to people outside of their own environs indicates that they have not yet reached a mature level of thinking. Their human potential has not yet been reached. Only some people develop to the point where they are concerned for those suffering and who remain largely "invisible." It is these individuals who have extended their commitments beyond their own self-interests. They tend to *act* on their awareness and sympathies. In the words of Berger, they become "less malleable"—or subject to the whims of things like the media or even their own immediate desires, "more self-assertive"—or willing to take the initiative rather than waiting for opportunities to drop in their lap, and "more characteristically human"—reaching the socially and morally responsible potential set before all human beings. It is these few who become fully human and humane.

However, as indicated in the preceding chapters, very few people have reached this maturity in their development of social affinity. While many may realize that the world continues to turn while they are not looking, the world does not get their attention except insofar as it affects them directly. Their focus is limited to what is directly in front of them. As soon as the "object" is gone—such as coverage of famine in Ethiopia—their attention moves on to something new. These individuals are governed primarily by self-interest, especially as this quality is represented by the proximity and distance variables described in chapter 8. While, as we see in the last section of this chapter, it is important to address one's own personal concerns and balance that with a concern for others, they have not asserted their individual agency in order to *actively* shape their own consciousness, sentiments, and actions. Instead, they remain "malleable" and easily shaped by larger groups, institutions, and cultures. In the words of Eisenberg, they are not yet "fully human" in that their concern has not yet extended "beyond family and beyond nation to mankind."

One may ask whether the small number of those who have become fully human in their development of social affinity is characteristic of humanity: Is it a human universal that so few people reach full maturity in terms of social affinity? Or is this deficit more characteristic of our own culture of individualism within the United States? The answer to these and other questions will form the basis of this chapter. First, we will consider the individualism and lack of moral obligations endemic to our culture. Then, we will move beyond these questions and look at the relevance of what we have learned about social affinity to such topics as urban planning and community and the globalization of the economy. Finally, we shall conclude with the question of "Who is my neighbor?" and the potential for individuals to bridge the personal and the global.

How Unique to U.S. Culture is the "Out of Sight, Out of Mind" Mentality?

As already mentioned in previous chapters, in the modern world there are innumerable claims upon our social affinity. In this study, we have only focused on social affinity in the context of social issues, so the multiplicity of claims upon our affinity is especially pronounced when one considers that all the social issues out there are just one means of understanding social affinity. We get "bad news" from all over the world every night on our news broadcasts, not to mention all the other sources of information in our environment. Within the context of "globalization,"[1] we are put into contact with an increasingly broad range of problems and "issues;" and yet our social consciousness, our reserves of sympathy, and our perceived ability to act are still bounded by a mentality that is highly reminiscent of premodern, village-centered society—a focus on what is merely local. The affinity we have available to us can in no way match the claims placed upon it, so we are forced to choose where our affinity will lie. And our choice is usually restricted to those concerns that have a direct impact on ourselves and our closest loved ones.

Thus, the notion of a "global community" is highly problematic. This is a term that seeks to convey the idea that we as individuals are brought closer to the multitudes that populate our world via television, radio, newspapers, telephone, the Internet and so on. As noted in the introduction, the whole world is at our fingertips, but our grasp remains the same. Our consciousness, our sentiments, and our actions have not expanded to meet the great and more varied claims placed upon them. Our capacities for these qualities have remained much the same as they were prior to globalization. Thus, it is not surprising that individual interests—what we find "interesting"—are so narrowly focused on the proximate and easily tangible.

In the late 1800s and early 1900s, the "Renaissance Man"—the person whose experiences and interests included "everything"—was idealized. However, "everything" was much more circumspect at that time. In today's world, it is highly difficult, if not impossible for an individual to give attention to his or her personal life and loved ones as well as the global claims placed upon himself or herself. Thus, those global claims that *are,* in the end, given attention are also the ones most congruent with the individual's personal life. One's social location in terms of social, spatial, and temporal proximity plays a major role in where and for whom an individual's social affinity lies.

One may ask whether this dynamic between social location and the extension of social affinity is a universal human characteristic, or whether it is a distinct product of our U.S. culture of individualism and self-interest. While the data presented in earlier chapters is limited to Americans, it is possible to hypothesize that this dynamic affects people worldwide insofar as they are a part of the process of globalization. However, our culture of individualism aggravates the importance of social location because it plays right into the self-interest reflected in the proximity variables. Given our culture, it is easier to legitimate restricting our moral concerns and obligations to the parameters of our self-interest: "If it affects me and/or those close to me, I am interested; otherwise, while I may sympathize with your predicament, I cannot help." In other words, we tend to restrict our broader or global concerns to those things that affect our personal lives in some way.

Past research supports the idea that Americans are less likely to apply conceptions of "moral obligation" to situations that do not affect them than are people of other cultures. For example, in a highly suggestive study, Miller, Bersoff, and Harwood (1990) compared Americans with Hindu Indians regarding their perceptions of social responsibility. In this study, subjects in both India and the United States were interviewed regarding several hypothetical helping situations. The researchers point out that "Indian subjects were found to maintain an extremely broad view of interpersonal moral duties," applying feelings of moral obligation to family, friends, and strangers alike. Moreover, "the primary criterion for categorizing social responsibilities in moral terms was the existence of some unmet need." By comparison, "American subjects considered a *smaller domain* of social responsibilities as moral obligations" (1990: 137; emphasis mine). The judgment of Americans was heavily influenced by the social proximity of the person in need. Strangers—those who are most socially distant—were the least likely to elicit feelings of moral obligation whereas family members were the most likely.[2]

The researchers attribute these differences in perception of moral obligation to the cultural differences of the two populations. They compare the Indian and American cultures as follows:

The wide scope of interpersonal moral obligations observed among the Hindu Indian sample, for example, appears to reflect the sociocentric emphasis of Hindu Indian cultural conceptions and practices. In such a cultural framework, the starting point of morality is the social whole, of which the individual forms an interdependent part. Obligations to serve the social whole through responsiveness to the needs of dependent others, then, tend to be regarded as fundamental moral commitments. In contrast, the more narrow scope of interpersonal moral obligations observed among American subjects may be seen to reflect the cultural premise that the autonomous individual constitutes the fundamental social unit. Such a perspective is evidenced, for example, in the high cultural value placed on independence and privacy and in the Western philosophical assumption that individuals exist prior to social institutions. Within this cultural system, individual freedom of choice tends to be weighed against the highly desirable, but competing, value of beneficence. (1990: 137)

Within the Indian culture, the social whole is given paramount importance, and individual self-interest, while still important, is subordinated to the benefit of society. By contrast, in American culture, the self-interests of the individual are given priority. The result is that Americans are less likely to feel obligated to those who are removed from the individual's circle of interest because they have less "self-relevance." The farther away a person in need is, the less likely an American will help out of moral obligation. But even the most proximate individuals may not elicit such feelings of obligation if their need is not perceived as great—as in, for example, a family member needing directions to an unfamiliar store (1990: 138–139).[3]

Thus, the impact of social location in terms of proximity and distance is much more pronounced among Americans, and this is largely due to our culture of individualism. However, this does not mean that social location has no relevance in other cultures. In fact, it did exert some influence among the Indian population in the study. The researchers cite the example of Indian adults who "categorized minor-need stranger obligations in moral terms less frequently." While the effect of social distance was weaker, it was present nevertheless (1990: 139).

Another interesting finding of this study, which further underscores the role played by American culture in aggravating the relevance of the social location variables, has to do with those situations of need that were not obviously a matter of moral obligation nor a matter of personal choice. In these ambiguous situations, Americans attempted to combine "the notion of an objective obligation . . . with the notion of individual freedom of choice" (1990: 139). The researchers call this a "personal-moral" category for looking at situations of need, and it was utilized exclusively by Americans. The usage of such a category reflects the mixed feelings Americans have about social responsibility.

> Although maintaining that it is highly desirable to fulfill social responsibilities, Americans . . . also tend to experience such responsibilities as *in conflict* with individual freedom of choice. The personal-moral category may be seen to express this ambivalence. In particular, in using such a category, Americans simultaneously express (a) a commitment to meet the needs of dependent others through claims that social responsibilities are objective and (b) a commitment to personal liberties through assertions that it is the agent's own business whether to fulfill social responsibilities. (1990: 140; emphasis mine)

In other words, there is much tension between the individualism of our culture that seeks to maximize self-interest and the vestiges of older moral values, such as the ideal of "loving one's neighbors as oneself." As discussed in more detail later, Americans are pulled in both directions and find that it is difficult to resolve these conflicting values. In sum, while the influence of social, spatial, and temporal proximity and distance are universal in that they affect the feelings of social affinity across a variety of cultures, research lends credence to the view that their effect is more pronounced in a culture such as we have in the United States—a culture that places self-interest above the interests of society.

Of course, Hindu Indians are only one example of a culture exhibiting collectivist tendencies with wider circles of moral obligation, and the United States represents only one example of a culture dominated by individualism. Social psychologist Harry Triandis compares many different cultures in terms of their collectivism and/or individualism. Cultures that share the collectivist tendencies with Hindu Indians include China, where "a person who is not responsive to those around him [or her] is considered self-centered" (1995: 91); southeast Europe (Italy and Greece); the Philippines; Latin Americans, Hispanic Americans; Africans "south of the Sahara;" Arabs; Balinese; and Japan, although this culture seems to be moving toward individualism (1995: 89–95). Triandis also includes "urban villagers," which is a term referring to those who live in tightly knit, urban communities (Gans 1962).

At the same time, the United States is not alone in its individualism. Triandis points out that Ancient Greece may have had individualistic tendencies, although it is difficult to say for certain. Contemporary Germany, France, Great Britain, the Netherlands, Scandinavia, Canada, Australia, and New Zealand all exhibit individualistic tendencies, some more than others (1995: 95–99 and 104). However, the individualism of the United States, first pointed out by Alexis de Tocqueville (1835), appears to be the most extreme due to, among other factors, "British influence, affluence, the open frontier, and social and geographic mobility. Most immigrants must have been more individualistic than [the other members of their respective cultures], since moving requires breaking with traditional behaviors" (1995: 98).

Ironically, the "rugged individualism" that is so valued in our culture is more the result of an idealization of our history than it is an accurate reflection of it. Author Travis Charbeneau argues that the image of the lone frontiersman conquering the wild West is more myth than reality. Such a "rugged" individual would not have been able to survive. The way in which the American West was "won" (setting aside the moral qualms one might legitimately have toward the butchering of Native Americans in the path of westward expansion) was through communal efforts. Charbeneau points to phenomena such as wagon trains and barn-raisings as evidence of the interdependence rather than independence necessary for survival. For example, regarding wagon trains, "if your fellow traveler's wagon got washed down the Big Muddy, you were expected to help out—and he did the same for you" (1992: 132). In other words, Americans are misguided in placing such importance on individual freedom and independence: "Community, not the lone gunslinger, is what *really* tamed the Wild West, and a sense of national community is what we need to revitalize our country. . . . Our interdependent American heritage . . . is exactly what's required to survive and prosper in the increasingly interdependent national and global community" (1992: 132–133).

Unfortunately, the allure of rugged individualism has overshadowed the importance of community-based obligations and has given license not only to subordinating social concerns to self-interests but actually harming society.

[The] "pioneering loner" today translates into rapacious corporations and institutions hungry to devour anything, from each
other to you and me to the whole planet. Our "loner" now has
not only an iron will but also iron bulldozers, chain saws, and
oil-drilling platforms. Our "loner," now invariably in the company of a cavalry troop of lawyers and lobbyists, can gobble up
whole city neighborhoods, acquire great enterprises in "hostile
takeovers," raid the banking and health-care systems, pollute the
countryside, elbow his way up to a prime feeding spot at the
Pentagon trough, and generally sacrifice the national interest—
all on the altar of "rugged individualism." (1992: 132–133)

While it is possible to utilize the pursuit of self-interests in generating
social participation, the negative consequences of such "rugged" individualism for society are tremendous.

As an additional example of the prominence of self-interest and individualism in American society, consider the current trend of linking affinity
with consumerism. Affinity itself is being "packaged" and marketed by
banks offering "affinity credit cards." The idea behind these affinity cards is
that "a third party endorses the card. . . . In return it usually recieves a small
percentage of the value of each card transaction" ("Sticky Fingers" 1996:
94). Such cards are meant to represent where the cardholder's affinities lie.
While many of these cards are geared toward nonpolitical and nonsocial
causes—such as the "Elvis Presley Mastercard," which benefits the Elvis
Memorial Foundation—some are intended to reflect civic values. In this
vein, many universities now sponsor credit cards and receive a small percentage of all purchases made with these cards for funding and scholarships.
Local governments and even special interest groups also sponsor and benefit from these cards: the city of Boston sponsors the "Boston Community
Card" in order to "raise a little revenue for special projects without raising
taxes or fees" (Chacón 1996: 21) and gay and lesbian charitable, nonprofit
organizations and scholarship funds benefit from the "Community Card"
and the "Rainbow Card"—the latter of which is endorsed by tennis star
Martina Navratilova. American Express has also advertised contributions for
the "fight against hunger" when making purchases with their card.

While these affinity cards do demonstrate the interest the holder has
in the causes supported by the sponsors, "the amount raised seldom
amounts to much" (Chacón 1996) given that the donated percentage of
purchases is so small. Moreover, and as described in previous chapters, they

work in much the same way as Milgram's "specialized instutions" by inter-ceding on behalf of individuals. In effect, they can serve to alleviate any sense of moral obligation the individual may have had to become active in her or his community. By substituting consumerism for actual involve-ment, the usage of affinity cards—by themselves, without any other form of action—plays into the hands of individualism and self-interest and undermines opportunities for the emergence of social affinity.

As already alluded to when distinguishing between collectivist and indi-vidualist cultures, Triandis attributes the shift toward individualism to a vari-ety of factors, including the affluence of a society that can package and market affinity. Other factors in this shift include a variety of variables associated with modernization: "changes in ecology (how people make a living), . . . mobility (both social a geographic), and movement from rural to urban settings. . . . [Moreover], these societies that are exposed to the mass media become more individualistic because the mass media messages are designed to create plea-sure rather than inspire people to do their duty" (1995: 83).

However, as noted before, the media does more than turn our atten-tion away from our duties toward others. To belong to the media age is to be exposed to the overwhelming and potentially limitless scope of moral claims upon the individual. Thus, the link between modernization and globalization can wreck havoc on our sense of moral obligation. Triandis points out that moving toward a world market provides a situation con-ducive to the emergence of individualism. In this kind of situation,

> the size of the groups one is dealing with changes from narrow, such as the nuclear family, to broader collectives such as extended family and the tribe, to still broader collectives such as co-religionists and members of the same political party, to still broader collectives, such as the state, and finally one is dealing with the world market and humankind. As one is relating to broader groups, one has more choices; hence I-factors [variables associated with individualism] are larger. Furthermore, the indi-vidual's emotional involvement with the collective is likely to diminish as the collective becomes very large. Thus, we expect individuals attached to very large collectives to be highly indi-vidualistic. (1995: 87)

The research of Triandis, when put together with the research presented here indicates that the social location variables and individualism exist in a dialectical relationship: globalization (i.e., increases in social and spatial distance) encourages a shift toward individualism while individualism exacerbates the role of the social location variables in prompting individuals to compartmentalize their lives from those around them.

In the sections that follow, we see how our culture of individualism and the social location variables of proximity and distance combine into a lethal mix that wrecks havoc on the sense of social responsibility and moral obligation that holds society together. However, there are also means for overcoming the limits of social location and creating an environment that is conducive to the emergence of social affinity from the local to the global levels.

Urban Planning and the Breakdown of Community

Robert Moses is considered to be among greatest American builders in the twentieth century—designing everything from parks and highways to housing and urban renewal. Throughout his career, stretching from 1924 to 1968, he billed himself as being outside the purview of politics, claiming to have never made a deal (Caro, 1974: 16–19). He constructed an image of himself as a man of the people and the "antithesis of the politician." The press and public opinion backed him up so well that almost no one dared to try to undermine his policies with regard to urban planning. Then governor of New York Franklin Delano Roosevelt tried, but was forced to concede in the face of "acclaim for Moses that rolled not only through New York but across the country" with the result that Moses was "embedded more firmly than ever in the public consciousness as the fearless defier of politicians" (1974: 16–17). His image held sway even after he left the limelight:

> The vast majority of the public accepted the legend as fact. And even those skeptics who were disposed to test its truth had no facts with which to make the test, because the records . . . and the mouths . . . were so effectively sealed. (1974: 17)

Moses was perceived as a hero, and the reality of that view could not be swayed. But his public persona was based on a lie: concern for the people. Underneath the veneer was a more unsavory picture. One commentator had this to say about the reality beneath the image:

> "He doesn't love the people. . . . It used to shock me because he was doing all these things for the welfare of the people. . . . He'd denounce the common people terribly. To him they were lousy,

dirty, people, throwing bottles all over Jones Beach. . . . He loves the public, but not as people. The public is just *the* public. It's a great amorphous mass to him; it needs to be bathed, it needs to be aired, it needs recreation, but not for personal reasons—just to make it a better public." (1974: 318)

For Moses, a "better public" was one in which the "common people" were cleansed away, and he made every conceivable effort to make this happen.

While he continued to portray an apolitical stance, the impact of his work was highly political, not only in its means but also in its ends. For example, to make room for his projects, Moses evicted close to half a million people from their homes, the vast majority of whom were poor and black and/or Puerto Rican. When he built housing for these populations, he contributed to the ghettoization of New York City by effectively isolating various minority and low-income groups. In the wake of those he evicted, Moses built playgrounds for the rich—from upscale neighborhoods to recreational facilities (1974: 20). Moreover, Moses intentionally built the city and its surrounding environs in such a way as to minimize access by the poor and nonwhite ethnic groups to these playgrounds of the wealthy—even to the *public* parks.

Perhaps the most telling example of this is found in the parkways that Moses constructed. These parkways were constructed in such a way as to allow a highly specific segment of the population *in* to these playgrounds and to keep another, equally specific segment of the population *out*. The poor and lower middle classes of New York were highly dependent on public transportation. To make it more difficult for these groups to gain access to state parks, Moses limited rapid transit to these areas. For example, he vetoed a proposal by the Long Island Rail Road to construct a branch spur to Jones Beach (1974: 318). Moses's efforts did not stop there. The very structure of his parkways prevented easy access by these "undesirable" groups. He intentionally built the bridges over the Long Island parkways too low for buses to pass beneath them, effectively forcing all buses to use local roads, "making the trips discouragingly long and arduous" (1974: 318). Given that only one-third of New York City's population had access to cars, fully two-thirds of the people were prevented from enjoying these public parks (1974: 546).

Building the parkway bridges low was indeed an example of Moses' foresight in trying to keep intact his original concept of the area through which those roads ran—lovely Long Island—

as a serene and sparsely populated suburban setting, a home for the relatively small number of people wealthy enough to live there, a playground for the larger but still restricted number of people wealthy enough to drive there and play in the parks he had built there. (1974: 952)

When it came to blacks, Moses was particularly insidious, using the "separate but equal" ideology of his time to its fullest degree. He made it difficult for buses chartered by black groups to obtain the necessary permit to enter state parks, particularly his favorite, Jones Beach. Instead, these groups were allowed access only to the most remote parks on Long Island. Because "Moses was convinced that [blacks] did not like cold water, the temperature at the pool at Jones Beach was deliberately icy . . ." (1974: 319). Nonetheless, in keeping with his public image, Moses vehemently denied all attempts to divert "undesirables" from "his" playgrounds.

Moses was highly conscious of the impact of our physical environment on social relations. Through the layout of his parkways, neighborhoods, and parks, he intentionally made it very difficult for people from different racial and class backgrounds to interact with one another. While segregation was not such a blatant policy in New York as it was in the South, the end effect was the same: through policy or through urban planning, "undesirables"—whether racial or class-based—were set apart and distanced from "polite society." To maximize the social distance between these groups, the spatial distance was increased. The gulf between black and white, rich and poor was strengthened by minimizing the contact and interaction between these groups.

While one might think that we as a society have come a long way since the time of Robert Moses and segregation, these same dynamics are at work today. While our culture idealizes the notion of community, the reality is that we prefer to be in community only with those who are as similar to ourselves as possible. We prefer not to cross the socially enforced boundaries of race, class, ideology, and so on and, as a result, we close off the possibility of becoming socially or even relationally referenced toward those who are different from ourselves. Out of self-interest, we prefer to leave our boundaries intact. When these boundaries are breached, the result is phenomena such as the "white flight" of the past and what one author currently describes as the "secession of the successful" (Vanderpool 1995).

In recent years, there has been a virtual assault on public spaces— those places where people from diverse populations and backgrounds freely interact with one another. For example, public playgrounds across the country are deteriorating. Parents have begun replacing trips to the park with trips to private, indoor playgrounds such as the Discovery Zone (Sarasohn 1992: 130). Moreover, parks and playgrounds are not alone. Public libraries, according to the American Library Association, have had to "shorten hours, freeze new book acquisitions, lay off staff, and cancel special services such as story hours, bookmobiles, and adult literacy classes" (1992: 130). Museums, too, are feeling the crunch of insufficient funding, having to raise their admission charges, reduce programming, and even sell part of their collections to private collectors (1992: 130).

Economist and former Secretary of Labor Robert Reich points to two areas in particular that are suffering this assault on public spaces: infrastructure and public education. In the past, public investment in these areas was justified in terms of its benefit to the whole of society. However, "in more recent years, as [the privileged classes] have come to depend less on other Americans, the traditional justification has apparently lost some of its potency" (Reich 1991: 253). For example, the infrastructure of public highways and streets—particularly city roads—and public transportation upon which so many working and lower class people depend are not so important among a privileged class that now relies more on private telecommunications and air travel. As a result, federal funding of infrastructure has not kept pace with the expansion of the U.S. economy. "And much of what the federal government *has* underwritten in recent years has been dedicated to downtown convention centers, office parks, research parks, and other amenities utilized mostly by [the middle and upper classes]" (1991: 254–255).

Public education has also suffered. While the demands on public education have increased, the United States is still far behind other nations such as Canada, Japan, and Germany in terms of spending for education (1991: 255–256). Moreover, the federal government contributes only 6 percent of the costs of primary and secondary school education. The balance is shouldered by each state and local community. Thus, wealthier states and communities are able to provide more funds for public education than are poorer states and communities. The result is a great disparity in the quality of public education from one locality to another (1991: 274–276; see also Kozol 1991). Moreover, fewer people are able to afford a college education and private schooling while these same schools proliferate among those who can afford them.

Trends such as these result in the "homogenizing" of society: those one encounters in one's daily routine are very similar to oneself in terms of race, class, and other socially defining characteristics. Mike Davis, in his critically acclaimed book, *City of Quartz,* describes this phenomenon as "the architectural policing of social boundaries" (1992: 223). Oftentimes, this architectural segregation is done in the name of "security." As crime rates rise in urban areas, people—usually white and middle to upper-class—have sought to "insulate" themselves from those areas and people— usually the poor and persons of color—associated with crime. Apartment complexes, entire neighborhoods, and even supermarkets and malls are surrounded with high walls and fences and are policed by private security with the help of myriads of video cameras. In effect, these residential and commercial areas are "able to privatize local public space, partitioning themselves from the rest of the metropolis, even imposing a variant of neighborhood 'passport control' on outsiders" (1992: 246). One Los Angeles suburb has gone so far as to close "its parks on weekends to exclude Latino and Asian families from adjacent communities. One plan under discussion would reopen the parks on Saturdays only to those with proof of residence" (1992: 246). Social activist and poet, Daniel Berrigan, in commenting about a gated and privatized neighborhood in uptown New Orleans said that those who live there are not locking others out so much as locking themselves in.[4] In essence, the walls and locked gates are metaphors for the social consciousness of those dwelling within these areas: they remain closed off and distanced from the rest of the population, insulated from the realities of daily living for the underprivileged classes.

Even urban centers are subject to this process of homogenization. In addition to the disappearance of public space, Davis points out that,

> The Downtown hyperstructure [of Los Angeles] is programmed to ensure a seamless continuum of middle-class work, consumption and recreation, without unwonted exposure to Downtown's working class street environments. Indeed the totalitarian semiotic of ramparts and battlements, reflective glass and elevated pedways [of current urban design], *rebukes any affinity or sympathy* between different architectural or human orders. (1992: 231; emphasis mine)

The boundaries and distance placed between classes and races makes it more difficult for individuals to establish any degree of social affinity for others. Self-interest or, at best, the interests of those most like ourselves, is paramount. Our society has become sheltered from much of its inherent diversity as walls have gone up between its different populations. Such a trend further aggravates our tendency to focus on the proximate, the similar, and the familiar and undermines the emergence of social affinity and the very fabric of society.

Critics argue that the homogenizing of our public spaces and the secession of the successful from the rest of society is detrimental not only to the social fabric of society but also the very democratic processes upon which our society is built. In the 1800s, urban planners—aware of the relationship between public spaces and democracy—actively promoted *"mixing* classes and ethnicities in common . . . recreations and enjoyments" (Davis 1992: 227). However, this mixing of diverse peoples is currently out of fashion, and the implications for democracy are disturbing.

> Many commentators argue that the "security" of privatized space is being bought with a high price—that as public space goes, so goes democracy. "This trend runs counter to the traditional American faith in free speech and assembly as the cornerstone of constitutional democracy," writes Wally Bowen. . . . "As public space disappears, so do opportunities for average citizens to be active in public life." Sociologist Richard Sennett argues . . . that "the classic ideal of a public space was that it was a place of truth. It was where people understood other people in society by talking to them."
>
> This poses a scary question: If democracy depends on interacting with others, and if the public space where this interacting can occur is disappearing, then what is the future of democracy? . . . The Constitution is predicated on a sense of "we the people," but if we no longer experience a plural sense of citizenship, then where are "we" headed? (Gerloff 1993: 48)

Not only is democracy threatened by the divisions within society that are promoted by modern urban design, but our democratic law now reinforces these divisions.

"Out of sight, out of mind" is now a part of public policy. Nowhere is this desire to distance ourselves from those who are unlike "us" more apparent than in our current treatment of the homeless. While the homeless are being discouraged from loitering by such aspects of the urban environment as barrel-shaped bus benches—that are impossible to sleep on—and automatic sprinklers that turn on at random times throughout the night in public parks—again to discourage sleeping (Davis 1992: 233)—such passive efforts are only the tip of the iceberg. In many communities throughout the country, homelessness is actually being criminalized: "At least 50 cities are considering or already have adopted ordinances that specifically target the behavior of homeless people" (Pascale 1994: 38). For example, in June of 1994, the city of San Francisco passed Proposition J, which makes it "illegal to linger for more than 60 seconds within 30 feet of an automatic teller in use" (1994: 38). While the reasoning for the law has to do with "security," already discussed, such an ordinance is clearly directed at the homeless. Business owners are especially supportive of these ordinances and have even "made their continued support [to nonprofit organizations serving the homeless] contingent upon" the nonprofits' support of these ordinances (1994: 39).

Occasionally, city leaders have considered deporting the homeless altogether. Davis notes that the leaders of Los Angeles have considered "deporting them to a poor farm on the edge of the desert, confining them in camps in the mountains, or, memorably, interning them on a derelict ferry at the Harbor." Ironically, the reason deportation proposals have not passed is not because of concern for the homeless or the morality of such a "solution;" instead, it rests on self-interest: "[S]uch 'final solutions' have been blocked by council members fearful of the displacement of the homeless into their districts" (1992: 232). Critics charge that the reason that these ordinances and deportation proposals are proliferating is that merchants believe that "*visible* poverty, not criminal behavior, may be the greatest threat to business in the 1990s" because it discourages shopping (1994: 39; emphasis mine). The solution espoused is not to address the problems of poverty underlying homelessness, but to make it invisible so that American consumers will not allow their conscience to interfere with their spending habits.

Our culture maximizes the "Out of sight, out of mind" mentality inherent in the social location variables of social, spatial, and temporal distance, and this tendency has reached its most pernicious dimensions when it is actively pursued by social policy and urban planning. However, there are also some hopeful countertrends, such as the promise posed by New Urbanism, which is emerging among architects and city planners, and grassroots community initiatives to revitalize neighborhoods as well as foster the sentiment of community. These efforts are aimed at counteracting the distancing effects by bringing together diverse elements of the population. Moreover, they empower individual citizens in such a way that they are more likely to pursue civic participation and develop a sense of social interest that complements self-interested motivation.

New Urbanism and Grassroots Neighborhood Initiatives

The term "New Urbanism" refers to an alternative movement among city planners and architects who devote themselves "to creating new community space that is dense, diverse, and convenient—in a word, urban" (Gerloff, 1994: 28). In the past, this movement was heavily criticized by the architectural establishment as being a "romantic, Disney-like exercise in nostalgia" as well as for its use of "obsolete, discredited forms." Today, however, it receives much more acceptance. Those espousing New Urbanism tend to view the urban environment from a systems perspective in which pedestrian, mass transit, and automobile traffic are all taken into account while including "environmental, housing, and employment concerns" (Shaffer and Anundsen 1993: 104). Communities designed within the New Urbanist paradigm emphasize diversifying the neighborhood by including homes, town houses, and apartments that vary in cost in order to cater to different classes. They include parks and playgrounds as well as small businesses, offices, and services such as a post office and library all within close walking distance. Moreover, public transportation is easily accessible. The architectural style of the community is integrated but not of the "cookie-cutter" tendency that characterizes most suburbs.

What is perhaps more important than the physical layout of these communities is the social interaction generated by the physical layout of the community and the *process* of establishing such a community. Shaffer and Anundsen demonstrate that the difficulties this New Urbanist philosophy has had in being accepted in the planning and architectural community has actually worked to the advantage of the communities themselves. For example,

> Part of the problem is the need to revise old zoning restrictions and overcome people's natural resistance to change. To speed this process, designer/builders are giving public presentations, incorporating local architects with a sense of the area's history and personality into design teams, and inviting citizens and officials to comment on the developing project at each step of the way. Citizens who yearn for community-friendly neighborhoods help by making their voices heard in planning meetings and pressing for necessary zoning changes. (1993: 105)

In other words, these communities emerge out of a process that gets everybody involved, from the planners themselves to the citizenry who will live there. The process brings people together who might otherwise have never paid attention to one another and gives them a common and concrete goal. In effect, as self-interests become intimately tied with common interests, the boundaries of social distance are broken down. Given the opportunity to listen to the perspectives of others allows individuals to exercise their capacities for empathy and role-taking. In other words, social affinity is fostered.

The results of this process of establishing communities are especially apparent in the many grassroots neighborhood initiatives that have sprung up across the country as efforts to revitalize already existing urban areas. Urban renewal often elicits images of the destruction of community through the displacement of minority and immigrant populations from their old neighborhoods in order to make way for new, high-rise urban centers. For example, in the city of Boston, the West End was a low-rent "urban village" situated near the central business district. The Italian and Jewish communities that lived there were displaced in order to make room for a new "Government Center" (see Gans 1962). However, another Boston example shows that revitalizing the city does not have to imply the destruction of community.

The Dudley Street Neighborhood Initiative (DSNI) is a grassroots organization set up as a response to the deterioration of the Dudley Street neighborhood in Roxbury—another section of Boston (see Medoff and Sklar 1994). When local factories left the area, the Irish working class also relocated with the help of federal and state funding. In their place, blacks, Hispanics, Cape Verdeans, and other racial and ethnic groups moved in, taking advantage of affordable housing costs and out of necessity due to red-lining by banks (i.e., banks restricting where minorities can live in order for them to qualify for mortgages). The banks and Boston city government—dominated by Irish Americans—turned their backs on the area, allowing it to deteriorate. Many buildings were eventually abandoned and many of those burned to the ground, leaving behind vacant lots that became depositories for trash and illegal dumping by Boston businesses and industries.

The initial revitalization efforts were sponsored by white businessmen coming into the neighborhood and presenting a plan. Some residents reacted negatively to this, saying that "It's always people from downtown or somewhere who come in and tell you what your neighborhood needs." Moving beyond these complaints, area residents founded the DSNI, which included a board with representatives from the neighborhood itself. Each ethnic group in the community was allotted three seats on the board and the rest of the seats were for local businesses, charities, religious institutions, and so on. In short, DSNI extended across a diverse segment of the Dudley Street population and gave the residents a powerful voice. After polling residents, DSNI began a "Don't Dump on Us!" campaign and began to clean up the empty lots in the area. Eventually, they were backed by Boston Mayor Raymond Flynn, who provided some funding and equipment. The residents themselves did the work of cleaning and demonstrating in an effort to stop illegal dumping. They reclaimed a park from drug dealers by organizing regular activities in the park for children every day of the week. They even persuaded the police department to sign an agreement to be present at the park each day.

The largest project taken on by DSNI was the redesigning of the neighborhood. DSNI carefully chose planners who shared their concern for community input. In the end, more than two hundred residents were involved in coming up with the revitalization plan—a plan that included low and moderate income housing as well as parks and a community center. After much struggle and community effort, they convinced the city of Boston to support the plan with public funds. In other words, the revitalization project came from the "bottom up" rather than the "top down." The most bold move by DSNI was to request eminent domain from the city in order to acquire all of the empty lots that were not already owned by the city. While such a motion was controversial because unprecedented—never before had eminent domain been granted to a neighborhood organization—it was eventually approved. Over the course of the next few years, the housing construction has progressed and many residents have become proud new homeowners. As the construction has continued, DSNI has instituted additional neighborhood events—such as an annual multicultural festival and youth volunteer opportunities—to bring residents together. For the organizers of DSNI, the most important part of what they have accomplished is the fact that diverse and previously distant peoples were brought together and empowered through community organizing efforts. The residents were given hope and a collective vision. Self-interests and collective interests were merged.

The story of the Dudley Street Neighborhood Initiative is not unique. The Banana Kelly Neighborhood Improvement Association of the South Bronx of New York City and Vision 2000 of Chattanooga, Tennessee, accomplished similar goals—the latter encompassing the entire city (Shaffer and Anundsen 1993: 94–102). In all cases, the benefits extend beyond the physical reconstruction of the neighborhood. A community spirit that unites diverse and otherwise distant peoples emerges. For example, in Chattanooga, "racial and class conflict have always been a part of the city's makeup. The Vision 2000 project lowered some long-standing barriers between blacks and whites as well as brought together [the upper-middle class] and inner-city residents. A municipal human relations committee has been established, but perhaps more important is the increased connection among people" (Walljasper 1994: 16). The emergence of social affinity has been nurtured in an environment that bridges social, spatial, and temporal distance and that brings self-interest and social interest together. Individualism has been tempered with a "communitarian" perspective.

Many people—social thinkers and average citizens alike—have lamented the loss of community and civic values that came with the dominance of individualism. Some of those dissatisfied with this current state of affairs have begun to band together under the rubric of "communitarianism"—a movement "based on an effort to balance individual rights with community responsibilities" (Winkler 1994: 105). Such an effort begins with "[shoring] up the moral foundations of our society," especially through the family, schools, communities, and the national society (Etzioni 1993: 248). For example, with regard to the community, communitarians espouse much of what was just described, aiming to "make our physical environment more community-friendly. . . . An era dedicated to a return to we-ness would value and promote design that is pro-community" (1993: 127–128).

Much of the focus of the communitarian movement is to keep decision making and social planning as local and proximate as possible:

> Generally, no social task should be assigned to an institution that is larger than necessary to do the job. What can be done by families should not be assigned to an intermediate group—school, etc. What can be done at the local level should not be passed on to the state or federal level, and so on. There are, of course, plenty of urgent tasks—environmental ones—that do require national and even international action. But to remove tasks to higher levels than is necessary weakens the constituent communities. (Etzioni 1993: 260)

By keeping these social tasks proximate, social affinity is fostered. The social, spatial, and temporal distance between individuals, groups, and peoples is minimized. Opportunities for social participation as well as the other dimensions of social affinity are maximized. Moreover, individuals are more likely to see the direct results of their actions and feel empowered and further motivated as a result—points that were made in chapter 7. When individuals are brought together, they begin to see that their self-interests overlap with those around them and they begin to think in terms of collective interests, supporting the communitarian perspective that "recognizes both individual human dignity and the social dimension of human existence" (1993: 253).

However, while it is very important to begin expanding individuals' social consciousness beyond the self and toward local concerns, it must not stop there. In this sense, keeping everything at the local level is a double-edged sword. After all, we live in an increasingly global world in which decisions are made that have far-reaching effects, and communitarians have failed to adequately step beyond the most proximate concerns and focus on social agents larger than individuals. For example, the communitarian stance on social justice is that, "[f]irst, people have a moral responsibility to help themselves as best as they can" and, second, "responsibility lies with those closest to the person, including kin, friends, neighbors, and other community members" (Etzioni 1993: 144). Restricting social justice to the most proximate reflects the very same self-interest criticized in this and the preceding chapters. And even more importantly, while communitarians admonish individuals for forgetting their social responsibilities, organizations and institutions are just as guilty of pursuing their "self"-interests to the point where the rights of others are trampled in order to meet the goals of these organizations. Such a critique of communitarianism is especially apparent when considering the globalization of the economy.

The Global Economy: Prospects for a "Global Village"

The emphasis of communitarians on individual social responsibility does not account for the current trends of globalization. Brecher and Costello, authors of the book *Global Village or Global Pillage* (1994), point out that the globalization of the economy has concentrated economic power within the hands of a few hundred multinational corporations and organizations such as the World Bank and International Monetary Fund (IMF). In the past, American corporations were integral parts of their respective communities, providing jobs and some semblance of security. However, it has always been the case that, in order to maximize profits, it is in the interests of corporations to keep wages low. As international commerce was made easier with new technology, it was then possible for large companies to seek cheaper sources of labor. It became more profitable to set up factories in "undeveloped" or "developing" parts of the world. Not only were wages cheaper, but the companies did not have to grapple with unionization of the work force, stringent environmental laws, and so on.

Today, workers all over the world must compete in a global labor market in which those who are paid and protected the least are the first to be employed. Many corporations turned their backs on local communities in favor of the greater profits to be found when "setting up shop" internationally:

> All over the world, people are being pitted against each other to see who will offer global corporations the lowest labor, social, and environmental costs. Their jobs are being moved to places with inferior wages, lower business taxes, and more freedom to pollute. Their employers are using the threat of "foreign competition" to hold down wages, salaries, taxes, and environmental protections and to replace high-quality jobs with temporary, part-time, insecure, and low-quality jobs. Their government officials are justifying cuts in education, health, and other services as necessary to reduce business taxes in order to keep or attract jobs. (1994: 3)

The result of increased corporate mobility has been what Brecher and Costello call "downward leveling:" "a disastrous 'race to the bottom' in which conditions for all tend to fall toward those of the poorest and most desperate." In effect, the globalization of capital has created a "lose-lose" situation for the world's labor force: workers are forced to settle for the worst of working conditions, the lowest salaries and benefits, and the least protections or settle for no job at all.

In a global economy, decisions are made in the boardrooms of private, multinational corporations and organizations. The vast majority of the world's population has no say in determining global economic policies. Even national governments are often coerced by these private interests: in order to bolster their own economies, governments are willing to loosen their labor and environment protections. Moreover, when dealing with international financial institutions, such as the World Bank and IMF, or trade agreements, such as the General Agreement on Tariffs and Trade (GATT) and the North American Free Trade Agreement (NAFTA), national laws are superseded by the rules of these organizations and trade agreements. And if governments themselves are often the victims of coercion, then the democratic process is compromised in that ordinary citizens have no voice in determining the policies that affect their lives. Brecher and Costello call this process in which elites dictate the policies of the global economy, "globalization-from-above" (1994: 79).

In terms of the social location variables of proximity and distance, there is very little connection between those who make decisions and those who must live with the impact of those decisions, between the elite board members and the workers themselves. For the most part, members of the board have little or no contact with the average worker and often will never see the factory floor, especially when one considers the fact that workers and factories are spread all over the globe. Instead, board members see balance sheets and accounts. The distance, both social and spatial, is immense and the human factor is lost in between: "Numbers don't die, people do" (Keen 1991: 84). The greater the corporate or organizational hierarchy, the greater the distance between those at the top and those at the bottom and the greater the difficulty in establishing the bonds of social affinity. Consciousness, sentiment, and action are undermined at the root of their development. Moreover, when one considers the losses in environmental protections, it is possible to see the influence of temporal distance as well. With a focus on short-term gains at the expense of long-term planning, the environment upon which all the world's people depend is compromised. The future of human survival is placed at risk, but the voices of future generations cannot be heard in the present and so they elicit little or no feelings of social responsibility on the part of those making decisions.

Because national governments have been largely ineffectual in the face of organizations that have a global reach, there is often a "pervasive feeling of powerlessness in the face of unaccountable global forces" (1994: 5). Without a global reach of their own, social movements have also been outflanked by the process of globalization. While in the past there was a relatively coherent Leftist agenda working for the betterment of labor within national boundaries, today even national movements have fragmented into smaller and more specialized movements. This fragmentation of the Left is very apparent in the United States and is reflective of the primacy of narrowly defined interests over collective interests. In the past, the Left was united in its focus on labor and class issues. However, it overlooked other forms of social oppression, such as racism, sexism, and heterosexism. Thus, from the 1950s to the 1970s, the Left began to splinter among those who preferred to fight for the more specific issues that affected themselves. The result was the emergence of "identity politics" (Schwerner 1995). Blacks fought for their own civil rights, and soon women and gays and lesbians followed suit. Identity politics also gave way to single issue movements, such as the abortion and right-to-life movements, the environmental movement, animal rights movement, and so on.

This fragmentation of the Left had the initial benefit of "[broadening] the base of Left activism" (Schwerner 1995: 33). Whereas the old Left had attracted primarily the working class, these new social movements drew the support of the middle classes as well. In other words, it was "critical because it allowed for a multiplicity of voices that had been excluded from earlier leftist discourse" (1995: 44). By narrowing the scope of these social movements, it became possible to cater to the self-interests of diverse people and encourage them to take action based on those interests. On the negative side, however, self-interest as a source of motivation has now overshadowed the collective interests at stake when addressing social issues. The uniting vision of the old Left was largely abandoned: "because these movements [under the umbrella of identity politics] lacked a common vision and connection, they became isolated from each other as well as from the wider culture" (1995: 33). It is this common vision that was so central to the activism of Jason—discussed in chapter 7—and that distinguishes him from a person like Sherri, whom we also met in chapter 7 and who did not even think about the connection between poverty and hunger until she was interviewed, despite the fact that she was raised in a family with a focus on "faith, peace, and justice."

Thus, the focus on the proximate and what is perceived as "relevant"—in short, the focus on self-interest even in one's activism—while important in eliciting more widespread involvement, has robbed us of any means of effectively dealing with issues—such as globalization—that are not easily reducible to the language of self-interest. The proliferation of social issues is overwhelming and, when one includes a global perspective, the effect can be paralyzing. However, there are alternatives to the fracturing of activists into movements centered around a single identity or specialized cause and that foster a sense of common interest. As we saw in the previous section, neighborhood-based community organizing has the potential to bring diverse people with diverse interests together for a common goal. There is also much potential for similar results at the global level.

Brecher and Costello argue that activists need to globalize their efforts in much the same way that multinational corporations have done in order to adapt to a global economy. While globalization is important and unavoidable, "globalization-from-above" has proved destructive to the interests of workers and the environment. This "downward leveling" has produced a set of common interests for many movements around the world. While they acknowledge that "resistance is still highly fragmented" and that "fragmentation is easily exploited by those who would make different workforces, peoples, and communities compete with each other in the 'race to the bottom'" (1994: 84), there are also, "[n]ew transnational networks . . . arising, based on such common interests" (1994: 8). The authors describe numerous examples in which diverse interests were brought together in order to oppose or modify, for example, free trade agreements such as GATT and NAFTA. In opposing NAFTA, for example, environmentalists and trade unions—traditional opponents—were brought together by their larger common interest. Thus, while in one sense the adage of "Think globally, act locally" is quite true in that local involvement nurtures feelings of efficacy and brings neighbors together, the opposite is also true.

> Said U.S. family farm advocate Mark Ritchie, a key initiator of international small-farm networking, "We learned to reverse the old slogan, 'Think globally, act locally.' We learned you have to act globally to succeed locally—you have to go to Brussels to save your farm in Texas. It was really important for farmers in different parts of the world to see their common circumstances and to develop win/win approaches, rather than being played off against each other." (1994: 96)

In other words, it is no longer enough to *think* globally. It is important to extend one's consciousness, sentiment, *and* action beyond the limits of one's locale.

As the previous chapters indicate, developing a sense of social affinity that extends beyond one's immediate environment is assisted by drawing links between the self and others. Thus, Brecher and Costello advocate a form of "globalization-from-below" in which linking diverse interests is a central strategy in the creation of a more just world within the context of globalization: "[this strategy] requires a high level of cooperation among people who are diverse and distant and who have conflicting as well as common interests. . . . [A]t the core of [this strategy] lies the work of overcoming divisions by constructing links" (1994: 107). They advocate linking self-interest with common interests. For example, "when people in one country support the right of workers to organize and strike in other countries, they are helping others, but they are also helping themselves by ensuring that they will not have to compete with those forced to work in degraded conditions" (1994: 107–108). It is also important to link the global to the local by (1) "[clarifying] the connections between the immediate conditions people face and the global processes that are affecting them"; (2) "[linking] local struggles with global support" by resisting "downward harmonization where you are and help[ing] others resist it where they are"; and (3) "[linking] local problems to global solutions" such as international codes by which international corporations and financial institutions must abide (1994: 108–109). Brecher and Costello conclude that, "the key to moving people from political apathy to political participation is to make political participation a vehicle for improving daily life" (1994: 116–117).

While mainstream communitarianism overlooks the need for global community and corporate accountability, there are critics who advocate attention on these very concerns. Left communitarianism, for example, presents an alternative that maintains the importance of social responsibility while incorporating a global perspective. As sociologist Charles Derber points out, "[c]ommunitarianism must propose a structural politics that forthrightly addresses the economic foundations of our problems. It must, for example, challenge the system of income distribution that in recent years has promoted an extreme division of rich and poor incompatible with community. . . . Left communitarianism steps in and offers a way to wrestle capital and power away from multinational corporations and federal bureaucracies into the bosom of the community" (1995: 207; see also Derber, 1994: 111–117). While not going so far as to dispose of capitalism itself, Left communitarianism seeks to replace the free-market model, which is the current *modus operandi*, with what is called a "social market:"

> [T]he social market offers a practical communitarian alternative to the free-market model, incorporating in varying degrees and in different ways (1) a social accounting system by which . . . corporations [may] measure the human costs of their policy and to factor social costs and benefits into economic decisions; (2) accountability mechanisms to ensure that businesses are responsive to community interests; (3) distribution mechanisms that ensure a high level of equality in income and wealth; (4) social investment strategies, such as the use of pension funds to build affordable housing and promote community development; and (5) forms of economic participation and governance, such as employee ownership, that institutionalize the logic of democratic community inside business itself. (1995: 208)

By making it clear that each individual has a personal stake in the practices of a globalized economy and by empowering her through the democratization of the policy-making process within such a context, it is possible to foster the awareness that the ends of self-interest are most effectively reached when social interests are also addressed. Just as grassroots neighborhood initiatives bring diverse people together for a common cause, empowering them and giving them hope, a global economy that is shaped by the participation of workers throughout the world will promote the "upward leveling" advocated by Brecher and Costello, that is, "raising the standards of those at the bottom and thereby reducing their downward pull on everybody else. . . . [Upward leveling means] a cumulative increase in both power and well-being for the poorest and least powerful—poor and working people, women, marginalized groups, and their communities. The advancement of those at the bottom is crucial to blocking the race to the bottom" (1994: 9).

It is through this same process of giving individuals a personal stake in the globalized economy that a broad sense of social affinity will emerge. By linking self-interests with social interests, the social consciousness of individuals and their ability to empathize and role take with otherwise distant others will be expanded. Empowering individuals by giving them a voice in shaping broad economic policies will reinforce their participation. When individuals are enabled to recognize through direct, personal experience that, in order to maximize one's self-interests it is also necessary to promote social interests, the social, spatial, and temporal distances that narrow the vision of individuals will be more easily overcome. Only by linking the self and society will the idea of "neighborliness" be extended beyond those who are most proximate, and only then will a broad sense of social affinity among the world's peoples be nurtured. Without this crucial sense of social affinity, the most promising dimension of globalization—the potential for a true global "village"—will prove to be its greatest liability by keeping individuals under the thumb of corporate self-interest.

Who Is My Neighbor?

In a globalized world, it is no longer enough to think of neighbors as those who share some small locality. It is essential to extend one's social consciousness, sentiment, and action beyond the immediate and the proximate. As was noted in chapter 2, "To be modern is to face the consequences of decisions made by complete strangers while making decisions that will affect the lives of people one will never know. The scope of moral obligation—especially at a time when issues of possible nuclear war, limitations on economic growth, and ecological destruction are public concerns—seems to be without limits" (Wolfe 1989: 2–3). In a modern world such as ours, one's self-interests are often better served by addressing the social interests that also benefit one's immediate *and* distant neighbors.

Considering the fact that U.S. history is so imbued with Christian sentiments, the value of loving one's neighbor as oneself has been central in the moral development of the majority of Americans. However, as we have seen throughout this and earlier chapters, such a social value is in tension with the underlying individualism of our culture. We are being pulled in two opposite directions: toward compassionate outreach to others and toward the maximization of our own self-interests. Many Americans are aware of this tension and recognize that, overall, self-interest is winning the tug-of-war.

Among those whose stories are presented throughout the preceding chapters, a world in which everyone loved their neighbor is seen as an ideal. Ashleigh describes what such an ideal world would be like: "The world would be a better place if people loved their neighbor as themselves. You wouldn't hurt people around you because you wouldn't want yourself to be hurt. So, if everyone obeyed this idea of 'love thy neighbor as thyself,' I think that there wouldn't be as much violence, there wouldn't be as much hunger, there wouldn't be the widespread . . . whatever. It would be a lot different. The world would be a different place." Such an ideal has not yet been reached and many of those interviewed lament the fact that so few Americans seem to actually follow such a precept even though they may say they believe it. Diane also praises the ideal and, by relating it to the Planned Parenthood shooting described in the previous chapter, shows how far we are from realizing that ideal: "I think it's a beautiful and idealistic statement and if people actually lived that way, it would be a lovely world. It just kills me that there are Christians who kill people because they work in an abortion clinic. Christ wouldn't be out here shooting people. It's ironic that the ones who think they are so thoroughly devoted to God are the ones who are breaking God's rules, such as this one [of loving one's neighbor]." Patrick also recognizes that few Americans actually do love their neighbors, and presents us with his reason as to why:

I don't think that [precept] holds true anymore, to be honest. I think it's become a free-for-all in society. It's more of a "You better do it to

them before they do it to you" type of thing. This "love your neighbor"
stuff is good in theory, but it's not practiced. People like to say it. Peo-
ple like to read it. People like to hear it. However, when it comes down
to it, people are not going to practice it because if you do something like
that, you're going to get trampled in society. You're going to be taken
advantage of.

In our society, as deep as the Christian identity of many people runs, self-interest and individualism clearly have the upper hand over the value of loving one's neighbor as oneself.

The ways in which individuals interpret the maxim of "loving one's neighbor" are also revealing. While 41.7 percent of those interviewed ($N = 36$) interpret it in terms of treating others equally or in the same way one would like to be treated—in other words, as another form of the Christian maxim of "do unto others as you would have them do unto you"—the next most common interpretation (held by 16.7% of the sample) is to treat others with respect.[5] For example, Erica makes this interpretation:

I think the idea of loving your neighbor is very important. I think you
need to understand that, even though someone doesn't believe the same
things you do or doesn't have the same background, they deserve the
same respect as anyone else. I think it's just basic. People are people and
there's nothing that makes you better than anyone else, be it your skin
color or your financial situation or the world that you live in.

The word "respect" implies feelings of "esteem" or even, as is implied by Erica, "concern." However, it also means "to refrain from interfering with."[6] In other words, "I'll keep my hands off of your affairs." Such an interpretation is not surprising given the value placed on individualism in our society. Overall, Americans believe that everyone can and should be able to take care of themselves, a view that is closely tied with blaming others when they fail and land "at the bottom of the heap" (Ryan 1976).

Moreover, such a perspective is not only the purview of conservatives. Liberals, too, refrain from interfering in an almost "laissez faire" way. The most obvious example regards attitudes toward gays and lesbians, a highly controversial population within our society. Those who are tolerant but not accepting of such a "lifestyle" can be heard saying, "as long as they keep it to themselves." In other words, "your gay or lesbian identity (and especially behavior) are okay so long as we don't have to see it." What both the liberal and conservative versions of "not interfering" have in common is that they serve to distance the individual from those he or she "respects." The other is held at arm's length. The possibility for social affinity is cut off because the social distance between the two parties is maximized. The trend of interpreting "loving" one's neighbor as "respect" supports the individualism of our culture and further underscores the tension between the competing values of compassionate outreach and self-interest.

Making the issue even more complicated, as described earlier, is the increasingly global context in which Americans find themselves. We are no longer simply being challenged in terms of loving our neighbor: the very concept of "neighbor" is open for debate. In a world frequently described as a "global village," who exactly is our neighbor? When asked, only 27 percent of those interviewed interpreted "neighbor" as meaning literally "everyone," no matter how distant they are. Lloyd takes this position:

> *People too often think of neighbors in terms of proximity and knowledge of someone. To me, neighbor means someone that you're in coexistence with. It doesn't matter where they are—the fact that they're existing is enough because that idea of loving your neighbor as yourself was there before that person and is going to be there after that person. So, when that person is there, you take advantage of it and you know that they're there and that they're your neighbor regardless.*

Unlike Lloyd, the remaining 73 percent of the interview sample described our neighbor as those with whom we come into direct contact or who are proximate to ourselves,[7] reflecting our modern, global condition and our own American culture. Art explains why he thinks that most people do not include "everybody" when they conceive of their neighbor:

> *In the big picture, our neighbors should be all humans, but in the real picture it's just the opposite. When I was a kid in suburbia, I knew all my neighbors and I could go in their house and have a glass of Kool Aid if my mother wasn't home or something. Now it seems like people don't know those who live next door. We're a society of strangers. Everybody's so busy, and there's so much mobility and fear. People may join clubs, but if a neighbor living next door doesn't share any of their interests, then they don't have anything to do with him. In the old days, even though my father might have absolutely nothing in common with the neighbor and even if he privately thought the neighbor was sort of a dummy, he would still make an effort to talk to him across the fence periodically simply because he did live next door and that was how you*

*were supposed to conduct yourself. You were supposed to have some rap-
port with your neighbors in the old days. Now, if somebody's not in
your little circle of associates of common interest, then you don't even
say "hi" to him.*

Art expresses the same regret at the loss of "neighborliness" as Ashleigh and
Diane. However, he also speculates as to why this has occurred. With
modernity and the increased mobility of our global world, our culture has
changed in such a way that self-interest takes precedence over the social
standards of "the old days" and we restrict the term "neighbor" to those
who are in our own "little circle."

Silva is one of the majority who views the concept of neighbor only
in terms of those with whom we come into direct contact: "Our neighbor
is the person we walk beside when we walk down the street. Our neighbor is the person who lives next door. Our neighbor is the person we talk
to on an elevator. Our neighbor is that classmate that's beside us. It's everyone around us." The characteristic that distinguishes those like Silva is that
they perceive as neighbors only those who fall within their own life sphere,
as if their lives are *the* social epicenter.

Such a point of view is reminiscent of the belief that the sun revolved
around the earth. The self and its interests are first and foremost in the
mind. While self-interest only forms the subtext of the quote by Silva,
Veronica makes this focus on the self explicit:

*I don't know about that statement [of loving our neighbors as ourselves]
just because you can't love someone equally. You can't treat them equally.
You have to have better standards for yourself. We're in a society where
you have to be one up on everybody else. That's just how it is. It should-
n't be that way, but it is. So, if you're going to "love thy neighbor as you
love thyself," then you're just going to be stuck and you're not going to
get anywhere and you're not going to have a good life for yourself. I think
you do have to really try to treat people equally, but you also need to
know your own value. I don't think it means treating them equal to
yourself. I think it means treating them like you treat everybody else.*

While Veronica believes we should treat everyone else equally, her individual self is clearly higher on her hierarchy. Individualism has the "edge" over
social compassion.

However, an individual does not have to sacrifice himself or herself
for the common good in order to live a moral life. It is possible to strike a
balance between the individual and society. Achieving such balance begins

when the individual is able to keep his or her own interests in mind while *simultaneously* stepping outside of those parameters to perceive the interests of others. For example, of those who first described "everyone" as their neighbor, and who later qualified their answer by limiting who "everyone" was, two individuals specified that their own community came first. Kesia takes such a perspective when she says that her neighbors include "just anyone, in an overall sense: boy, girl, black, white. It doesn't matter. But in the more narrow-minded sense, I'd be more apt to help the people of my own community before I go to someone else's community and help them. That's just a given." Kesia does not think in terms of self-interest so much as community interest when it comes to defining her neighbor. She has begun stepping outside the bounds of her own life sphere.

Three more of those who qualified their initial answer of "everyone" gave priority to those who are "less fortunate." Martin also steps outside of his self-interest by defining our neighbor as, first and foremost, those who are in need: "Who our neighbor is depends on what sense. In the general sense, everybody is our neighbor. But in the hunger sense, whoever is on the 'other side.' Since I'm on this side of hunger and I'm not hungry right now, my neighbors are those on the other side. On the race issue, it would be people on the other side of the color line. Or the person with AIDS on the AIDS issue." Both Martin and Kesia, while still focusing on their individual selves, manage to devote some of their attention beyond their own, personal interests.

Those who are most successful at achieving balance between their views of their neighbor as being those most proximate on the one hand, and including everyone on the other, are able to appreciate the interconnectedness of their own lives with the lives of other people. While such interconnectedness is most obvious in one's closest and most proximate relationships, these individuals also recognize that their lives are a part of a much larger picture in which the lives of everyone are interconnected. Jason describes this quality in more concrete terms:

> *Loving your neighbor begins with your personal interactions, your individual relationships with people—being a kind person. . . . Then there's the question of how you are with the macro stuff. How do you support policies which love our neighbors? You come into contact with the whole rest of the country when you vote. There's a contract on America and people are voting for policies that are going to make people go hungry. People need to think at this policy level too.*

Almost as an afterthought, Jason adds, "You've got to love yourself, too." In the end, Jason keeps three different levels in mind when responding to the precept of loving one's neighbor as oneself: he directs his love toward himself, toward those in his immediate relationships, and toward those who are more abstractly interconnected with his own life. Given what Jason says here and what he has said in chapter 7, it is clear that the proximity variables associated with social location are minimized by his playing an *active role* in exercising his social affinity toward others.

Lloyd is also able to transcend the abstract qualities of thinking of one's neighbor as "everybody," no matter what the social, spatial, or temporal distance. In thinking about the relationship between the self and one's neighbor, he says,

> *Someone has to have a very special nature whereby they* know *themselves and are at* peace *with themselves to such an extent that they are able to give that pure self-interest up so that someone else can have the same thing. It can reach a point where I don't have to know you to do this for you. I don't even have to have anything but the most basic knowledge about what's going on. I don't even have to have the experience. I don't even have to feel it. I just have to be connected in some way to be able to do that. It could even reach a point where I would give up my life or what I have for someone whom I don't even know. But it has to start with me in order for me to connect with someone else and in order for someone to connect with yet another person and for these connections to just hit these points all over the world.*

While he is adamant about the importance of the self in the process of establishing social affinity with others, Lloyd has moved well beyond self-interest in his views on loving one's neighbor and describes the more spiritual dimension of recognizing the interconnectedness of all the world's people. At a more basic level, he seems to take the perspective of the saying that no one is an "island"—a value that is in direct opposition to the individualism of our culture. For Lloyd and Jason, the individual is one important element in a much larger whole known as society.

It is individuals like these and all those who have broken the boundaries between themselves and others—particularly the socially referenced—who have overcome the allure of self-interest and the relevance of proximity. In other words, it is important to note that the relevance of self-interest and one's social location is not absolute in their effect because they are constructed and interpreted through our cultural lens of individualism.

As individuals, we have the capability to act as agents, making choices and decisions that necessarily alter any strict deterministic models of behavior. It is possible for an individual to transcend the "constraints" of spatial, temporal, and social distance. Jean Bethke Elshtain regards this ability to transcend one's interests and social location as an integral part of citizenship: "I can't get to know every one of over 200 million fellow citizens. But I can imagine certain things about how some people are compelled to live. And I can care about it, even though I don't know them, I don't deal with them face to face. To the extent we cut ourselves off from that empathic ability, we cut ourselves off from certain aspects of citizenship" (Snell 1995: 71).

However, the ability to transcend the proximity and distance variables of social location may be either positive or negative. In the positive sense, individuals may transcend the *distance* between self and an "other." Such transcendence was especially apparent in the discussion of empathy and role-taking in chapter 6. Consider as an additional example the person who has identified with the suffering of starving children on another continent, even though he has never seen or spoken with such a child for himself but has only heard of the condition of these children. He has overcome both the spatial and social distance that serve to separate him from these children. The distance between "one" and an "other" is transcended.

Recalling that it is possible to manufacture social distance, there is also a negative case to such transcendence. This individual capacity was most obvious in the construction of social consciousness—especially in the idea of filtering out information—discussed in chapter 5. We also saw, in the previous chapter, how Curtis distanced himself from the experiences of gay men and lesbians by dehumanizing them. In that instance, he overcame the proximity—the similarity between his experiences with discrimination and theirs—between himself and this population of "others." Thus, transcending one's social location can work both ways. However, it is in part this ability to transcend distance and proximity that makes us human.

Herein lies the promise for realizing a sense of community within a global context: individuals may step outside of the constraints placed upon them by their culture, society, and group memberships and act as free agents. By doing so, they have become "fully human" in the same sense described by Eisenberg in the opening quote of this chapter. In short, it is through the collective efforts of those who take an active role in society that we may realize the *virtues* of a "global village" as well as its benefits—a world in which neighbors do love one another as they love themselves. Given this individual ability to overcome distance and even proximity, a strictly deterministic model of social affinity in which individuals are mere automatons reacting to social forces beyond their control is inappropriate. While self-interest and one's social location are compelling in their influence, the social world is not so cut-and-dried as some analysts might hope. In fact, it is human transcendence more than human predictability that holds the interest of the researcher and gives hope to the activist.

The Empirical Approach
to Social Affinity

Unique opportunities and challenges were posed in researching social affinity. In the first place, the empirical approach to studying this topic allowed for the opportunity to actually mimic the theory in my data collection. Thus, there is an interesting mirroring effect between the theory and the methods used. This is the topic of the first section of this Appendix. Moreover, in order to fully explore social affinity, it was necessary to pay attention not only to social participation, but to nonparticipation as well. And yet, those who do not participate in the social world outside the boundaries of their immediate lives are also unlikely to take part in social research. Methodologically, this posed an interesting problem. In the second part of the Appendix, I present my strategy for attracting the noninvolved as well as the results of this strategy. Throughout the Appendix, I have utilized extensive endnotes. For those with a strong methodological inclination, the vast majority of these notes present the details of the data collection and analysis.

Theoretical and Methodological Mirroring

The methodological approach to social affinity presents a fascinating parallel with some of its most basic tenets. It is clear that variations in social proximity and distance play a major role in the emergence of affinity within the individual and, as a researcher, I was highly attuned to the ways in which the methods of data collection were reflective of this dynamic. In other words, my methodological approach mirrored the differences between social distance and social proximity and the resulting impact on the emergence of social affinity. While social scientists argue that the researcher's methodological approach should arise naturally from the purpose of the study and its research questions, in very few instances is this methodological approach actually reflective of the theoretical perspective from which it is supposed to emerge.

In studying this topic, I relied primarily on two sources of data: a survey followed by a series of semistructured intensive interviews.[1] The data collection was guided by several interrelated research questions: What is it that gives a person an affinity toward those experiencing a given situation versus a person who has a distinct lack of such an affinity and may even be labeled "apathetic?" In other words, what is it about a person's life situation and experience that places him or her at a specific point along the continuum between apathy and social affinity? Related to this, what are the conditions that promote or hinder the development of social affinity? And finally, what does it mean to have an affinity for others and how is such an affinity experienced?

The first stage of the data collection involved the distribution of a survey questionnaire to a purposive sample[2] of students and nonstudents.[3] Four-hundred twenty-six people responded to the survey.[4] The surveys included detailed demographic data, an empathy scale,[5] and questions on three issues of social concern: hunger, AIDS, and the issue the respondent identified as being most important.[6] The purpose of this primarily quantitative method of data collection was not for conducting an elaborate and complicated statistical analysis for the purpose of generalization to the entire population of the United States so much as it was used as a filter for obtaining a purposive sample of interviewees. However, to the respondents, it still exhibited all the characteristics of a traditional survey.

While entering the data from these surveys, it struck me that it mirrored the impact of social distancing on the development of social affinity. In the context of a survey that is not administered *by the researcher* in a face-to-face setting, anonymity—a signifier of social distance—is maintained. There is no personal contact between the researcher and the respondents, and so their personhood has no relevance to the data collected except insofar as it is hinted at by the answers to the questions themselves. However, since most of the possible responses to survey questions are standardized, most of that which is unique to the individual is wiped out. Survey respondents are highly aware of this depersonalization. The lack of personalization can be both beneficial and detrimental in terms of self-expression.

On the positive side, depersonalization can inspire greater self-confidence: it frees the respondents to "say" things about themselves that they might not have been willing to bring up on their own in a face-to-face encounter with a complete stranger or even with someone who already knew them. This is particularly true when it comes to the most personal or controversial topics. Sexual behavior is the most obvious example. Our cultural norms have encouraged reticence when discussing such matters. Given these norms, anonymity is highly liberating. Consider the examples of the priest and the bartender who hear the "confessions" of individuals struggling with sexual issues. In the traditional church, the possibility of a nameless and faceless confession to a priest and the added benefit of the silence of the confessional have allowed individuals to express their innermost secrets. While not all those seeking absolution for their sins may take advantage of the anonymity of the confessional, the freedom of choice is enhanced when compared with environments that are not conducive to such anonymity. The same dynamics are at play with the bartender in a city far distant from one's home. While the bartender may not be nameless and faceless, there is some assurance that, if one chooses, one need not ever see this person again. Thus, in the case of the priest, the bartender, and the social scientist, the promise of anonymity allows greater freedom in self-expression. In this way, surveys have the distinct advantage of eliciting information that might not otherwise be obtainable.

On the other hand, depersonalization has a negative side. Some respondents exhibit apparent dissatisfaction with the nature of such a cold relationship. The fact that surveys rely primarily upon closed-ended questions with only a limited number of possible choices means that the respondents must force their highly individual experience into a radically generalized response category. From this perspective, the use of a survey is highly constraining upon the respondents. They are no longer free to express the unique nuances of their situation. Thus, the social distance that may be liberating in one instance also confines the respondents within the parameters of a highly structured question. As a result, those respondents most adamant about the uniqueness of their experience tended to rebel against the constraints placed upon them.

Nearly a quarter[7] of the respondents broke out of the confines of the questions and wrote in the margins of the survey, explaining their responses or lack of response to various questions. These unsolicited comments represented an attempt on the part of the respondents to assert their identity and unique circumstance. These "marginal comments" took several forms: (1) an explanation or justification for a particular response, (2) modifying a question, (3) expressing uncertainty with regard to a question or its answer, (4) "X"ing out a question altogether, and (5) general comments and reflections.

There were many occasions where respondents would explain the response they gave and the circumstances that made it true *for them*, thus claiming a degree of uniqueness. One respondent marked both "yes" and "no" when responding to the question as to whether hunger affected her own life. She marked "yes" because it was true "in the sense that it really worries me." She marked "no" because, as she noted, "I'm not suffering from hunger myself." Another respondent explained why her attitude toward the hungry had changed for the worse when she noted that the ". . . food and money donations never seem to go where they're supposed to!" In many instances of this form of marginal commentary, the respondents justified the answer they gave. However, it was also interesting to note that in no instance did respondents feel the need to justify their prosocial behavior. Instead, they justified actions or inactions that might be looked down upon by others. For example, after indicating that she did not take part in a fund-raiser nor give a donation to an organization addressing hunger, one respondent justified her answer by explaining that this was "Not because I didn't want to. I'm disabled and on a fixed income right now." In another instance, a respondent answered "No" to whether she has ever taken part in a fund-raising event for an organization addressing hunger, and then explained why when she said, "I was away all year, but have done so in years past." In some instances, the respondent actually qualified the choice made, specifying circumstances in which the response would or would not hold true. While she noted that she was very sympathetic toward persons with AIDS, one respondent qualified her answer by indicating that her sympathy was for children. In a similar vein, another respondent noted that she was "somewhat unsympathetic" in her current attitude toward persons with AIDS and asked, "How did they get it?"

Some respondents modified the questions themselves, such as in adding an additional choice. These changes in the question were usually meant to address the special circumstances or attitudes of the respondent. For example, instead of indicating whether her attitude toward the hungry had changed in a positive way or a negative way, one respondent wrote in "Both" and explained why: "I am more upset by the reality of it, but I am offended by beggars on the street more than I used to be." Another respondent, while checking off "Working Class" with regard to his class background, at the same time crossed out all of the choices to this question and wrote "Happy" as his option in the margin. As a third example, when answering to the question "Have you been active in doing something about this issue?", yet another respondent modified the "No" response—which she checked—so that it would read "Not Yet! . . ." In some instances, respondents modified a question—usually one in which they were asked to list their top three issues—by adding an extra space for a fourth issue, presumably because of the difficulty in listing only three. For example, after listing "Crime," "Homelessness," and "Cultural/Racial Tensions" as her top three issues that will affect future generations, one respondent added a line for a fourth response: "AIDS & Cancer."

There were some instances where the respondent did not understand a question or the directions for responding to it. Oftentimes, this form of self-expression took the form of just a question mark drawn in the margin. In other instances, the respondent actually wrote out his or her question. For example, after scratching out all the possible responses to the statement "Seeing people with AIDS on TV upsets me," one respondent says, "I do not understand the question; it upsets me to know people are dying needlessly. It does not upset me to see AIDS activists protesting." Another respondent, when asked to list the top three responses to the question "Who would you say is affected by hunger?", put a question mark and said, "I don't get this question. I mean, the people who are hungry, obviously?!"[8]

There were a few respondents who refused to answer a question altogether. This was more than just skipping the question such that it would be coded as missing data. Instead, the question itself was "X"ed out—in which case it is difficult to interpret the reason for it—or an explanation for a nonresponse was given. For example, one respondent "X"ed out several questions, including the one about his sexual orientation—which may imply that he objects to the question, that he does not know the answer, or that he objects to categorizing something which he may perceive as ephemeral. He also "X"ed out a question indicating income level—again the reason is unclear. In several instances, respondents refused to indicate their racial background. At the same time, they made sure it was known they were leaving it blank on purpose by writing something such as "N/A [Not Applicable]" or "I never answer this question!"

Finally, some respondents merely offered general commentary in response to a closed-ended question, reflecting on their personal experiences and values. For example, one woman listed "prejudice/nonequality" as the top social issue affecting her life. In the margin, she notes that, "Since my partner is a woman, our marriage will not be recognized by the state or country; we do not get equal rights—insurance benefits, tax breaks, or even get to be considered family by hospitals, etc." As an interesting contrast, another woman not only checked the "straight" category when asked about her sexual orientation, she actually starred it and, drawing arrows to the "Bisexual" and "Gay or Lesbian" categories, said "Not right!!! I'm totally against them." These comments present a personal position on a highly controversial issue.

Additional marginal comments also reflected on issues that, while not necessarily a topic of heated controversy, are open to a wide variety of viewpoints. After indicating that "everyone" is affected by hunger as all three of her top choices, one respondent explained why: "When you walk around and see people with signs who will work for food, it makes you upset!" Many people agree with her and many do not. On the other hand, another respondent expressed strong agreement with the statement, "Seeing people who are hungry on TV upsets me." She then noted that "Those commercials (the Sally Struthers ones) tend to desensitize me," a reaction many people may experience and yet be unwilling to admit.

Marginal commentary, such as the examples just presented, reflect the attempt of the survey respondents to step outside the constraints of the question format in order to express their individuality in some way. In making these comments, the respondents were reacting against the impersonal nature of the survey method of gathering data and clamoring for the freedom of self-expression. Even so, for the researcher who is sifting through these surveys, it is difficult to say that he or she *knows* the respondent. Any affinity that the researcher might otherwise feel for a particular respondent has been hindered in its development by the constraints of the survey method. However, when respondents break through those constraints, faint glimmerings of the person behind the questionnaire may be detected so long as the researcher is paying attention them.[9] Thus, surveys are quite paradoxical in that they simultaneously hinder and promote this freedom of self-expression. Interestingly, most of the examples of marginal commentary given were written by women. Indeed, women were much more likely to offer such commentary than were men.[10] At the same time, those individuals who stepped outside the constraints of the survey were also much more likely to volunteer for an interview,[11] leading to the idea that the quality of being willing to express one's own opinions and circumstances is also a quality that encourages participation and voluntarism.

As already noted, the surveys were used to screen interviewees. At the end of the survey, I asked for interview volunteers. Those who volunteered numbered 148, constituting 35 percent of the sample.[12] This provided a sufficient pool for purposive sampling. Thirty-six individuals were then interviewed with regard to their personal backgrounds, experiences, and values as well as the issues of hunger, AIDS, and the issue they felt was most important. An attempt was made to balance the sample in terms of gender[13] and to include as many minorities as possible.[14] However, the major focus with regard to the purposive sampling was to balance those interviewed in terms of their activism or inactivity with regard to each of the three social issues. In other words, approximately half of those interviewed were active with regard to hunger and half were not; half were active with regard to AIDS an half were not; and half were active with regard to the issue of their choice while half were not.[15] In addition, when it came to the issue of most importance to the respondents, every attempt was made in selecting interviewees to make these issues as varied as possible. Thus, these issues included everything from violence and the breakdown of the family to racism and education.[16]

As the central source of data, these interviews provided a welcome contrast to the impersonal nature of the quantitative data. In situations where social proximity is paramount, personal identity is important and relevant to the situation (Berger, Berger, and Kellner 1973). The intensive interviews reflected this personalization. However, paralleling the depersonalization of survey methods, the more personal nature of intensive interviews is also beneficial and—ironically—detrimental to self-expression.

The unique experiences, histories, and stories of the interviewees were the focus of this aspect of the methodological approach. No longer was it possible for there to be pure anonymity. I knew their name and they knew mine. We shook hands, sat face-to-face, and were able to "size each other up." Because anonymity was no longer possible, confidentiality was assured. In fact, because some of what was said was so deeply personal, I doubt that such openness could have been achieved without such assurance. In contrast with the surveys, explanations for particular responses formed the heart—the substance—of this particular mode of data collection. Thus, the unique, the individual, and the personal all characterized this second stage of the research process and represented a high degree of social proximity. I felt a close bond with each of those I interviewed. Even if I disagreed with their opinions, I came to appreciate their perspective and value their personhood.

This is especially interesting when one considers that those I interviewed and with whom I achieved a degree of closeness were, at first, "anonymous" individuals who had filled out my survey. It is not that I did not know their names; however, I did not know who they were as people. There were a number of times when I was surprised by the person I interviewed because of the lack of pertinent information in the survey. For example, my initial impression of Melissa Devlin, a woman whose top issue was animal rights, was highly distorted by the fact that she listed this issue first. In my mind's eye, all of the stereotypes concerning animals rights activism (e.g., paint and fur coats) and activists (e.g., crunchy granola types), I am afraid to say, created an image that was a far cry from the reality of her own unique views. Another time, there was a woman—Joann Mansfield—whose appearance surprised me because she listed "Hispanic" as her race and yet looked like any other white student on campus; this impression was formed *despite* the fact that I look just as white as others and yet I too list "Hispanic" as my race. In another instance, I knew from looking at Julius Gambarini's survey that he was a conservative. It became apparent in the course of the interview that he and I disagree with one another on a number of issues. However, because I was interviewing him and was "forced" to sit and listen rather than argue, I learned that we actually hope for many of the same goals for society. It is just that we approach those goals differently. Thus, the process of interviewing those who had previously been unknown to me proved to be one of constant surprise and discovery. For me, it was quite an exciting process.

Yet the personal nature of the face-to-face interview can also be detrimental to some forms of self-expression. The anonymity of the survey allowed individuals to bring up information about themselves that they might not share with others on a regular basis—or ever. On the other hand, the interview setting, while prompting some degree of self-revelation, is bound to curtail the expression of some of the most personal dimensions of the self. This is due to two factors. In the first place, the respondent may not be comfortable in revealing some aspects of their lives to someone they have just met, no matter how personal the context. Unfortunately, being the researcher myself, I am not privy to any examples of such self-censorship. Secondly, the researcher himself or herself may not be comfortable in raising particular questions. For example, I tended to avoid discussing sex in the interview but was not shy about asking questions on this topic in the survey.[17] On the other hand, whereas the strict parameters of the survey and the clearly defined questions within it inhibited the respondents from expressing their individuality, the context of the intensive interviews allowed for the exploration of even the finest details.

Moreover, it allowed the freedom to bring up topics, which, while related, were not in the original game plan. In fact, some of these "tangents" proved to be invaluable to the research.

Thus far, I have been referring to the personalizing and depersonalizing nature of data collection. When it comes to data *analysis,* there is a different story.[18] Analysis of even qualitative intensive interviews is by its very nature an attempt to generalize at least as far as the sample.[19] Thus, the individuality of each case is wiped out in the analysis process in an attempt to come up with a single, coherent "explanation" of the behavior of all the research participants as a group—an explanation that applies to all cases regardless of their unique circumstances. Thus, the process of data analysis—for both quantitative and qualitative data—takes the path of social distance; and for those who place high importance on objectivity, this actually takes the form of conscious distanc*ing.* Because of this quality of social distance, I think we as researchers and consumers of research need to be careful. This is one reason for the increasingly strict nature of research ethics. Otherwise, there is the possibility of ethically suspect research in which "the ends justify the means" (i.e., there is so much emphasis on the data collected that the short-term *and* long-term well-being of the participants is overlooked).[20] But even the most ethical research—in terms of the letter of the law—can be morally suspect. While the actual dehumanization of research participants is no longer possible when following the guidelines for ethical research, the "wrenching" of general theories from individual experiences can prove to be hazardous to all involved. This is especially apparent in research that has direct or even indirect policy implications or is used for ethically suspect purposes.

All of this lends more value to the qualitative tradition of presenting individual and unique examples in support of general theoretical statements. This form of data presentation puts the personhood of those studied back into the results obtained. Readers are thus able to "see" and understand the perspectives of the people behind the theory and are able to appreciate both the uniqueness and the generality contained in what they have to say. The research has thus been "humanized." This is why I not only used extensive quotations but also gave each interviewee a pseudonym and presented narratives in which it is easier for the reader to get to know them in depth.

As noted, social scientists have argued that one's methodological approach should arise naturally out of the theoretical perspective taken. By combining both quantitative and qualitative data, the former noted for its anonymity and depersonalization—social distance—and the latter known for its humanizing tendencies—social proximity—this methodological approach not only arises out of the theory, but actually *mirrors* it. I developed actual *relationships* with those I interviewed and my affinity with them was high. I felt *responsible* for the way in which each of them was portrayed in my analysis. With the surveys, I could be much more objective and discriminating. I did not feel a twinge of guilt when I calculated averages, knowing that they were not representative of any one person. My sole concern was with what these averages represented overall. In this way, accountability is diminished, raising all sorts of ethical questions with regard to research that is so depersonalizing.

By using both a quantitative and a qualitative approach, I was able to balance the depersonalizing and the personalizing effects of data collection, thus strengthening the research overall. Such balance is very important. In a society where polls and statistics pull so much weight, we need to remember the abstracting, alienating, depersonalizing nature of these numbers. This is why, and I applaud the tendency, in major policy decisions, major interest groups attempt to boost their facts and figures with personal stories. For example, statistics on AIDS are rather formidable and convincing. However, as discussed in chapter 5, there are many conflicting values caught up in this issue, values that may get in the way of beneficial social policy proposals. That is why the major source of federal funding for AIDS was named after Ryan White—a child, an innocent. Ryan's personal story was well publicized and followed. He was someone with whom the vast majority of the population could identify and sympathize. His name lent a rather technical, abstract, and impersonal piece of legislation a personal and human aura. Without this personal touch, the controversy over AIDS would have split public and legislative support, arguably preventing its passage. Thus, it is very important not to lose sight of the human side of empirical data, whether quantitative or qualitative. By including both forms of data, it is possible to achieve a balance between social scientific rigor and the human dimension underlying the "results."

Attracting the Noninvolved

Social activism presents an ideal forum for studying social affinity. However, in looking at activism, social scientists tend to focus more on the activists. This comes at a time when the activists themselves decry the dearth of people willing to remove their heads from the sand and actually participate in society rather than coast through life assuming that *someone* out there will get things done. For this research, it was deemed just as important to consider *noninvolvement* in studying social affinity as it was to consider *involvement* in civil society: Why are people *not* involved? At the same time, this presented an interesting dilemma: how does the researcher attract the participation of people who are already not participating in the society beyond the tight borders of their personal lives? Given that self-selection biases affect even the best attempts at randomized sampling—resulting in a sample of people who, by their very participation in the study, were more likely to volunteer their time in other forums as well—it became important to include those individuals who might not otherwise select themselves for inclusion in a study in the first place.

The solution to this problem, however, was immediately apparent when pretesting the survey and intensive interviews. As already noted, the surveys were distributed through purposive sampling utilizing a "network-convenience" approach in a number of different venues. The pretesting of the survey was conducted in the same manner. One-hundred twenty-three surveys were distributed and forty-three were returned, giving an initial pretest return rate of 35 percent. However, the return rate was dramatically different for those surveys distributed in a class where extra credit points were offered for participating in the study and/or where some class time was devoted to filling out the survey. In this instance, the return rate was over 80 percent,[21] a significant difference. It was thus apparent that the students needed some kind of incentive to fill it out—which may be understandable given the length of the survey: eighteen pages.

The point was further underscored by a story that one of the pretest interviewees told me after his interview. Garrett Gilmore mentioned that his roommates had asked him on his way out the door where he was going. He told them that he was going to be interviewed and so they asked him whether he would be getting anything out of it. When he mentioned that he was (interviewees were given two free movie passes for their participation), they thought that was great. The unstated implication was that they would not have bothered otherwise. Garrett said that he would have done the interview anyway, but that the incentive was a nice bonus. Since the people who would be most likely to participate without incentive would probably also be the ones who were already concerned with social issues, I needed a way to attract people like Garrett's roommates—those who would not otherwise participate in the study. With this in mind, offering an incentive would be like casting a wider net, making participation more appealing for this group of people.[22]

Given that not all of my survey contacts were in a position to offer incentives for participation, such as extra credit, I decided to offer incentives to *everyone* who participated in the study. The decision was made to hold a raffle. For every survey returned, the respondent would be entered into a raffle with three prizes: one $50 and two $25 gift certificates from a music store. In addition, all of those who were interviewed would continue to receive two free movie passes. This information was included on the cover letter and the raffle ticket was included with the informed consent form.[23] The end result was a survey return rate of 47 percent.[24] Thirty-five percent of those who filled out the survey also volunteered for an interview.[25] Offering the raffle and movie passes was successful in raising the response rate, effectively casting a wider net. As intended, this wider net caught those who were not involved as well as the involved. For example, 57 percent[26] of the respondents fell into the categories of low or no activity with regard to the hunger issue—77 percent[27] with regard to the AIDS issue and 55 percent[28] with regard to the issue of their choice.[29] On the other hand, 43 percent of the respondents exhibited moderate to high activity with regard to hunger—23 percent and 45 percent for AIDS and the issue of their choice, respectively. Thus, overall, the noninvolved were just as likely to participate in the study as were the involved, giving the sample a good and necessary balance between these populations.[30]

Not surprisingly, the return rate varied for the different contacts. The variables accounting for these variations included (1) whether it was a student or a nonstudent population and (2) whether—for students—there was the added incentive of extra credit. Interestingly, the social context of the distribution had little impact, suggesting that use of the "network-convenience" method of purposive sampling was not problematic. Let's consider each of these points in turn.

The return rate for those surveys distributed to the nonstudent population was also high, although not quite as high as for students. Again, the overall return rate was 47 percent. The return rate for nonstudents was 40 percent.[31] Obviously, this population did not receive extra credit. However, they were still included in the raffle and were given movie passes when interviewed. Thus, given that the pretest return rate—for which there was no raffle—was 35 percent, this incentive also had a positive effect on the return rate for nonstudents. Even so, the added incentive of extra credit—since grades are often in the forefront of student's minds, at least in the classroom setting—had the power to raise the return rate in those instances where extra credit was offered to 69 percent,[32] the highest overall rate for any group.

Thus, for those students given the survey in the classroom, there was a significant difference in the return rates for those students who were offered extra credit and those who were not. The average return rate (ARR) for students in the classroom setting was 62 percent.[33] However, for those surveys that were distributed to students who were not offered extra credit, there was only a 24 percent ARR[34]—a significantly lower percentage than the rate of 69 percent for students overall or the 40 percent ARR for nonstudents. Moreover, the range of return rates for those students not offered extra credit extended *up to* 44.0 percent,[35] while for those who were offered extra credit, the range *started* at 44.19 percent and extended upwards from there. In other words, students were the population least likely to fill out a survey unless they were given the survey in the classroom setting and offered extra credit.

Only one of my survey contacts achieved a 100 percent return rate. He distributed his surveys in two different classes. One was an Introduction to Sociology course and the other was a methods course in psychology. He did not teach either of these courses. Instead, the professors teaching these courses gave him permission to distribute the surveys in their classes and gave him class time in which to distribute and explain the surveys. They even allowed the students to complete the surveys during class while the contact waited for them. In addition, at least one of these professors asked that my contact relate the administration of the survey to what was being covered in the class. Thus, the context was entirely conducive to achieving a high return rate. The students had nothing to lose by returning the surveys—not even their personal time. In fact, considering that they were entered in a raffle for their participation, they had everything to gain.

This example would seem to indicate that the social setting in which surveys are distributed has an enormous impact on the return rates. However, the assumption is misleading. For example, when one compares those students who received the survey within the context of the classroom—62 percent ARR—versus those who received it outside of that setting—24 percent ARR,[36] it seems that the structured nature of the classroom setting has a tremendous impact. Based on this conclusion, one might hypothesize that this effect may be due to the fact that the surveys were distributed in the classroom by a teacher—an authority figure. Outside the classroom, the surveys were distributed by other students.

Again, this conclusion is misleading because, if one compares the ARR for those students who received the survey outside the classroom with those students who received the survey in the classroom but with no offer of extra credit, there is no difference. The average return rate in *both* cases is 24 percent. Thus, when using a "network-convenience" method of sampling, the variety of distribution contexts has little, if any, impact on the return rates. Instead, the primary factor was the incentive offered for participation. The more incentives that were offered, the higher the return rate was likely to be, particularly for students.

This finding suggests that in our society, we are motivated in our actions by what we can "get out of it"—a strong indicator of the individualistic ethic that permeates our culture. Interestingly, as indicated by the ARRs for students who did not receive extra credit (23.77%, $N = 547$) versus non-students (39.60%, $N = 101$), this phenomenon seems slightly stronger for students. When considering that students also tend to be younger—the average age was twenty years,[37] compared with thirty-two years for nonstudents[38]—several possible factors come to mind. First of all, the individualism in our culture may be stronger with the college-age population, lending credence to the idea of the "me generation." Secondly, a stronger sense of individualism may be more a function of age, maturity, and moral development than of one's generation. Lastly, this quality may arise out of student culture. While it is not possible to prove or disprove these possible explanations with the data gathered for this study, they do make interesting hypotheses for further research. Given that individualism and self-interest are shown to have a major impact on the emergence of social affinity, such research will further illuminate the topic.

Beyond the question of varying degrees of individualism, the fact that incentives are necessary for increasing participation has tremendous implications. Even when taking into account the fact that filling out a survey or being interviewed for a study is quite different from getting involved in social issues, research participation is still a form of *participation* in the social world outside of the confines of one's own life space. If incentives are needed in order to increase participation, then those organizations presenting opportunities for such participation would do well to make incentives available. Those who already participate without such offers would in all likelihood continue their work and in many cases would probably not even pursue the incentives. On the other hand, those who, while not unwilling to participate, do need an extra push to get them going, may be drawn toward participation. Of course, one—and usually this is one who freely participates already—may lament the idea that it takes such incentives to get many people on their feet. However, given that it will take time to temper extreme forms of individualism—assuming anyone is working toward that end—it is more effective to work *with* the culture rather than against it. In fact, as this study suggests, getting people involved for whatever reason—incentive or not—is likely to work against that very individualism that makes incentives beneficial in the first place. As discussed in chapter 7, once people get involved, they come to realize that participation *in itself* is highly rewarding and are likely to continue their involvement and grow from the experience.[39] In this way, they experience the internal transformation so central to the development of social affinity. As more and more people are transformed in their orientation toward life, the culture of individualism will be challenged by a value system that recognizes not only the rights of individuals but also their social responsibilities.

Transcript of a Commercial for the Christian Children's Fund

The two voices in this commercial are a speaker who appears on the TV screen and a narrator who is never seen—the viewer only hears his voice. The commercial begins with the speaker who has a serious look on his face. In the background, there are scattered children, standing in what appears to be a village, looking at the camera. The image is in color. The speaker is a white man who is balding and who has white hair and beard. The children all have black, straight hair and darker skin.

SPEAKER: Before nightfall, 40,000 children will *die* from hunger and disease. Fifty-five will die before I finish talking.

At this point, ominous music begins and the image changes to black and white. A series of still photographs are shown. The photographs show children in a poverty-stricken environment. The first one looks close to starving. He is lying on his side in an almost fetal position, ribs showing, and his arms are quite thin. This photo remains on the screen for a couple of seconds. Several of the pictured children are crying. All are nonwhite. One photo shows a child and an adult together. The last photo is of a girl with dirt on her face and nose. Her hair is messy. This photo remains on the screen several seconds longer than that of the other children, including the photo of the first child.

NARRATOR: They're dying because—to most of us—they're nameless, faceless masses, too numerous to help. But they *each* have a name and they *can* be helped, one by one. If you can set aside seventy cents a day, twenty-one dollars a month [the words "70¢ a day" and $21 dollar a month" flash consecutively on a black screen as these words are spoken], then please call this number and sponsor a child like María [at this point the phone number—1-800-493-9900— is displayed over the black-and-white picture of a girl who is smiling]. María might be a statistic now [a smaller photo of a white woman is displayed to one side of the screen] if it weren't for Angela Toath, a homemaker from Michigan.

The image on the screen reverts to color and shows the speaker and the little girl beside him. She smiles shyly and glances out of the corners of her eyes in a self-conscious manner. The speaker is now smiling and he periodically looks away from the camera and toward the girl. Children are walking across the background, entering a building. It appears that they are going to school since they are wearing backpacks. The music has changed to a delicate melody played on a piano, almost like a music-box.

SPEAKER: Before Angela sponsored María through Christian Children's Fund, the situation was very bad. María and her mother were alone and frightened. María's father had been kidnapped [close-up of the girls face. She smiles slightly. The phone number remains on the screen.]; and with no source of income, it's pretty tough to get along in this part of the country. But María *will,* thanks to Angela. Now they share pictures, letters, their joys, sadness. [Close-up of the speaker.]

The ominous music and the black-and-white still photos of children return to the screen.

NARRATOR: Thousands of children, *just* as precious as María, die every day—not because people are heartless, but because we feel powerless. [At this point, the photo is not of a child but of a crowd of indistinguishable people on an open plain with dust hovering in the air. It looks very dry, arid, hot]. How many times have you heard child mortality statistics [again a photo of a child, this time apparently in a hospital since he has tubes taped to his head] and thought, "The problem's so big. What can I do?" [These phrases flash on the screen—white on black. The phone number is gone.] *You* can do plenty. [The phone number returns with a picture of a black boy.] You can pick up the phone and save *one* child. [Another close-up of a boy's face appears, still in black and white.] That's a great feeling. [The black-and-white photo of the boy turns into a color image.] Meet José [the image is no longer a still photograph as the camera recedes from the face of the boy to gradually include the speaker next to him. The piano melody returns.], sponsored by Scott Levins [a small photograph of a white man appears to one side of the screen, next to the boy], a Florida technician.

SPEAKER: José is just getting over pneumonia, which is *usually* fatal here. [The camera continues to recede. The speaker is talking with a serious expression on his face. In the background is a group of children all facing an adult woman of the same ethnicity. She is having them touch their toes. One can also hear their voices.] You see, where José lives, there's no clean water, no medicine, nothing but poverty. But with Scott's twenty-one dollars a month, Christian Children's Fund is able to give José good food, clean water, warm clothes, and the penicillin that saved his life. [The speaker glances from the camera to the boy and back again, several times.] The only thing we can't save you from is your school work! [As he says this, the speaker is looking at the boy, smiling, and mussing up his hair with a playful pat on the head. The boy turns his head to the speaker and smiles.] Christian Children's Fund can do a lot with your twenty-one dollars.

Once again the image on the screen is a black-and-white close-up of a girl's face—one that has been seen two times now during the commercial. She has dirt on her cheeks and nose and her hair is messy. The other children shown appear only once and in rapid succession. Her photo again remains on the screen several seconds longer than the other photos. This time, the music is still the melody of the piano, which continues to the end of the commercial.

NARRATOR: Remember, your phone call can make a *wonderful* difference in the life of a child.

The image returns to the color motion picture of the speaker. He is kneeling with a crowd of children around him. He has his arm around one of the girls. The children face the camera, although not all are looking directly at it.

SPEAKER: The number for Christian Children's Fund is on your screen. Please call it.

The image now shows a black background with a quote—in white—taken from *Money* magazine: "One of the ten best-managed large charities in America." Below it, in yellow, appears the title of the organization—Christian Children's Fund—together with the phone number, which has remained on the screen since last mentioned in this description.

NARRATOR: We'll send you the name and photo of a child you can sponsor.

APPENDIX C
Social Issues Frames

	Overview				Supporting Arguments			Mobilizing Potential	
Frame	*How Issue is Defined*	*Who Is Responsible?*	*Solution*	*Symbols or Portrayals*	*Causal Roots*	*Consequences*	*Cultural Resonances*	*Mobilizing*	*Demobilizing*
Individual Frame	matter of individual responsibility	individuals alone	help the deserving and allow undeserving to fend for themselves	guilt vs. innocence (of those affected by the issue), i.e. "innocent children" vs. "licentious adults"	personal failings such as illicit behavior	only the irresponsible themselves pay for their actions	individualism	Can lead to charity for the *deserving*, or a focus on taking care of one's self—as in AIDS education.	Most often demobilizing since individuals are accountable only to themselves.
Bureaucratic Frame	matter for the experts	experts in the relevant field	allow the experts to do their job as they see fit	"we live in a highly complex world"	outside of the average individual's control	without the experts, we would all be helpless in the face of the issue	the Division of Labor, belief in human progress, technofixes	Could be mobilizing if see the need to provide support for the experts (i.e. money) or if people are upset with the experts.	Could be demobilizing if individuals assume only experts are capable of addressing the issue.

(continued on next page)

	Overview			Supporting Arguments				Mobilizing Potential	
Frame	How Issue is Defined	Who Is Responsible?	Solution	Symbols or Portrayals	Causal Roots	Consequences	Cultural Resonances	Mobilizing	Demobilizing
Structural Frame	issue is a result of structural problems or a symptom of deeper problems in society	no one in particular—the "system" is to blame	optimize or change "the system"	guilt vs. innocence (of the system itself); references to "It"	The system is inappropriate for current circumstances	the public is at the mercy of the system	democratic participation for the greater good of all; social responsibility	Could be mobilizing within a social movement or advocacy approach.	Could be demobilizing if paired with feelings of powerlessness or division of labor among social movements (i.e. identity politics).
Universal Frame	this is an issue which should be of concern for everybody	everyone is, but no one in particular	???	ripples in a pond	???	everyone is affected	"We are the world"	May lead to charitable work, especially among those who feel "guilty," so long as the issue is "in" and it is convenient.	Most often demobilizing since no one person or group has responsibility.

(continued on next page)

	Overview					Supporting Arguments		Mobilizing Potential	
Frame	How Issue is Defined	Who Is Responsible?	Solution	Symbols or Portrayals	Causal Roots	Consequences	Cultural Resonances	Mobilizing	Demobilizing
Social Ethics Frame	this is an ethical/moral issue	I am	taking personal responsibility for getting involved	guilt vs. innocence (of those witnessing the effects of the issue); justice and equality	individuals not taking responsibility for society	if we all don't take responsibility, we all lose	social responsibility, moral obligation	Most often mobilizing; the question is at what level? Some may move toward structural activism, others toward charitable outreach to all those affected, or some combination of the two.	Can be demobilizing if focus is on *own* moral behavior (i.e. tendency toward individual frame) or if this moral obligation is interpreted as seasonal (i.e. Christmas).
Conspiracy Frame	issue is a result of attempt by few to exploit and maintain control over the many	those in power are at fault	overthrow those in power	guilt vs. innocence (of those in charge); references to "They"	mismanagement of the system by those in power	those without power will be the ones hurt	concern for the underdog	Could be mobilizing with revolutionary potential.	Could be demobilizing if paranoia leads to concern for *own* welfare above that of others.

Notes

2. The Roots of Social Affinity

1. It is interesting to note that Tönnies and Durkheim applied the terms "organic" and "mechanical" in opposing ways. Tönnies's use of organic referred to the wholeness of premodern community and Durkheim's use of the same term referred to the mutual interdependence of individuals—analogous to an organism's biological system—within modern society.

2. Of course, outright domination is still present, particularly toward marginalized groups, peoples, and nations.

3. I have here concentrated upon the typology of Ferdinand Tönnies. However, Durkheim too believed that the individualism of modernity, breaking down social solidarity, would lead to "the decay of society" (Durkheim 1984: xiv). In addition, keep in mind that these theorists are painting the world in broad strokes. While Tönnies stated that there are still elements of *Gemeinschaft* in *Gesellschaft*, he did not elaborate on the point. Thus, we must keep these elements of community in mind when reading about the shortcomings of complex societies.

4. "Moral obligation" is a term that serves the same function as Tönnies's "mutual obligation" and Maybury-Lewis's "interconnectedness."

5. In this statement, Tönnies is prefiguring social psychological thought concerning the distinction between "ingroups" and "outgroups"—to be discussed later.

6. This suggests that spatial and temporal proximity are of secondary importance, whereas social proximity may be hypothesized as being of greater importance. However, as is noted later, I also hypothesize that the

relative importance of each depends upon the simplicity or complexity of the society being studied.

7. I have intentionally used Vander Zanden's textbook material because it has integrated much original source material in an easy-to-understand format, one that reduces the complexity here. For citations of this original source material, please refer to the textbook.

8. There is another body of literature that says that "opposites attract." However, this literature focuses on complementary *personality* rather than social variables and actual marital choices, not on the creation of selection possibilities. Thus, the two perspectives may themselves be complementary.

9. In the literature on social psychology, prejudice is considered an attitude and, like all attitudes, includes three components: a cognitive, an affective, and a behavioral component (Vander Zanden, 1987: 465–466). We tend to perceive "others" in particular ways, usually involving the use of stereotypes, and this cognition evokes particular emotional responses—in the case of outgroups, they are typically negative. Based on our cognitive and affective responses to a particular group of "others," we exhibit a tendency to act negatively to that group. Note, however, that this is only a tendency and does not necessarily follow from the first two components; yet, when it does occur, this negative action is likely to involve discrimination. In any case, "prejudiced individuals easily retain evidence that confirms their negative attitude while ignoring or discounting evidence to the contrary. The hallmark of prejudice is that the negative belief persists despite contrary evidence" (Vander Zanden, 1987: 467; see also Darley and Gross, 1983).

10. The principles of ingroup/outgroup divisions also operate between different cultures and nationalities. When different groups are brought together within a single state, the result is the creation of "minorities"—or more broadly speaking, the "other," i.e., those without power in society—and the problems that arise from the friction between dominant ingroups and subordinate outgroups and between subordinate groups themselves, problems "which are not inherent in the mere existence of human differences" (Vander Zanden, 1987: 410).

Viewed from within, "others" are special types of "ingroups" with an "outgroup" status relative to the rest of society. Notice how similar are the characteristics of a minority—described here—to the characteristics of an ingroup:

> Members of a minority experience an intense social and psychological affinity with others like themselves. They possess a

primal sense of kinship, a solidarity springing from the roots of a real or mythical common ancestry in ages past. Frequently, they are so strongly bound together by a common identity that all other differences and conflicts become submerged in a spiritual loyalty and allegiance to the "people"—"my people:" the Jews, Turks, blacks, Armenians, or Greeks. (Vander Zanden, 1987: 463; also note how the word "affinity" is used)

While internally an "ingroup," they are considered an "outgroup" by those holding power within society. At the same time, the members of the majority are perceived as "others" by the members of the minority group, so these dynamics work both ways. In either situation, it is the differences between the groups that are foremost in our minds, and "others"—whether they are the majority or the minority—seem alien to us. As such, "others" are often met with a certain degree of prejudice, a point that recalls the sentiment of mastery described by Maybury-Lewis.

11. At this point, it may be apparent that I have freely used the first person plural in my writing—"we," "our," etc. While this may not be the best writing technique, I strongly believe that this is necessary given the purpose of this research. When we use third-person examples—"they," "one," etc.—we immediately set a barrier between ourselves and the actions being described. A major part of the point in this research is that we—all of us—must start accepting our *social responsibility*—responsibility for what goes on in our world, even if we are not the direct perpetrators. Use of the first person plural—*collective language*—demonstrates the sense of responsibility that is central to social affinity.

12. It is important to note that while many participants in this study shocked the victims, even at the highest levels, many were not actually comfortable doing so. Yet the dynamics of the situation prompted them to set aside their moral compunctions and continue administering the shocks. It is alarming to see how disparate our values and our behavior can be, given the situation, particularly the spatial factors that are often beyond our control.

13. Of course, in everyday life, people are largely unaware of the social psychological dynamics and subjective variables involved in our social relations. However, this is also a part of the problem. With understanding, we have the potential to *overcome* many of these dynamics, although such potential does not necessarily translate into actual behavior.

14. This definition comes from *Webster's Ninth New Collegiate Dictionary* (1984). Here and in several other chapters that follow, I have utilized

dictionary definitions in lieu of specifically sociological definitions in order to convey both the nuances and the connotations of the term in question.

15. I have used the terms "one" and "other" in order to avoid the cumbersome alternatives to sexist language. Constantly repeating "him or her," "he or she," and "his or her"—stylistically speaking—leaves much to be desired. While it is also possible to couch my arguments in terms of "they" and "them"—using the genderless plural form—such an approach does not allow me to refer to specific individuals (who are the units of analysis in this research).

Secondly, the use of the word *other* has some theoretical value when considering a topic such as this. The term has received much attention in recent feminist theory because it suggests that those so labeled are in some way marginalized by mainstream society. Because the theory of social affinity incorporates the notion of proximity/distance—especially with regard to *social* proximity/distance—the connotations of the word "other" are entirely appropriate. The "other" refers to those individuals whom we *perceive* as distant or removed from ourselves and the circles of our lives—socially, spatially, and/or temporally.

16. This distinguishes empathy from sympathy, in which the affective state is *congruent,* not identical. Also, sympathy consists of feelings of sorrow or concern for another's welfare. We feel bad for them, but we do not feel what they are feeling. Also, we are not so much experiencing an emotion of our own so much as *responding* to the emotion of another (Wispé 1986, and Gruen and Mendelsohn 1986).

17. Both "empathy" and "apathy" derive from the Greek word "pathos" or "passion." Empathy thus means "with passion" and apathy means "without passion."

18. Obviously, this model reflects a value-oriented position within the social sciences. However, given the subject matter, I believe that such a position is incumbent upon the researcher. I am not alone in taking such a position. Other social scientists have done the same in their unapologetic pursuit of social justice. Gordon W. Allport, the author of the social psychological classic *The Nature of Prejudice,* is but one example.

3. The Construction of Social Issues, Part I

1. In the sample for this study, 26 percent of the respondents knew someone who was HIV positive whereas 14 percent knew someone who

has gone hungry ($N = 426$). Moreover, of those who knew someone who had experienced hunger, 41 percent said that this person was an "acquaintance" or other distant individual they had reached out to at least in their consciousness (the subject of chapter 5), such as "my clients," the people at the shelter where they worked, or even a "work partner." With regard to those who knew an HIV-positive individual, 66 percent indicated the person was an "acquaintance" or other distant individual. In other words, respondents were more likely to reach beyond their immediate social circle when thinking about the AIDS issue and those it affects. Thus, they included references to very distant individuals largely unknown in a direct way, such as "a friend's parent," "my boyfriend's brother," or even "my best friend's, [half]-sister's father."

2. This and the following quotes and statistics are from *Sports For Hunger* of Waltham, Massachusetts. *Sports for Hunger* is a nonprofit fundraising organization which gets youth involved in the hunger issue by fundraising while playing sports they enjoy.

3. Chronic or persistent hunger is commonely understood as a physical state of malnutrition over a sustained period of time.

4. Unless otherwise noted, this and the following figures pertaining to AIDS in the United States are as of January 1, 1996, and are from the United States Centers for Disease Control and Prevention. Figures provided by the AIDS Action Committee of Massachusetts, Inc.

5. HIV stands for Human Immunodeficiency Virus, the virus that causes AIDS.

6. Massachusetts Department of Public Health. Figures provided by the AIDS Action Committee of Massachusetts, Inc.

7. Global Programme on AIDS, World Health Organization. Figures provided by the AIDS Action Committee of Massachusetts, Inc.

8. This and the following narratives have been edited in such a way as to eliminate the interview questions. In this way, the "narrative" style is maximized. Moreover, this and all narratives and quotations from the interview data that appear in this and the following chapters have been edited for ease in reading. The repetitions, incomplete and grammatically incorrect sentences, and false starts that characterize spoken language are difficult to follow when translated to written format and so were modified while maintaining the original meanings and intent of the interviewees.

9. For ease in presentation, I use the terms "social issue" and "social problem" interchangeably here and throughout the following chapters.

10. Silva's belief that street performers are homeless and hungry is

false. Some are, but many are not. Within the wide range of motives for playing music on the street, some view it as their full-time job, for others it is a supplementary source of income while doing something they enjoy. Others are music students looking for an opportunity to earn extra money while they practice. So, the belief that street performers are also homeless and hungry is an overgeneralization.

4. Construction of Social Issues, Part II

1. Diane points out that, "If we're talking about people who are homeless, I assume also that they are hungry, that they have no resources. I spend a lot of energy and attention towards homelessness, so I feel like I'm covering both bases."

2. See Rotello, Gabriel. "Ralph Reed: Antichrist or Revolutionary Reformer?" *OUT* magazine, August 1996, p. 68. Rotello points out that Ralph Reed, the former executive director of the Christian Coalition, actually disagrees with such a perspective while acknowledging it as a part of the history of the religious right. For a more detailed explication of Reed's perspective, see his book *Active Faith: How Christians are Changing the Soul of American Politics*. New York: The Free Press, 1996.

3. See Rosenhan, D.L. "On Being Sane in Insane Places," in C. Clark and H. Robboy, eds., *Social Interaction*. New York: St. Martin's Press, 1992.

4. Social consciousness, sentiment, and action have their roots in the social psychological literature on altruism and prosocial behavior. Batson's (1987) model of altruism, for instance, focuses on perception, empathy, and a behavioral response. This link with Batson is discussed in more detail at the end of chapter 7.

5. The "Other Side of Silence"

1. See Webster's *Ninth New Collegiate Dictionary.*

2. Karl Weick actually restricts the concept of sense-making to those instances where there are incongruities in perception—conflicting facts (1994: 2). However, much of his theory is equally applicable to consciousness in general because, in order for us to be aware of our world, we also have to make sense of the cues we pick up from that world.

3. From a personal communication with Madelyn Rhenisch, based on her experiences as a volunteer with a hunger hotline at a statewide hunger advocacy organization.

4. See Appendix B for a transcript of just such a hunger commercial.

5. Mention of the movie *Philadelphia* was much more likely during the early part of the data collection since the movie release was more recent at that time. As time progressed, it was less likely to be brought up, highlighting the fact that the effects of such media filters do wear off with time.

6. See Appendix C for a summary chart of these filters. The columns referring to the "mobilizing potential" of each frame are discussed in chapter 7.

7. However, as we see at the end of chapter 7, social consciousness is not necessarily the first element of social affinity to emerge. There are times when action precedes the emergence of consciousness.

6. A "Sentimental Journey"

1. These "individuals" do not even have to be a part of "real life." Recall the reactions to the characters in the movie *Philadelphia* mentioned in the previous chapter. Fictional characters such as those in the movie, while not a part of "reality" beyond the big screen, are products of society and can be responded to with the same sentiments one might feel toward a nonfictional individual. Thus, the distinction between what is fiction and what is reality is highly permeable.

2. In addition to the examples from Durkheim and Smith that follow, see Simmel's discussion of "Faithfulness and Gratitude" (1950: 379–395).

3. For this reason, social psychologist Steven Gordon finds it advantageous to distinguish between "emotions"—our bodily experience of our feelings—and "sentiments"—which reflect the social and cultural dimensions of those same feelings. He defines sentiments as "a socially constructed pattern of sensations, expressive gestures, and cultural meanings organized around a relationship to a social object, usually another person" (1990: 566).

4. There has been much controversy over the relative merits of the terms "sympathy" and "empathy" (see Kohn 1990; Clark 1987; Eisenberg and Miller 1987; Wispé 1986; and Gruen and Mendelsohn 1986) and no

clear agreement with regard to how they are to be used. Because empathy has been more readily identified with role-taking (with the exception of Clark), and because of the centrality of taking the perspective of the other in our consideration of social affinity, this is the term that will be used. However, Clark's analysis of emotions will also play a central role in this chapter. Therefore, when referring to her work, I will use the term "sympathy" in accord with her own usage.

5. This may, in part, explain why the expressions of sadness and sympathy were so prevalent among my interviewees. These words may have been said for my benefit as an interviewer and because they are expected in our society when discussing such social issues as hunger and AIDS.

6. Again, Smith used the term "sympathy," which today has the same connotations as our usage of "empathy."

7. Eisenberg and Miller also point out that a full range of emotions—from positive to negative—are available for empathy, not just sorrow (1987: 92). This further distinguishes empathy from sympathy. However, it is for this very reason that Clark abandons the term in favor of sympathy. She points out that "empathy with one's competitor in a sporting contest or in a competition for promotion on the job is necessary for malicious glee, just as it is for sympathy. . . . In short, empathy is necessary but not sufficient for sympathy" (1987: 295).

8. While the terminology used here is the same as that of Kohn, he lends a slightly different focus to them in his analysis than what follows. Figure 6.1 is an adaptation of Kohn's chart, showing the link between these forms of other and the typology presented in chapters 3 and 4.

9. The reader cannot help but notice that both individuals serving as examples of the socially referenced are female. In fact, much research has pointed to the notion that women are more likely to engage in role-taking and to empathize with others. Kohn points out that "on certain issues related to empathy, evidence for a gender difference—presumably a socialized one—seems fairly solid" (1990: 123; see also Feshbach, 1982; Hall, 1978; and Larrieu and Mussen, 1986). In my own statistical data, there was some difference in empathy between men and women. While the overall mean empathy score was 1.375 (on a scale from -4 to $+4$, where the higher the numerical value, the greater the empathy; $N = 426$). For men, the mean score was .818, compared with a score for women of 1.647. However, when comparing the percentages of the socially referenced who were male versus female, there was virtually no difference. Two separate studies con-

ducted by Nancy Eisenberg and Randy Lennon, in which the researchers reviewed over 120 studies on empathy, found that gender differences are actually an artifact of how empathy is measured. When measured in a self-report format, as in my survey, women tend to score higher than men. However, when measured through facial expressions and even physiological responses, men and women are equal (Eisenberg and Lennon 1983; Lennon and Eisenberg 1987). Moreover, even when differences were found, as in the research cited earlier, it generally indicates that these differences between men and women are rather small.

Another line of research suggests that differences in empathy and role-taking are more a function of one's power relative to others. Reminiscent of the work of feminist standpoint epistemologists (Harding 1991), Sara Snodgrass's work (1985) suggests that those in a subordinate position find it more necessary to role-take and empathize with those who are in a more powerful position—it is a simple matter of survival. This research seems to suggest that class—at least insofar as it relates to power—is also related to empathy and role-taking: those in a lower class are more likely to engage in empathy and role-taking. On the other hand, some research shows that "the person whose own needs seem more pressing than those of the other is also relatively unlikely to attend fully to that other person" (Kohn 1990: 122; see also Strayer 1987). My own survey shows that empathy scores increase with one's class, *except* for the upper class, which is closer to the working class in their mean scores (see Table 6.1). This body of research is reflective of Abraham Maslow's (1954) "Hierarchy of Motives," in which an individual must meet their basic biological needs—food, water, sleep, etc.—and their needs for safety and security before they can move on to their social needs. In other words, those in the lower classes who need to struggle with their own needs for survival are *less* likely to

TABLE 6.1.
Distribution of Mean Empathy Scores According to Class ($N = 426$)

Economic Class	Mean Empathy Score
Lower class	1.000
Working class	1.071
Lower middle class	1.387
Upper middle class	1.447
Upper class	1.138

engage in empathy and role-taking and the prosocial behaviors associated with them. Thus, these two branches of social research regarding class and empathy are somewhat contradictory and are yet to be resolved with any degree of definitiveness.

10. Gordon argues that relationships—and, by inference, especially those that are closer and longer lasting—provide a context for "emotional arousal" (1990: 575–577). One of these he calls "reminiscent arousal" in which we reminisce over past relations. He specifies several additional sources of emotional arousal, including interruptions or novelty in the midst of our routines ("Arousal from interruption or novelty"), our own monitoring of our emotions ("validative arousal"), anticipation of future events or relations ("anticipatory arousal"), and empathizing with other's emotions ("empathic arousal").

11. The case of Reuben, whose aunt is HIV positive and for whom he has no sympathy whatsoever, is a notable exception. In this instance, his moral stance on illicit drug use acts as a filter in the same sense as described in chapter 5. Any sentiment he may have felt for his aunt is effectively filtered out.

12. Despite the arguments that these emotions of fear, anger, surprise, and so on are biologically based, the *social meanings* given to social issues like hunger are oftentimes a root source of these apparently biological emotions. Part of Silva's fear stemmed from her awareness that discussing her experiences with hunger would not be socially acceptable among her peers. Thus, even emotions of apparent biological origin have social dimensions (see also Karp 1996).

13. Clark specifies an additional rule: "claim some sympathy." If an individual rarely claims sympathy, others are not likely to believe it when he or she does claim sympathy. As Clark explains, "one who never claims or accepts sympathy from another over a period of time in a stable relationship may simply come to be defined as an inactive member of the interaction network. . . . When roles have solidified and become habitual, an out-of-character claim for sympathy may not 'compute'" (1987: 309).

The reason that this rule was not included earlier is that, in the context of social issues, the very *existence* of these issues is a claim to sympathy. Although a claim is more obvious if an actual solicitation occurs, the very nature of a social issue as a *problem* places a sympathy claim on all who learn of that issue whether they have been directly solicited or not. However, this rule is still informative in the context of social issues.

Clark points out that making a claim for sympathy "crystallizes the statuses and roles of those in the relationship along a *superordinate-subordinate* dimension. Mutual exchanges of sympathy commonly symbolize equality, whereas one-way gifts of sympathy usually signify inequality" (1987: 310). In the context of social issues, there is no "mutual exchange" in the literal sense. While the presence of social issues is an implicit claim to the sympathy of the individual, the individual cannot claim sympathy of an issue. Even when one brings the level of analysis down to the individual on both sides of the equation, the person who is suffering from hunger, for example, is not in an equal position with the person from whom sympathy is asked. There is an inherent power difference between these two individuals (Bergin, Coutsoukis, and Vela-McConnell 1994), and the claim to sympathy posed by the hungry, or by hunger in general, solidifies this disparity in power between the solicitor and the individual in a position to offer sympathy.

On the other hand, the fact that an exchange of sympathy "crystallizes" the relationship is central to the heart of social affinity. It is through these claims to sympathy that the social ties between disparate individuals develop, forming the basis of the social fabric that holds society together. In this light, both making a claim to sympathy and offering sympathy are central to the health of society.

14. I am here using the term "overinvestor" in a way that is slightly different from that described by Clark. She defines a sympathy overinvestor as someone "who give[s] sympathy to others who have deviant sympathy biographies" (Clark 1987: 313), that is, those who break the sympathy rules. I use the term "overinvestor" in the sense of someone who shows what is viewed as "too much" sympathy to others regardless of their level of "deservedness."

7. A Call to Action

1. The complete frequency distributions are shown in Table 7.1. The figures presented in the table reflect a composite of three different variables for the hunger and AIDS issues. Respondents were asked three yes/no questions: (1) whether they participated in fund-raising, (2) had made a donation, and (3) volunteered their time to each issue in the past year. The breakdown for each of these variables is shown in Table 7.2.

TABLE 7.1.
Levels of Activity by Issue

Hunger (N = 407)		(N)	AIDS (N = 425)		(N)
Not Active	20.9%	85	Not Active	52.2%	222
Low Activity	35.6%	145	Low Activity	24.7%	105
Moderate Activity	21.4%	87	Moderate Activity	14.1%	60
High Activity	22.1%	90	High Activity	9.0%	38
	100.0%	407		100.0%	425

TABLE 7.2.
Participation Sorted by Type of Participation and Issue

Hunger			AIDS		
Fund-raising (N = 426)		(N)	Fund-raising (N = 425)		(N)
Yes	41.8%	178	Yes	23.8%	101
No	58.2%	248	No	76.2%	324
	100.0%	426		100.0%	425
Donation (N = 426)		(N)	Donation (N = 425)		(N)
Yes	75.1%	320	Yes	44.5%	189
No	24.9%	106	No	55.5%	236
	100.0%	426		100.0%	425
Volunteering (N = 407)		(N)	Volunteering (N = 425)		(N)
Yes	27.3%	111	Yes	11.5%	49
No	72.7%	296	No	88.5%	376
	100.0%	407		100.0%	425

2. I do not mean to imply that socialization is not an important factor in the lives of the individuals representing the other forms of activism and nonactivism. In fact, socialization and role models are very important in this process. However, for the purposes of this research, I have chosen to emphasize different factors in an effort to contribute additional knowledge to the field of sociology rather than merely expand on one line of theory and research.

3. For the sake of simplicity in describing the linear model of motivation, I leave our sentiments out of the equation at present. However, it should be remembered that consciousness—our perception of the social

problem—does have an impact on our sentiments and that our sentiments too, as described in chapter 6, have an additional impact on whether or not we take action. All three aspects of social affinity—consciousness, sentiment, and action—are considered together in chapter 8.

4. See Appendix C for a summary of the mobilizing potential of each of the frames discussed.

5. Another way in which this frame can be demobilizing is when the individual is conscious of the division of labor among social movements (i.e., identity and issue-specific politics) and begins to despair that the efforts of activists are being spread too thinly to effectively promote any kind of real structural change. In other words, their feelings of powerlessness have moved beyond their own selves and have encompassed their attitude toward activists and activism in general. The topic of identity and issue-specific politics are taken up again in chapter 9.

6. Recall that in chapter 5, I speculated as to an additional conspiracy frame. Such a frame also has two possible outcomes in terms of mobilization. As already described, this frame defines an issue as a result of the exploitation of the many by a few in power. Given that the way to solve the problem is to overthrow those few in power, this frame is oftentimes mobilizing toward a revolutionary form of activism. On the other hand, the conspiracy frame could also be demobilizing if paranoia leads to concern for one's *own* welfare above the welfare of others.

7. The Gay and Lesbian Speakers Bureau is an organization that provides guest speakers—upon request—to area institutions and organizations desiring sensitivity training on gay and lesbian issues.

8. For further discussions of the ties between affiliation in church groups and prosocial behavior, see Jackson et al., 1995; Wuthnow, 1990 and 1991; and Hodgkinson, 1990.

9. In his article, Batson is more concerned with establishing that an altruistic motive is separate and distinct from an egoistic motive and thus devotes his attention to research testing what he calls the "altruism-empathy hypothesis." While the debate between the egoistic and altruistic perspectives is not new, Batson points out that social scientists have traditionally espoused the egoistic explanation of prosocial motivation. However, if altruism is a separate motive, it would establish the importance of social psychological research on that topic—a departure from the traditionally accepted egoistic view. Batson notes that, if altruism cannot be satisfactorily separated from egoism, "then parsimony favors an exclusively egoistic view" (1987: 115). I disagree with this assertion. My research suggests that, indeed,

empathy *and* self-interest are relevant to prosocial behavior. By pursuing Batson's agenda, everything regarding empathy would be dismissed as unimportant because self-interest is easier to demonstrate. However, upon examination of the data presented here, it is apparent that *both* sources of motivation are important to understand because neither one of them is universal. Some people display more self-interest, others more empathy. The majority show elements of both. Given this, it is important to examine the interactions between both sources of motivation—a task that began in chapters 5 through 7 and that is pursued in chapters 8 and 9.

10. By broadening empathy to sentiment, it is possible to incorporate important elements of both egoistic motivation and altruistic motivation because "sentiment" includes a greater range of emotions. Within his egoistic model (there are actually two models, but for ease of presentation, we will focus on only one), we are motivated to reduce our "vicarious emotional response of personal distress" (1987: 84). In other words, there is still an emotive element in such egoistic motivation. However, the emotions in the egoistic and altruistic models are different. Batson associates the emotions of empathy with being "sympathetic, moved, compassionate, tender, warm, and softhearted." On the other hand, the emotions leading to egoistic motivation include being "alarmed, grieved, upset, worried, disturbed, perturbed, distressed, and troubled" (1987: 98), emotions that, as we saw in chapter 6, while they are not the most likely to motivate one to reach out to those affected by social issues, still do play an important role. The fact that both sets of emotions are relevant to our consideration of social affinity underscores the importance of simultaneously considering self-interest and altruism when studying prosocial behavior.

11. This is an adaptation of the model presented by Batson (1987: 84).

12. Only two rather than three entry points are suggested because neither logic nor the data presented here suggest that one may begin the process with sentiment. In order for us to experience sentiment, we first need some form of stimuli. We need to perceive or become aware of something before we can experience an emotive reaction to it. In other words, social consciousness precedes social sentiment, although action may or may not precede social consciousness.

13. In addition to these partisan concerns, disputes have arisen as to which issues would and would not be approved for such mandatory volunteering. As Martin notes, "in one community, service to Planned Parenthood was approved but service to an anti-abortion group was not" (1996: 16). Given that most social issues represent particular interest

groups, such "territorial" disputes are not surprising. In addition, legal questions have been raised about mandatory service. Martin describes cases brought by three North Carolina high school students who claimed that such a requirement constituted slavery. However,

> all three cases have failed in courts. In denying the North Carolina slavery case, U.S. District Judge Frank W. Bullock cited the argument made by the American Alliance for Rights and Responsibilities that service-learning is an educational initiative that prepares students for participation in society. (1996: 16)

Clearly, this debate will continue for some time.

8. From "Compartmentalizing" to "Breaking the Boundaries"

1. Curtis is referring to a gay and lesbian organization formed in response to the wave of hate crimes perpetrated against members of the gay and lesbian community. The members of this group patrol areas frequented by gay men and lesbians in an effort to deter such crimes.

2. Curtis also displays glimmerings of the individual frame, defining the issue in terms of individual responsibility, as in when he says, "There's so many skills that you see, and yet they're not being used properly. Those skills could help raise up our community. But no, they're helping degrade our community. . . . These people have to see that they do have skills." The proper or improper utilization of one's skills is a clear reference to an individual's accepting responsibility for themselves. However, Curtis's next statement acknowledges that these individuals are being constrained by their circumstances: "But they also *need the means* to go to college" [emphasis added]. Without sufficient means, individuals have less control over their own fates. Thus, the structural frame receives primacy in Curtis's social consciousness.

3. The actual name of the clinic has been changed as well as some details of the event in order to further protect Diane's identity.

9. Becoming "Fully Human"

1. Some social commentators refer to globalization in purely economic terms—"the shorthand term we will use for [the] globalization of

capital" (Brecher and Costello 1994: 4). Indeed, as multinational corporations flourish and national economies become increasingly interdependent, the economy is central to the globalization process. However, I use
the term in a broader sense that includes the role of technology and the
media. Through the Internet, for example, we are able to "connect" with
people all across the globe so long as they also have the resources for utilizing this technology.

2. The magnitude of need was also a relevant factor for the American subjects: life-threatening situations of need were much more likely to
be accompanied by feelings of moral obligation than were non-life-threatening situations. However, this factor was mediated by the social proximity of those in need. For example, non-life-threatening situations of need
were seen as moral obligations *if* the person in need was a dependent family member. The magnitude of need had little effect on the feeling of obligation by the Hindu Indians.

3. The researchers distinguished between three degrees of need:
minor, moderate, and extreme need. Providing directions was a minor need
incident. A sample moderate need incident is "Not giving aspirin to someone who is suffering from a painful migraine headach on a bus ride,
because you do not want to bother looking for the bottle of aspirin you
are carrying." A sample extreme need is "Not administering mouth-to-
mouth resuscitation to someone who has stopped breathing, because you
might get dirty administering the procedure" (Miller et al. 1990: 143).

4. From a personal communication with Daniel Berrigan.

5. One of these individuals who define "loving one's neighbor" as
showing respect also included elements of the idea of treating others
equally as well as helping those in need. Of the total sample, 13.9 percent
interpreted the precept exclusively in terms of helping those in need.
Another 8.3 percent combined the equality and helping interpretations. Of
those interviewed, 11.1 percent defined "loving one's neighbor" more literally in terms of love or compassion. The remaining 8.3 percent gave
ambiguous interpretations or did not interpret it at all.

6. Definitions taken from *Webster's Ninth New Collegiate Dictionary.*

7. The percentages are based on a sample of thirty-three. For the
remaining three interviews, this data is missing. Of the 73 percent in the
latter category, 41.7 percent ($N = 24$) initially said "everyone," but then
qualified their answer by saying, for example, "my community first."
Three individuals (12.5%) said "everyone, but particularly those who are
less fortunate."

Appendix A. The Emperical Approach to Social Affinity

1. While the survey and the intensive interviews were the primary sources of data, they were not the only ones. In addition to these sources, I relied on field observation and content analysis of personal reflections and organizational records. Each source of data was tied specifically to the case study issues of hunger and AIDS. Prior to the inception of this research, I worked with two colleagues—Platon E. Coutsoukis and Patricia Bergin—on a study of street solicitors, particularly the homeless. While the homeless and the hungry are not necessarily one and the same, they often are and are certainly linked in the minds of most of my interviewees. Thus, where it was applicable, I drew upon the data gathered in this project. The data collection began with twenty-six hours of field observation in Harvard Square (Cambridge, MA)—in which we focused on the observable dynamics of interaction between street solicitors and passersby—and continued with thirty-two brief interviews with passersby. The interviews focused on how the passersby felt about the solicitors, who they felt was responsible for their welfare, how they responded to the solicitors, and why. Finally, additional data was gathered from the written responses of fifty-six social psychology students to the question "How do you react when someone asks you for money on the street?"

The data pertaining to the case study issue of AIDS was obtained specifically for this research. A *systematic sample* of two hundred active volunteer applications was obtained from the files of a major AIDS service and advocacy organization. (The total population of active volunteers at that time was 3,009. A sampling interval of fifteen was used. Thus, there is an approximate standard error of less than 8 percent at the 90 percent confidence level for this sample.) The reason for sampling the application forms was that they included information that was quite insightful with regard to the research questions in this study. For example, volunteers were asked the following questions: (1) "What is your desired level of involvement? (periodic or regular?)," (2) "Discuss any experience you have had in dealing with HIV or AIDS," (3) "What needs of your own do you expect to fulfill as a volunteer?," and (4) "What prompted you to volunteer?" A complicating issue with regard to this data source was the fact that there were several different versions of the application form used at different points in the history of the organization. For example, the older version of the application did not ask for any demographic information, thus limiting my analysis for the longer-term volunteers. However, much of the information was still intact and useful.

Thus, this research was based on a variety of data sources—a survey; a series of semi-structured intensive interviews; field observations; another series of interviews, this time quite structured; and content analysis of both organizational records and individual reflections. These methods were highly complementary of one another. Where one method of data collection failed due to its inherent limitations, the advantages of another would offer a compelling substitute. In short, it was possible to engage in triangulation. When this method is employed, "consistent findings among different data collection methods increase the credibility of research findings" (Nachmias and Nachmias 1987: 208–209). This is because results obtained from multiple methods reduce the risk of drawing erroneous conclusions. At the same time, "discrepancies [in results] call for clarifications and further research" (1987: 209). The consistencies between the multiple sources of data used in this research support the credibility of the theory of social affinity. Perhaps this was because, despite the quantitative nature of the survey data, an inductive approach was taken. In this way, all sources of data were allowed to work together to enrich the theoretical framework and our understanding of social affinity.

2. A purposive—or "judgmental"—sample oftentimes is used in qualitative research (Bogden and Biklen 1992: 71–72). This sampling proceedure is defined as "a type of nonprobability sample in which you select the units to be observed on the basis of your own judgment about which ones will be the most useful or representative" (Babbie 1992: G5).

3. I consider this research to be inductive rather than deductive in nature. Despite the fact that I utilized a survey, I did not engage in traditional sampling techniques utilized for quantitative research. The sampling procedure was a variation on the purposive sampling approach used in qualitative research. For lack of a term, I describe it as "purposive sampling through a network-convenience approach." In other words, I relied on a network of friends, colleagues, and acquaintances to distribute surveys in a variety of locations. This approach had the advantage of reaching a wider variety of individuals, some of whom had specific characteristics. For example, my initial surveys were distributed to students enrolled in sociology classes. Since this is most assuredly a nonrepresentative sample, extending my network of contacts allowed me to reach students who were enrolled in other fields, such as foreign languages or philosophy—classes that, being in the core curriculum, attract students of all majors, not just the humanities or social sciences. I was also able to sample students outside of classroom settings. Part of the sample was attained through a contact in

a university department of residential life. Again, this had the advantage of allowing a sample from a variety of majors. Other contacts I had were members of student organizations representing special interests, such as a student gay and lesbian organization and an AIDS group. This was necessary in order to increase the demographic diversity of the sample but also—in the case of the AIDS group—to recruit individuals with an interest in a specific social issue, an interest that was tremendously underrepresented in the sample up to that point and that was directed toward an issue that was central to the research. As the sample grew and more contacts were made who were willing to distribute the survey, the sample also diversified. For example, five very different colleges and universities in the New England area were represented, each of which attracts different kinds of students.

While relying on students is often criticized because they are atypical of society in general, I found this to be a distinct advantage. The college environment has been described by Madelyn Rhenish [personal communication] as an "identity crucible." In other words, it is here that individuals begin an intensive process of secondary socialization and re-formation of their identities. Prior to that time, individuals tend to reflect the values they were taught during primary socialization by their parents and close friends and families. By presenting a variety of alternative value systems, college provides an environment that is conducive to setting up a value system of the students' own making. Within this context, they are able to make conscious decisions about who they are going to be as individuals and how they view and relate to the society around them. Paul Loeb eloquently describes the relevance of this period in personal development:

> [C]ollege is a time when many students develop a base of cultural assumptions they will use throughout their lives. They set habits of speaking out or remaining silent, of engaging with difficult public issues or avoiding them, of embracing or mistrusting the power of ordinary citizens to have a political say. They embark on self-reinforcing paths in their careers, friendships, and goals. On or off campus, they will face similar dilemmas of engagement or withdrawal, similar issues to respond to, similar arguments for passivity. (1994: 368)

Because the concept of social affinity is so closely tied to an individual's values, college students provide a particularly rich population for exploring this topic.

However, I was also able to sample individuals outside of academic settings. Since students themselves are an atypical population, I decided it was important to include nonstudents as well. Moreover, my network of contacts who distributed surveys through a variety of work and friendship networks extended well beyond Massachusetts. Through this procedure, I was able to sample people from Rhode Island, Colorado, and Louisiana. Keeping a record of the location of each respondent allowed me to compare these populations with regard to the full range of variables in the survey to see where the differences and similarities lay.

Relying on connections for the distribution of the surveys also had its drawbacks. When a researcher relies on such contacts—contacts who received no monetary compensation—a certain amount of control over the data collection is lost. As was already mentioned, there were a variety of contexts in which the surveys were distributed. While this variety had its advantages, such variations were, at times, beyond the discretion of the researcher. Moreover, some of the contacts proved to be unreliable, failing to distribute all of the surveys they were given or failing to keep track of the actual number of surveys distributed. (In two cases, I had to rely on estimates of the number of surveys actually distributed, so the return rates may be slightly off.) Finally, one contact had additional burdens placed upon him by the fact that he was a resident assistant (RA) who was distributing surveys in his hall. His resident hall supervisor—herself an RA—asked whether the survey had been approved by the Housing Office. The survey had actually already been approved by the Office of Research Administration, which oversees research participation on behalf of *all* students, regardless of residence. In other words, approval came from "higher up" the organizational ladder. The head RA showed the survey to the Director of Housing who had several questions (quite unimportant questions that should not have prevented the distribution of the survey—although they were important to *him* because they allowed him to exert his authority) that he wanted answered before he would allow the survey to be distributed. Unfortunately, I now had two intermediaries between the director and myself. However, my contact advised me to get in touch with the director and answer his questions myself. I did so and was summarily chewed out for contacting him directly. Instead, I was informed that I should communicate with him via his subordinates. (A rather humorous and harmless example of the otherwise serious form of institutional distancing discussed in earlier chapters.) Thus, I was put back in touch with the head RA who agreed to write a memo on my behalf and then quickly forgot. In the end, my original contact had to write the memo and give it to the head RA who would then give it to the director. Eventually, the response wound its way back through the chain to my own ears. The survey would be distributed as planned. The lesson learned here was that, when asking favors, it is best not to go above anybody's head because their egos may get hurt. Instead, obeisance is required at every level!

4. The return rate was 46.81 percent.

5. The empathy scale I chose to include in the survey was the Questionnaire Measure of Emotional Empathy (QMEE), developed by Albert Mehrabian and Norman Epstein (1972). There were a number of different scales available, although the QMEE and the Hogan Empathy Scale were the only two with independent studies demonstrating their validity and reliability (Chlopan, McCain, Carbonell, and Hagen 1985). In comparing these two scales, it was found by the reviewers that they actually measure different aspects of empathy—aspects that displayed only a low correlation. The reviewers noted that the QMEE measured "vicarious emotional arousal" while the Hogan Empathy Scale focused more on "role-taking ability" and speculated that this focus tapped into the "adequate social functioning" of those measured (1985). The QMEE's focus on vicarious emotional arousal tended to give results closely related to the moral development of those measured: "high scorers on the QMEE are more *socially aware, volunteer more to help others,* and have *higher moral development* than those who score low on the QMEE" (1985; emphases mine). These were the qualities I sought to find in those who exhibit a high social affinity for the "others" in society.

From reviewing the development of Hogan's Scale (Hogan 1969), it is apparent that the scale ignores the *relations between* the "one" being measured and the "other." Hogan conducted a series of tests in which he correlated his scale with such other scales as the California Psychological Inventory (CPI), the Minnesota Multiphasic Personality Inventory (MMPI), and the Myers-Briggs Type Indicator. The resulting correlations showed that the Hogan Empathy Scale was correlated with these measures of one's psychological make-up. However, in the instance of the Myers-Briggs, the scale was highly correlated with extroversion/introversion (.63 and −.61, respectively), while the correlations for such dimensions as perception, intuition, and feeling were quite low (.10, .16, and .10 respectively). Considering that this scale was constructed from portions of the CPI and the MMPI, such results are not surprising.

It was also apparent that the Hogan Empathy Scale, while measuring psychological profiles, was inadequate in predicting whether those who have a high score adopt a "moral point of view" in actual practice (1969: 315). The QMEE, on the other hand, was shown to predict both helping behavior and nonaggressive behavior (Mehrabian and Epstein 1972). While the intuitive appeal of a measure of role-taking ability is clear—given the centrality of such an ability in the theoretical perspective of George Herbert Mead (1934)—the approach in constructing the Hogan Empathy Scale precluded its usefulness as a measure of social concern for the welfare of others—a necessary element in the empirical approach to social affinity.

6. The surveys for students and nonstudents were slightly different in terms of the demographic variables. This was done in order to tap into the different experiences of each population. Thus, nonstudents were not asked about their campus activities and so forth. Instead, they were asked about their work status. And while students were asked about their families of origin—under the assumption that the vast majority of them are still considered dependents by their parents and have not yet started families of their own—nonstudents were asked about their family of procreation.

7. The actual figure is 24.18 percent ($N = 426$).

8. This open-ended survey question was admittedly rather broad. In fact, a number of them were, as were many of the questions prepared for the intensive interviews. While some methodologists might find this problematic, I found it to be an immensely useful methodological tool. This is due in part to my theoretical background in phenomenology and the idea of the "social construction of reality" (Berger and Luckmann 1967); however, it also arose out of the theoretical background of social affinity. An image that helps in understanding the "social construction of reality" is to picture a spider making a web. The threads of the web are actually a part of the spider—something internal that is made external. Once the thread is external to the spider and is made into a web, the web takes on an existence that is separate from the spider. At the same time, the web is the spider's home of its own making and essence. Such is the social world around us and such is our own view of that world. (This analogy is taken from a personal communication with Bernard J. Lee, coauthor—with Michael A. Cowan—of *Dangerous Memories: House Churches and Our American Story*, 1986.)

Our social consciousness—the first element of social affinity—is a reflection of the way in which we perceive and understand the world around us. The categories we create or inherit within our minds affect what we see and what we do not see in the world around us, thus promoting or hindering the development of social affinity. The easiest way for a social scientist to perceive these mental constructions is to allow them free reign. If someone answers the question "Who would you say is affected by hunger?" with "the hungry themselves, obviously," it tells the reader something about that person, something that is entirely different from the person who says that *everyone* is affected by hunger, or the person who says "*I* am affected by hunger" even though she or he has never experienced it directly. All of these responses say something about the mental constructions and the social consciousness of the respondents. The first is one who looks at social issues, or at least the hunger issue, as having definite boundaries beyond which the issue has no impact. The second sees no such boundaries, and yet this too could be problematic in that an issue has a weird way of affecting "no one" at the same time that it affects "everyone." In other words, while we acknowledge its existence and its ramifications, the problem is seen as so huge it is beyond the purview of any single individual. Hence, no one takes responsibility. The person who responds in this way may be quite aware of this dynamic; on the other hand, she or he may also be its victim. In the latter case, the respondent is well aware that hunger affects more than just the hungry themselves. It is not a bounded issue. At the same time, there is the understanding that the issue has an impact on his or her own life. When this realization occurs, the road is open for accepting social responsibility because it is in that individual's interests to do so. Thus, vague and broad questions have a definite usefulness about them. They allow the social scientist to enter the worldview of the respondent or interviewee in a way that more bounded questions do not.

9. Unfortunately, the statistical methods used to analyze data usually prevent these glimmerings and hints from ever being legitimized as data. In fact, to the traditional statistician working in a deductive model, perceiving the uniqueness of any one respondent is directly at odds with the goals of the approach. Moreover, any single cases that do not fit with the others due to their uniqueness—termed "outliers"—are usually dismissed in the course of the analysis.

10. Of the female respondents, 27.28 percent offered marginal comments while only 18.12 percent of men did ($p<.05$, $N=426$). Again, there are many possible explanations for this outcome. As noted below, women are more likely to get involved than are men, and so this finding may be reflective of that tendency. Another explanation is that this is an opportunity that women have to fully express themselves and their feelings, behaviors for which men receive less encouragement and training through

socialization into traditional gender roles. On the other hand, it may be an issue of power. Whereas men have the power to express their opinions and have them heard on a fairly regular basis, many women do not. A questionnaire, completed in private, gives them the opportunity for such expression.

11. Of those making marginal comments, 53.40 percent also volunteered for an interview while only 28.79 percent of those who did not comment volunteered ($p<.0001$, $N = 426$).

12. The actual figure is 34.74 percent ($N = 426$).

13. Given that women tend to volunteer much more than men do, it was somewhat surprising that they were only slightly more likely to volunteer for an interview than were men. Thirty-five percent (35.89%; $N = 287$) of women volunteered for an interview, while 32.61 percent ($N = 138$) of men volunteered. (I hypothesize that this is due to the use of incentives for participation, to be discussed in the second section of this appendix.) However, because women constituted a larger portion of the sample (67.53% were women while 32.47% were men; $N = 426$), they constituted 69.60 percent of those volunteering for an interview while men constituted 30.41 percent ($N = 148$). Thus, in attempting to balance the interview sample between men and women, 44.44 percent ($N = 36$) of those actually interviewed were men.

14. Racial minorities accounted for 15.40 percent of the entire sample ($N = 426$) and 18.49 percent of those volunteering for an interview ($N = 148$). However, racial minorities constituted 19.44 percent of those interviewed ($N = 36$). In total, there were three blacks, three Hispanics, and one Asian who were interviewed. Moreover, an effort was made to include sexual minorities as well. While they constituted only 4.06 percent of the entire sample, 13.89 percent of those interviewed were gay, lesbian, or bisexual.

15. Based on this approach, there were eight different combinations of activity and nonactivity as represented in Table A1.1

16. A complete list of these top issues is as follows: abortion, AIDS, the budget deficit, the Cuban refugee crisis, education, family breakdown, genocide, government reform, gun control/violence, health care, racism/discrimination/human rights, unemployment, and welfare/poverty/homelessness. While it may seem that including those individuals who felt that AIDS and issues relating to hunger are redundant because they were the case studies common to all research participants, it was important to include them because not everyone felt that they were the most important issue.

TABLE A1.1.
Eight Combinations of Activity (Y) and Nonactivity (N)

	Hunger	*AIDS*	*Respondent's Top Issue*
1.	Y	Y	Y
2.	Y	Y	N
3.	Y	N	Y
4.	Y	N	N
5.	N	Y	Y
6.	N	Y	N
7.	N	N	Y
8.	N	N	N

17. This example highlights the fact that personalization and depersonalization is a two-way street. At the same time that respondents found anonymity liberating, so did I. And where interviewees enjoyed the personal nature of a face-to-face interview, so did I.

18. Under ideal conditions, analysis of interview data would begin as soon as data began to be collected and would continue throughout the data collection process. Unfortunately, the constraints of my methodological approach limited the amount of analysis that could be conducted at that time. As already noted, the individuals I interviewed were an actual subsample of those who were surveyed. As a result, the time delay between the survey and the interview had to be minimal, particularly with regard to the student sample. An extended time delay would result in higher levels of participant attrition. For example, I contacted several interview volunteers for appointments only to find that they had forgotten they volunteered for an interview or even that they filled out the survey in the first place. At the same time, there were several interview volunteers who had already left the area before I contacted them. When one considers that students often leave for the summer break or change apartments, not to mention graduate and move, it becomes apparent that the interviews had to be conducted as quickly as possible at risk of losing contact with those who volunteered for interviews. As an attempt to compensate for the lack of time for a detailed analysis of each case after the interview was completed, I made sure to immediately write a memo after each interview. The memo went beyond describing my impressions of the individuals and the interview overall. I made sure to relate them theoretically to those interviews completed prior to that time. In this way, at least the rudimentary

elements of analysis were pursued at the same time as the data were actually being collected.

19. The survey, of course, was analyzed using traditional statistical methods. However, including a number of open-ended questions in the survey did allow for a more qualitative approach. The qualitative data was analyzed following a traditional grounded approach (Glaser and Strauss 1967) and utilizing HyperResearch—a computer program for qualitative data analysis (see Hesse-Biber, DuPuis, and Kinder 1990, for a description)—as a research tool.

20. The experiment by Stanley Milgram on obedience to authority—already discussed in chapter 2—provides a good example of ethically suspect research. Other examples include Haney, Banks, and Zimbardo's study of a simulated prison (1973) and Humphreys' study of sex in public places (1970).

21. I do not recall the exact figure because, at the time, it did not occur to me during this pretesting phase to track the return rate for individual classes.

22. As in Garrett's case, not everyone needs some form of external motivation. Some are motivated by internal factors, such as what they might learn from the experience or because they find the topic interesting in the first place. This implies that there are different levels of motivation, extending from the intrinsically motivated to those who are motivated by incentive to those who are not motivated at all.

23. Of course, this presented the additional problem of people who might decide to complete more than one survey so that they would have more chances of winning. As a result, a detailed system of checking each survey and raffle ticket with all those previously received had to be developed.

24. The actual figure is 46.81 percent ($N = 910$). This return rate is especially notable given that the survey was eighteen pages in length.

25. The actual figure is 34.74 percent ($N = 426$).

26. The actual figure is 56.51 percent ($N = 426$).

27. The actual figure is 76.94 percent ($N = 426$).

28. The actual figure is 55.18 percent ($N = 426$).

29. Twenty-one percent (20.89%, $N = 426$) were not involved with hunger at all, and 52.24 percent of the sample were not involved at any level with AIDS.

30. One will note that these figures were less balanced when it came to the issue of AIDS—77 percent exhibited little or no activity with regard

to this issue while only 23 percent *were* involved. This is why it was necessary to tap into the student AIDS awareness organization when it came to purposive sampling.

31. The actual figure is 39.60 percent ($N = 101$).

32. The actual figure is 69.23 percent ($N = 286$, range = 44.19% to 81.94%).

33. The actual figure is 62.17 percent ($N = 460$, range = 0% to 100%).

34. The actual figure is 23.91 percent ($N = 322$, range = 0% to 44.0%).

35. Separate return rates were calculated for each of my contacts who distributed surveys. Thus, the range refers to those contacts who achieved the lowest to the highest return rate for that category.

36. The actual figure is 23.56 percent ($N = 225$).

37. The range is from 18 to 38, with only 2.96 percent of these individuals over the age of twenty-five ($N = 372$).

38. The range is from nineteen to fifty-five, with 69.63 percent of these individuals over the age of twenty-five ($N = 51$).

39. I use this strategy in my teaching, also in the form of extra credit. If students notice a public event, such as a lecture or a fund-raiser, they may announce it to the class. Those who attend the event and write a brief sociological analysis of the topic or the event itself can earn extra credit points. The idea is to get the students used to keeping their eyes open to what is going on around them and to actually attend these events. Most students find this a very rewarding experience, both personally and intellectually. Interestingly, if a student completes an extra-credit assignment, they usually complete more than just that one. It is almost like they initially develop a feel for it and then they become so comfortable with it that it almost becomes second nature. My intention is to foster this form of personal development to the point that it will continue even after the semester is over and extra credit is no longer offered. At that point, the students may be a bit more selective about the events they attend, but so long as they continue to participate, the goal has been reached.

References

Allport, Gordon W. *The Nature of Prejudice.* New York: Addison Wesley, 1954.

Alper, J. "The Roots of Morality," *Science* 85 (March 1985): 70–76.

Amato, Paul R. "An Investigation of Planned Helping Behavior," *Journal of Research in Personality* 19 (1985): 232–252.

———. "Personality and Social Network Involvement as Predictors of Helping Behavior in Everyday Life," *Social Psychology Quarterly* 53, no. 1 (1990): 31–43.

And the Band Played On. Randy Schilts. New York: HBO Video, 1993.

Ariés, Philippe. *The Hour of Our Death.* New York: Alfred A. Knopf, 1981.

Babbie, Earl. *The Practice of Social Research.* 6th ed. Belmont, CA: Wadsworth, 1992.

Batson, C. Daniel. "Prosocial Motivation: Is It Ever Truly Altruistic?" In *Advances in Experimental Social Psychology.* Vol. 20, edited by Leonard Berkowitz. San Diego: Academic Press, 1987.

Batson, C. Daniel, B. D. Duncan, P. Ackerman, T. Buckley, and K. Birch. "Is Empathic Emotion a Source of Altruistic Motivation?" *Journal of Personality and Social Psychology* 40 (1981): 290–302.

Batson, C. Daniel, and R. A. Gray. "Religious Orientation and Helping Behavior: Responding to One's Own or to the Victim's Needs?" *Journal of Personality and Social Psychology* 40 (1981): 511–520.

Batson, C. Daniel, K. O'Quin, J. Fultz, M. Vanderplas, and A. M. Isen. "Influence of Self-Reported Distress and Empathy on Egoistic Versus Altruistic Motivation to Help," *Journal of Personality and Social Psychology* 45 (1983): 706–718.

Bellah, Robert N., Richard Madsen, William M. Sullivan, Ann Swidler, and Steven M. Tipton. *Habits of the Heart: Individualism and Commitment in American Life.* New York: Harper & Row, 1985.

Benson, Peter L., John Dehority, Lynn Garman, Elizabeth Hanson, Martha Hochschwender, Carol Lebold, Roberta Rohr, and Jane Sullivan. "Intrapersonal Correlates of Nonspontaneous Helping Behavior," *The Journal of Social Psychology* 110 (1980): 87–95.

Berger, Kathleen Stassen. *The Developing Person Through the Life Span.* 2d ed. New York: Worth, 1988.

Berger, Peter L. *Invitation to Sociology: A Humanistic Perspective.* New York: Anchor Books, 1963.

Berger, Peter L., Brigitte Berger, and Hansfried Kellner. *The Homeless Mind: Modernization and Consciousness.* New York: Random House, 1973.

Berger, Peter L., and Thomas Luckmann. *The Social Construction of Reality: A Treatise in the Sociology of Knowledge.* New York: Anchor Press, 1967.

Bergin, Patricia, Platon E. Coutsoukis, and James A. Vela-McConnell. "An Analysis of Interaction Encounters Between Solicitors and Passersby in Harvard Square." Paper presented at the 64th Annual Meeting of the Eastern Sociological Society, Baltimore, March 1994.

Blanchard, F. A., R. H. Weigel, and S. W. Cook. "The Effect of Relative Competence of Group Members Upon Interpersonal Attraction in Cooperating Interracial Groups," *Journal of Personality and Social Psychology* 32 (1975): 519–530.

Bogdon, Robert C., and Sari Knopp Biklen. *Qualitative Research for Education: An Introduction to Theory and Methods.* 2d ed. Boston: Allyn and Bacon, 1992.

Booth, Alan, and Nicholas Babchuk. "Personal Influence Networks and Voluntary Association Affiliation," *Sociological Inquiry* 39 (Spring 1969): 179–188.

The Boston Globe, 21 August 1996.

Brecher, Jeremy, and Tim Costello. *Global Village or Global Pillage: Economic Reconstruction From the Bottom Up.* Boston: South End Press, 1994.

Breckler, S. J. "Empirical Validation of Affect, Behavior, and Cognition as Distinct Components of Attitude," *Journal of Personality and Social Psychology* 47 (1984): 1191–1205.

Byrne, Donn. *The Attraction Paradigm.* New York: Academic Press, 1971.

Caro, Robert A. *The Power Broker: Robert Moses and the Fall of New York.* New York: Alfred A. Knopf, 1974.

Chacón, Richard. "City Credit Card Offers Chance to Back Events," *Boston Globe,* 21 August 1996.

Chambré, Susan M. "Kindling Points of Light: Volunteering as Public Policy." *Nonprofit and Voluntary Sector Quarterly* 18, no. 3 (1989): 249–268.

Charbeneau, Travis. "Ragged Individualism: America's Myth of the Loner." *Utne Reader,* May/June 1992, 132–133.

Charon, Joel M. *Ten Questions: A Sociological Perspective.* 2d ed. Belmont, CA: Wadsworth, 1995.

Chlopan, Bruce E., Marianne L. McCain, Joyce L. Carbonell, and Richard L. Hagen. "Empathy: Review of Available Measures," *Journal of Personality and Social Psychology* 48 (1985): 635–653.

Clark, Candace. "Sympathy Biography and Sympathy Margin," *American Journal of Sociology* 93, no. 2 (1987): 290–321.

Clary, E. Gil, and Jude Miller. "Socialization and Situational Influences on Sustained Altruism," *Child Development* 57 (1986): 1358–1369.

Cooley, Charles Horton. *Social Organization.* New York: Scribner, 1909.

Coser, Lewis A. *Masters of Sociological Thought: Ideas in Historical and Social Context.* 2d ed. New York: Harcourt Brace Jovanovich, 1977.

Cuzzort, R. P., and E. W. King. *Twentieth-Century Social Thought.* 4th ed. Fort Worth, TX: Holt, Rinehart and Winston, 1989.

Darley, J. M., and P. H. Gross. "A Hypothesis-Confirming Bias in Labeling Effects," *Journal of Personality and Social Psychology* 44 (1983): 20–33.

Davis, Mike. *City of Quartz: Excavating the Future in Los Angeles.* New York: Vintage Books, 1992.

Derber, Charles. *Money, Murder and the American Dream: Wilding from Wall Street to Main Street.* Boston: Faber and Faber, 1992.

———. "Individualism Runs Amok in the Marketplace: Communitarians Can't Ignore the Economic Factors that Affect Community." *Utne Reader,* November/December 1994, 111–117.

Derber, Charles, with Karen Marie Ferroggiaro, Jacqueline A. Ortiz, Cassie Schwerner, and James A. Vela-McConnell. *What's Left? Radical Politics in the Postcommunist Era.* Amherst: University of Massachusetts Press, 1995.

Dickens, Charles. *A Christmas Carol.* New York: Dodd, Mead, 1935.

Dovidio, J. F. "Helping Behaviors and Altruism: An Empirical and Conceptual Overview." In *Advances in Experimental Social Psychology.* Vol. 17, edited by L. Berkowitz. New York: Academic Press, 1984.

Durkheim, Émile. *The Division of Labor in Society.* New York: The Free Press, 1984.

Eisenberg, Nancy, ed. *The Development of Prosocial Behavior.* New York: Academic Press, 1982.

Eisenberg, Nancy, and Randy Lennon. "Sex Differences in Empathy and Related Capacities," *Psychological Bulletin* 94 (1983): 100–131.

Eisenberg, Nancy, and Paul A. Miller. "The Relation of Empathy to Prosocial and Related Behaviors," *Psychological Bulletin* 101, no. 1 (1987): 91–119.

Eisenberg, Nancy, and Janet Strayer, eds. *Empathy and Its Development.* Cambridge: Cambridge Unversity Press, 1987.

Eliot, George [Mary Ann Evans Cross]. *Middlemarch: A Study of Provincial Life.* New York: New American Library, 1981.

Etzioni, Amitai. *The Spirit of Community: Rights, Responsibilities, and the Communitarian Agenda.* New York: Crown, 1993.

Feshbach, Normal Deitch. "Sex Differences in Empathy and Social Behavior in Children." In *The Development of Prosocial Behavior,* edited by Nancy Eisenberg. New York: Academic Press, 1982.

Festinger, L., S. Schachter, and K. Back. *Social Pressures in Informal Groups: A Study of Human Factors in Housing.* New York: Harper & Row, 1950.

Flacks, Richard. *Youth and Social Change.* Chicago: Markham, 1971.

Freud, Sigmund. "Beyond the Pleasure Principle," *The Standard Edition.* Vol. 18. London: Hogarth Press, 1920.

Gamson, Willam A. *The Strategy of Social Protest.* 2d ed. Belmont, CA: Wadsworth, 1990.

———. *Talking Politics.* New York: Cambridge University Press, 1992.

Gans, Herbert. *Urban Villagers.* New York: The Free Press, 1962.

Gergen, Kenneth J. *The Saturated Self: Dilemmas of Identity in Contemporary Life.* New York: Basic Books, 1991.

Gerloff, Robert. "Public Space Minus the Public: We Are Abandoning Democracy in our Desire for Personal Security." *Utne Reader,* January/February 1993, 46–48.

———. "The New Urbanism Takes Hold: Anti-Suburb Architects are Finally Getting Some Respect." *Utne Reader,* May/June 1994, 28–30.

Giddens, Anthony. *The Constitution of Society: Outline of the Theory of Structuration.* Berkeley: University of California Press, 1984.

Glaser, Barney G., and Anselm L. Strauss. *The Discovery of Grounded Theory: Strategies for Qualitative Research.* New York: Aldine de Gruyter, 1967.

Goffman, Erving. *Asylums.* Garden City, NY: Anchor Books, 1961.

———. *Frame Analysis: An Essay on the Organization of Experience.* Cambridge, MA: Harvard University Press, 1974.

Gonzales, M. H., J. M. Davis, G. L. Loney, C. K. Lukens, and C. M. Junghans. "Interractional Approach to Interpersonal Attraction," *Journal of Personality and Social Psychology* 44 (1983): 1192–1197.

Gordon, Steven L. "The Sociology of Sentiments and Emotion." In *Social Psychology: Sociological Perspectives,* edited by Morris Rosenberg and Ralph H. Turner. New York: Basic Books, 1990.

Greenberg, J., and T. Pyszczynski. "The Effect of an Overheard Ethnic Slur on Evaluations of the Target: How to Spread a Social Disease," *Journal of Experimental Social Psychology,* 21, 61–72, 1985.

Gruen, R. J., and Gerald Mendelsohn. "Emotional Responses to Affective Displays in Others: The Distinction Between Empathy and Sympathy," *Journal of Personality and Social Psychology,* 51, 609–614, 1986.

Hall, Judith A. "Gender Effects in Decoding Nonverbal Cues," *Psychological Bulletin* 85 (1978): 845–857.

Haney, Craig, W. Curtis Banks, and Philip G. Zimbardo. "Interpersonal Dynamics in a Simulated Prison," *International Journal of Criminology and Penology* 1 (1973): 69–97.

Harding, Sandra. *Whose Science? Whose Knowledge? Thinking From Women's Lives.* Ithaca, NY: Cornell University Press, 1991.

Heilbroner, Robert L., ed. *The Essential Adam Smith.* New York: W. W. Norton and Company, 1986.

Herman, Edward S., and Noam Chomsky. *Manufacturing Consent: The Political Economy of the Mass Media.* New York: Pantheon Books, 1988.

Hesse-Biber, Sharlene, Paul DuPuis, and Scott Kinder. "HyperResearch: A Computer Program for the Analysis of Qualitative Data Using the Macintosh," *Qualitative Studies in Education* 3, no. 2 (1990): 189–193.

Hochschild, Arlie Russell. *The Managed Heart: Commercialization of Human Feeling.* Berkeley: University of California Press, 1983.

Hodgkinson, V. A. "The Future of Individual Giving and Volunteering: The Inseparable Link Between Religious Community and Individual Generosity." In *Faith and Philanthropy in America: Exploring the Role of Religion in America's Voluntary Sector,* edited by Robert Wuthnow, V. A. Hodgkinson, & Associates. San Francisco: Jossey-Bass, 1990.

Hogan, Robert. "Development of an Empathy Scale," *Journal of Consulting and Clinical Psychology* 33 (1969): 307–316.

Holding Ground: The Rebirth of Dudley Street, prod. and dir. Leah Mahan and Mark Lipman, edited by Jon Neuburger. New Jersey: New Day Films, 1996.

Humphreys, Laud. *Tearoom Trade.* Chicago: Aldine, 1970.

Jackson, Elton F., Mark D. Bachmeier, James R. Wood, and Elizabeth A. Craft. "Volunteering and Charitable Giving: Do Religious and Associational Ties Promote Helping Behavior?" *Nonprofit and Voluntary Sector Quarterly* 24, no. 1 (1995): 59–78.

Jordan, Judith V. "Empathy and Self Boundaries," *Work in Progress,* No. 16. Wellesley, MA: Stone Center for Developmental Services and Studies, 1984.

Kadi, M. "Welcome to Cyberbia: Money Dictates Who Moves Into a Virtual Community," *Utne Reader,* March/April 1995, 57–59.

Kalliopuska, Mirja. "Relationship Between Moral Judgment and Empathy," *Psychological Reports* 53 (1983): 575–578.

Karp, David A. *Speaking of Sadness: Depression, Disconnection, and the Meanings of Illness.* New York: Oxford University Press, 1996.

Karp, David A., and William C. Yoels. *Sociology and Everyday Life.* Itasca, IL: F.E. Peacock, 1986.

Keen, Sam. *Faces of the Enemy: Reflections of the Hostile Imagination.* New York: HarperCollins, 1991.

Kohn, Alfie. *The Brighter Side of Human Nature: Altruism and Empathy in Everyday Life.* New York: Basic Books, 1990.

Kozol, Jonathan. *Savage Inequalities: Children in America's Schools.* New York: Crown, 1991.

Landis, B. *Ego Boundaries.* New York: International Universities Press, 1970.

Larrieu, Julie, and Paul Mussen. "Some Personality and Motivational Correlates of Children's Prosocial Behavior," *Journal of Genetic Psychology* 147 (1986): 529–542.

Latané, Bibb, and John Darley. *The Unresoponsive Bystander: Why Doesn't He Help?* New York: Appleton-Century-Crofts, 1970.

Latané, Bibb, and S. Nida. "Ten Years of Research on Group Size and Helping," *Psychological Bulletin* 89 (1981): 308–324.

Lauderdale, P., J. Parker, P. Smith-Cunnien, and J. Inverarity. "External Threat and the Definition of Deviance," *Journal of Personality and Social Psychology* 46 (1984): 1017–1028.

Lee, Bernard J., and Michael A. Cowan. *Dangerous Memories: House Churches and Our American Story.* Kansas City, MO: Sheed & Ward, 1986.

Lennon, Randy, and Nancy Eisenberg. "Gender and Age Differences in

Empathy and Sympathy." In *Empathy and Its Development,* edited by Nancy Eisenberg and Janet Strayer. Cambridge: Cambridge Unversity Press, 1987.

Levin, Jack, and Jack McDevitt. *Hate Crimes: The Rising Tide of Bigotry and Bloodshed.* New York: Plenum Press, 1993.

Loeb, Paul Rogat. *Generation at the Crossroads: Apathy and Action on the American Campus.* New Brunswick, NJ: Rutgers University Press, 1994.

MacLeod, Jay. *Ain't No Makin' It: Leveled Aspirations in a Low-Income Neighborhood.* Boulder, CO: Westview Press, 1987.

Markides, K. C., and S. F. Cohn. "External Conflict/Internal Cohesion: A Reevaluation of an Old Theory," *American Sociological Review* 47 (1982): 88–89.

Martin, Andrea. "Citizenship or Slavery? How Schools Take the Volunteer Out of Volunteering," *Utne Reader,* May/June 1996, 14–16.

Maslow, Abraham H. *Motivation and Personality.* New York: Harper & Row, 1954.

Maybury-Lewis, David. *Millennium: Tribal Wisdom and the Modern World.* New York: Viking Press, 1992.

McAdam, Doug. *Political Process and the Development of Black Insurgency, 1930–1970.* Chicago: The University of Chicago Press, 1982.

Mead, George Herbert. *Mind, Self, and Society: From the Standpoint of a Social Behaviorist.* Chicago: The University of Chicago Press, 1934.

Meadows, Donella H. et al. *The Limits to Growth: A Report for THE CLUB OF ROME'S Project on the Predicament of Mankind.* New York: Universe Books, 1974.

Medoff, Peter, and Holly Sklar. *Streets of Hope: The Fall and Rise of an Urban Neighborhood.* Boston: South End Press, 1994.

Mehrabian, Albert, and Norman Epstein. "A Measure of Emotional Empathy," *Journal of Personality* 40 (1972): 525–543.

Milgram, Stanley. "Behavioral Study of Obedience," *Journal of Abnormal and Social Psychology* 67 (1963): 371–378.

———. "The Experience of Living in Cities," *Science,* March 1970, 1461–1468.

———. *Obedience to Authority: An Experimental View.* New York: Harper & Row, 1974.

Miller, Joan G., David M. Bersoff, and Robin L. Harwood. "Perceptions of Social Responsibilities in India and in the United States: Moral Imperatives or Personal Decisions?" *Journal of Personality and Social Psychology* 58, no. 1 (1990): 33–47.

Mills, C. Wright. *The Sociological Imagination.* New York: Oxford University Press, 1959.

Moreland, R. L. "Social Categorization and the Assimilation of 'New' Group Members," *Journal of Personality and Social Psychology* 48 (1985): 1173–1190.

Moreland, R. L., and R. B. Zajonc. "Exposure Effects in Person Perception: Familiarity, Similarity and Attraction," *Journal of Experimental Social Psychology* 18 (1982): 395–415.

Morris, Alson, D. *The Origins of the Civil Rights Movement: Black Communities Organizing for Change.* New York: The Free Press, 1984.

Muson, Howard. "Moral Thinking: Can It Be Taught?" *Psychology Today,* February 1979, 337–346.

Mynatt, C., and S. J. Sherman. "Responsibility Attribution in Groups and Individuals: A Direct Test of the Diffusion of Responsibility Hypothesis," *Journal of Personality and Social Psychology,* 32, 1111–1118, 1975.

Nachmias, David, and Chava Nachmias. *Research Methods in the Social Sciences.* 3d ed. New York: St. Martin's Press, 1987.

Nader, Ralph. "Citizens and Computers: Using the Internet as a Tool for Community Organizing," *Utne Reader,* March/April 1995, 74.

Newcomb, Theodore M. "The Prediction of Interpersonal Attraction," *American Psychologist* 11 (1956): 575–586.

———. *The Acquaintance Process.* New York: Holt, Rinehart and Winston, 1961.

———. "Stabilities Underlying Changes in Interpersonal Attraction," *Journal of Abnormal and Social Psychology* 66 (1963): 376–386.

Nuland, Sherwin B. *How We Die: Reflections of Life's Final Chapter.* New York: Alfred A. Knopf, 1994.

Pascale, Celine-Marie. "The Criminalization of Homelessness: Cities Resort to Arrests Rather than Offering Real Help." *Utne Reader,* September/October 1994, 38–39.

Priest, Robert F., and Jack Sawyer. "Proximity and Peership: Bases of Balance in Interpersonal Attraction," *American Journal of Sociology* 72 (1967): 633–649.

Reed, Ralph. *Active Faith: How Christians are Changing the Soul of American Politics.* New York: The Free Press, 1996.

Reich, Robert B. *The Work of Nations: Preparing Ourselves for 21st-Century Capitalism.* New York: Alfred A. Knopf, 1991.

Rheingold, Howard. "The Virtual Community: Computer Networking

Can Help Bring Community Back to the Center of Modern Life," *Utne Reader,* March/April 1995, 61–64.

Ritzer, George. *The McDonaldization of Society: An Investigation into the Changing Character of Contemporary Social Life.* Rev. ed. Thousand Oaks, CA: Pine Forge Press, 1996.

Rosenhan, D. L. "On Being Sane in Insane Places." In *Social Interaction,* edited by C. Clark and H. Robboy. New York: St. Martin's Press, 1992.

Rotello, Gabriel. "Ralph Reed; Antichrist or Revolutionary Reformer?" *OUT,* August 1996, 66–69, 104–108.

Rutkowski, G. K., Charles L. Gruder, and D. Romer. "Group Cohesiveness, Social Norms, and Bystander Intervention," *Journal of Personality and Social Psychology* 44 (1983): 545–552.

Ryan, Charlotte. *Prime Time Activism: Media Strategies for Grassroots Organizing.* Boston: South End Press, 1991.

Ryan, William. *Blaming the Victim.* Rev. ed. New York: Vintage Books, 1976.

Sarasohn, David. "The Down Slide: The Demise of Playgrounds and Other Public Institutions." *Utne Reader,* March/April 1992, 130.

Schanberg, Sydney H. "Six Cents an Hour," *Life,* June 1996, 38–48.

Schilts, Randy. *And the Band Played On: Politics, People, and the AIDS Epidemic.* New York: St. Martin's Press, 1987.

Schwartz, S,. and J. A. Fleishman. "Personal Norms and the Mediation of Legitimacy Effects on Helping." *Social Psychology* 41 (1978): 306–315.

Schwerner, Cassie. "Beyond Socialism and Identity Politics: The U.S. Left After the Fall." In *What's Left? Radical Politics in the Postcommunist Era.* Amherst: University of Massachusetts Press, 1995.

Segal, M. W. "Alphabet and Attraction: An Unobtrusive Measure of the Effect of Propinquity in Field Training." *Journal of Personality and Social Psychology* 30 (1974): 654–657.

Shaffer, Carolyn R., and Kirsten Anundsen. *Creating Community Anywhere: Finding Support and Connection in a Fragmented World.* New York: Jeremy P. Tarcher/Perigee Books, 1993.

Sherif, M., O. J. Harvey, B. J. White, W. R. Hood, and C. W. Sherif. *Intergroup Conflict and Cooperation: The Robbers Cave Experiment.* Norman: Institute of Group Relations, University of Oklahoma, 1961.

Shibutani, T., and K. M. Kwan. *Ethnic Stratification.* New York: Macmillan, 1965.

Simmel, Georg. *On Individuality and Social Forms.* Donald N. Levine, ed. Chicago: University of Chicago Press, 1971.

Smith, Adam. *The Essential Adam Smith*. Robert L. Heilbroner, ed. New York: W.W. Norton, 1986.

Snell, Marilyn Berlin. "Turn Down the Volume," *Utne Reader,* November/December 1995, 71.

Snodgrass, Sara E. "Women's Intuition: The Effect of Subordinate Role on Interpersonal Sensitivity," *Journal of Personality and Social Psychology* 49 (1985): 146–155.

Speier, H. "The Social Types of War," *American Journal of Sociology* 46 (1941): 445–454.

Starbuck, William H., and Frances J. Milliken. "Executives' Perceptual Filters: What they Notice and How They Make Sense." In *The Executive Effect: Concepts and Methods for Studying Top Managers,* edited by Donald C. Hambrick. Greenwich, CT: JAI Press, 1988.

A Status Report on Hunger And Homelessness in America's Cities: 1991—A 28-City Survey. Washington, D.C.: The United States Conference of Mayors, December 1991.

Staub, E. *Positive Social Behavior and Morality: Social and Personal Influences.* Vol. 1. New York: Academic Press, 1978.

"Sticky Fingers." *The Economist,* 23 December–5 January 1995/1996, 94.

Strayer, Janet. "Affective and Cognitive Perspectives on Empathy." In *Empathy and Its Development,* edited by Nancy Eisenberg and Janet Strayer. Cambridge: Cambridge University Press, 1987.

Stuart, Reginald. "High-Tech Redlining: Are African-Americans Being Frozen Out of the New Communications Network?" *Utne Reader,* March/April 1995, 73.

Toi, Miho, and C. Daniel Batson. "More Evidence that Empathy is a Source of Altruistic Motivation," *Journal of Personality and Social Psychology* 43 (1982): 281–292.

Tocqueville, Alexis de. *Democracy in America.* New York: Random House, 1981 (1835).

Tönnies, Ferdinand. *Community and Society.* New Brunswick, NJ: Transaction Books, 1988.

Triandis, Harry C. *Individualism & Collectivism.* Boulder, CO: Westview Press, 1995.

Turner, Jonathan H. "Toward A Sociological Theory of Motivation," *American Sociological Review* 52 (1987): 15–27.

Underwood, B., and B. Moore. "Perspective-Taking and Altruism," *Psychology Bulletin* 91 (1982): 143–173.

Vander Zanden, James W. *Social Psychology.* 4th ed. New York: Random House, 1987.

Vanderpool, Tim. "Secession of the Successful: Homeownders' Associations Turn Neighborhoods Into Islands." *Utne Reader,* November/ December 1995, 32–33.

Vaughan, Diane. "Theory Elaboration: The Heuristics of Case Analysis." In *What Is a Case? Exploring the Foundations of Social Inquiry,* edited by Charles C. Ragin and Howard S. Becker. Cambridge: Cambridge University Press, 1992.

Walljasper, Jay. "Chattanooga Chooses: The Revitalization of This Once Dying City Shows Urban Decline Is Not Inevitable." *Utne Reader,* March/April 1994, 15–16.

Webster's Ninth New Collegiate Dictionary. Springfield, MA: Merriam-Webster, Inc., 1984.

Weick, Karl E. *Sensemaking in Organizations.* Thousand Oaks, CA: Sage Publications, 1995.

West, Cornel. *Race Matters.* New York: Vintage Books, 1994.

Wilder, David A., and Peter N. Shapiro. "Role of Out-Group Cues in Determining Social Identity," *Journal of Personality and Social Psychology* 47 (1984): 342–348.

Williamson, Marianne. *A Return to Love: Reflections on the Principles of a Course in Miracles.* New York: HarperCollins, 1996.

Winkler, Allan. "Communitarianism." *Utne Reader,* November/December 1994, 105–108.

Wispé, Lauren. "The Distinction Between Sympathy and Empathy: To call Forth a Concept, a Word is Needed," *Journal of Personality and Social Psychology* 50 (1986): 314–321.

Wolf, Kurt H., ed. *The Sociology of Georg Simmel.* New York: The Free Press of Glencoe, 1950.

Wolfe, Alan. *Whose Keeper? Social Science and Moral Obligation.* Berkeley: University of California Press, 1989.

Wuthnow, Robert. "Religion and the Voluntary Spirit in the United States: Mapping the Terrain." In *Faith and Philanthropy in America: Exploring the Role of Religion in America's Voluntary Sector.* San Francisco: Jossey-Bass, 1990.

————. *Acts of Compassion: Caring for Others and Helping Ourselves.* Princeton, NJ: Princeton University Press, 1991.

————. *What It Means to Volunteer: Lessons From America's Youth.* Washington, D.C.: Independent Sector, 1995.

Wuthnow, Robert., V. A. Hodgkinson, & Associates, eds. *Faith and Philanthropy in America: Exploring the Role of Religion in America's Voluntary Sector.* San Francisco: Jossey-Bass, 1990.

Zimbardo, Philip C. "The Human Choice: Individuation, Reason, and Order Versus Deindividuation, Impulse, and Chaos." In *Nebraska Symposium on Motivation.* Vol. 17, edited by W. Arnold and D. Levine, 1969.

Zinn, Howard. *You Can't Be Neutral on a Moving Train: A Personal History of Our Times.* Boston: Beacon Press, 1994.

Index